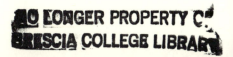

Accommodation
and
Resistance

Contributions to the Study of World History

The Myth of the Revolution: Hero Cults and the Institutionalization
of the Mexican State, 1920-1940
Ilene V. O'Malley

Accommodation and Resistance

The French Left, Indochina and the Cold War, 1944–1954

Edward Rice-Maximin

Contributions to the Study of World History, Number 2

Greenwood Press
New York • Westport, Connecticut • London

Library of Congress Cataloging-in-Publication Data

Rice-Maximin, Edward Francis, 1941-
  Accommodation and resistance.

  (Contributions to the study of world history,
ISSN 0885-9159 ; no. 2)
  Bibliography: p.
  Includes index.
  1. Indochina War, 1946-1954—France. 2. Communism—
France—History. 3. Socialism—France—History.
4. France—Politics and government—1945-1958.
5. World politics—1945-   . I. Title.
II. Series.
DS553.1.R53   1986   959.704′1   86-4624
ISBN 0-313-25355-2 (lib. bdg. : alk. paper)

Library of Congress Catalog Card Number: 86-4624
ISBN: 0-313-25355-2
ISSN: 0885-9159

First published in 1986

Greenwood Press, Inc.
88 Post Road West, Westport, Connecticut 06881

Printed in the United States of America

∞™

The paper used in this book complies with the
Permanent Paper Standard issued by the National
Information Standards Organization (Z39.48-1984).

10 9 8 7 6 5 4 3 2 1

In Memory of

FORREST ORAN WIGGINS

Wisconsin '38

Who Always Kept the Faith

Contents

Preface   ix

Introduction: The Legacy   1

PART ONE: THE LEFT IN POWER (1944-1947)

I.   Liberation (August 1944-September 1945)   11

II.   The French Return (September 1945-
March 1946)   23

III.   Negotiations (March-October 1946)   34

IV.   War (November 1946-March 1947)   42

V.   Cold War (March-December 1947)   52

PART TWO: THE LEFT DIVIDED (1948-1950)

VI.   Bao Dai (December 1947-March 1949)   65

VII.   The Peace Offensive (1949-1950)   75

VIII.   The Generals' Affair (1949-1950)   85

IX.   Internationalization (March 1949-
February 1950)   91

X.   Crusades (February-December 1950)   99

PART THREE: THE LEFT IN OPPOSITION (1951-1954)

XI.   De Lattre de Tassigny (December 1950-
January 1952)   110

XII.   Pigeons (January-December 1952)   116

XIII.   Henri Martin (1950-1953)   123

XIV.   Mendès-France and Ho Chi Minh (January-
         November 1953)   135

XV.   Dien Bien Phu and Geneva (November 1953-
         July 1954)   143

       Conclusion   150

       Bibliographical Essay   153

       Index   159

Preface

Communism, socialism and anti-colonial revolutions have been among the leading protagonists of the twentieth century. Sometimes they have been complementary, at other times opposed. During the First Indochinese War (1945- 1954), they were both. Communists in Vietnam were in the forefront of the anti-colonial struggle, while Communists and Socialists in France responded in a variety of convergent and divergent ways. Their story is complex and instructive.

The French Communists constitute the prime dilemma. Initially viewed through the prism of the Cold War, their support of the Vietnamese revolutionaries appeared unequivocal and their anti-war activities subversive and unpatriotic. In everything, they acted at the behest of Moscow. The Communists did not always object to these charges. Although they denied acting contrary to French national interests, they always claimed to be in the forefront of championing the causes of the colonial peoples.

The ambiguities in Communist colonial policies became more apparent as the Cold War thawed and more particularly during the Algerian War (1954-1962). Then, the events of May-June 1968 questioned anything truly radical in Communist history. Consequently, in the 1970's, certain left-wing historians, sometimes referred to as gauchistes, argued that, during the Indochina War, the Communists had significantly compromised their anti-colonial principles and had deliberately restricted their anti-war activities. The root problem was "Stalinism" (in France and in Russia).

Since then, more moderate historians have been less shocked and more sympathetic. The French Communists simply comprised the liberal wing of the "colonial consensus." Behaving like any other political party seeking power, they sought to integrate themselves with the rest of the French nation. Nationalist motivations inspired their behavior as much as Moscow's directives. They deliberately circumscribed their actions against the Indochina War, which, in the final analysis, were not terribly significant.

Through all this debate, Communist historians, while sometimes highly selective, have often ably defended their record. As a part of the government, the Communists faithfully supported the positions of the Vietnamese revolutionaries and resisted any compromises not imposed on them by the other ministers. Later on, they deliberately restricted only the most obviously subversive anti-war activities. Otherwise, they fought as vigorously as Cold War circumstances permitted and contributed significantly to the end of the war.

The French Socialists' approach to the First Indochina War has not elicited as much interest or passion. Few observers see more than some minor nuances in their positions. Prejudiced by the Socialist policies on the later Algerian War, left-wing critics see only an unswerving Socialist support of the Indochina War. More sensitive to the nuances, the Right argues that Socialist divisiveness and hesitation actually impeded the prosecution of the war. The Socialists themselves have claimed, not very convincingly, that they consistently opposed the war.

The Socialist story also has the air of a tragedy. While their support of the war was often reluctant, the opposition that they themselves mustered was ineffective and clearly removed from the main anti-war movements. Heavily entrapped in Cold War politics, on the defensive on most issues, and generally in serious decline, the Socialists were never able to chart an independent course on Indochina. Perhaps most damaging was the fact that their policies did not reflect the objective situation in Vietnam. Whereas the Communists could claim some heroic moments, few Socialists, despite some sincere efforts, found they could maintain their integrity on Indochina.

The French Communists and Socialists, of course, never acted in isolation. A number of individuals and groups (from the extreme to the moderate left), equally embroiled over Indochina, serve to put the policies of the Communists and Socialists into a fuller perspective. Moreover, while nationalist motivations were more important than previously thought, the First Indochina War did occur at the height of the Cold War and necessarily involved the foreign policies of the Soviet Union and the United States toward both Vietnam and France. Finally, since the French war was the embryo of the American, the dilemmas of the French Left during the First Indochina War should be instructive to Americans who both opposed and supported the Vietnam War.

*   *   *   *   *

    I would like to thank the following people specially for
their help and encouragement since this study first began some
fifteen years   ago: Harvey Goldberg and his <u>Atelier de
l'histoire sociale</u> at the University of Wisconsin; the Maximin
family for a thorough immersion in the world of French
colonial politics;   the Rice family for long endurance; Claude
Bourdet, Jean   Chesneaux, Daniel Mayer, Rosan Girard, Louis
Odru, Jean Pronteau, and several   other participants (who, I
believe,   for   various   reasons would prefer to remain
unmentioned) for intimate observations; Irwin Wall and Alain
Ruscio for sharing fruits of their own research; Dale Tomich,
Irwin Wall and Bill Hoisington for valuable comments on
various drafts; Mildred Vasan, Debby Dwyer and Loomis Mayer of
Greenwood Press for   expert   editing; Milan Reban for frequent
forums on French Communism; Solveig Olsen and Susan   Todd for
sound advice; Vivien Chan for supportive collegiality; the
International Student   and Scholar Office staff at North Texas
State University for delightful <u>camaraderie</u>; Maryam Salehian,
Sylvia Hsiao-wan Kao, and Cecilia Cervantes for special
encouragement; Clesbie Daniels of Bishop College and Thomas
Hoemeke and the International Education Committee at NTSU for
generous   research   and travel   opportunities;   Micheline
Rice-Maximin for everything.

Accommodation
and
Resistance

Introduction: The Legacy

Despite certain claims later on, neither the French Communists nor the Socialists had a single, unambiguous position on the colonial question prior to World War II. Viewed against a long and complex, sometimes contradictory tradition, the colonial policies adopted by the French Left during the First Indochinese War (1945-1954) become more understandable, if not necessarily more justified in the eyes of some people.

Writing before the main wave of nineteenth century European imperialism, Karl Marx and Friedrich Engels, in their fragmentary texts on the subject, unequivocally condemned colonialism for being an extension of capitalist exploitation. Essentially, they believed that most non-European civilizations were less advanced and that the independence of the colonies could only follow the victory of the European proletariat. Yet, Marx and Engels also gradually perceived that convulsions overseas might help stimulate revolutions in the Metropole, that certain colonial peoples might be able to take the lead in emancipating themselves and, skipping the capitalist stage of development, might move right on to socialism. They generally supported nationalist movements in Poland and Ireland and were sympathetic to anti-European reactions in India and China. (1)

The Socialists of the Second International (1889-1914) were much more involved in the colonial issue, but also more divided. A number of Socialist "revisionists" held that colonialism economically benefitted European workers and was a necessary tutelage for the "backward races." They proposed a progressive and humanitarian "Socialist colonial policy." More traditional Marxists countered that colonialism degraded peoples, whoever practiced it, and was fundamentally injurious to the interests of the European workers, and that, therefore, Socialists had a duty to emancipate the colonial peoples. The traditionalists prevailed in theory, but the Second International became basically revisionist in practice on the colonial question.

In any event, the Socialist reactions were complex. As humanitarians, most condemned the misery caused by colonialism but also did not want the colonized peoples to lapse back into "barbarism." (In France, they were particularly sensitive to the idea of a <u>mission civilisatrice</u> emanating from the French Revolution.) As Marxists, most Socialists condemned the capitalist exploitation of the colonies but also justified a rational use of world resources. As internationalists, they believed in the right of self-determination but also rejected anti-colonial reactions based on nationalism. As pacifists, they realized that colonialism was the source of world conflict but opposed revolutionary violence to end colonialism.

Jean Jaurès, founder of the French Socialist Party, <u>Section française de l'internationale ouvrière</u> (SFIO), did not believe that French civilization was superior, for example, to the Islamic civilizations. He was also acutely aware that colonial expansion threatened world peace and that the colonized peoples, already exhibiting a sense of national consciousness, would resist further subjugation. Yet, Jaurès did not oppose colonial rule in principle and never endorsed violent anti-colonial revolutions. He preferred for the Socialists to promote various reforms to help the overseas peoples to prepare for their eventual independence. (2)

V. I. Lenin, for his part, vigorously denied that the colonial peoples (including the peasantry) were incapable of radically changing their conditions by themselves. Citing the examples of Japan and China, he wrote a celebrated pamphlet, "Backward Europe and Advanced Asia." Yet, he still believed that the European proletariat remained the key to world revolution. Moreover, although he subscribed to the right of self-determination (saying it merited Socialist support), he also cautioned that the right to divorce did not imply the obligation to divorce.

By 1917, Lenin had interpreted imperialism as the fundamental cause of the World War, the root cause of the corruption of the European proletariat (and a prime reason for the collapse of the Second International), and a new source of (potentially revolutionary) contradictions in the capitalist system. Yet, he still held that Europe was the key and that a rebellion in Ireland was worth more than one in a distant colony.

Following their revolution in Russia, the Bolsheviks initially hoped to inspire further revolutions in Europe. When these failed to materialize, however, they were compelled to turn their attention to other theatres. While Lenin did not believe that the European revolution depended entirely upon the Asian, he did insist on the closest possible alliances. Hence, in 1920, the Comintern (Communist International), among its Twenty-one Conditions, instructed member parties to "support, not in words, but in deeds, every emancipation movement in the colonies," better educate the Metropolitan workers on the colonial question, nourish "fraternal feelings" between them and the colonial peoples, and promote "propaganda and systematic agitation" among the colonialist troops. (3)

The Parti communiste français (PCF), formed in 1920 from a majority of the old SFIO, initially followed the Comintern's precepts in theory but paid little attention to colonial problems in practice. The Soviet Union, while keenly concerned about certain areas of the colonial world, remained, for a long time, little interested in the fate of the French Empire. Therefore, the PCF's colonial policies developed pragmatically and largely autonomously. With their overseas implantation virtually limited to North Africa (until after World War II), the PCF saw that the peoples of the French Empire exhibited varying capacities for self-liberation and, therefore, contented itself with a search for a "realistic and effective" policy for a "complex and delicate" situation.

However, when in 1923 one of its Algerian sections (composed mostly of settlers) argued that a colonial revolution would only cause a relapse into feudalism and even barbarism, Leon Trotsky severely chastized the PCF before the Comintern. So did a young Vietnamese Communist, Nguyen Ai Quoc, one of the PCF's founders and the future Ho Chi Minh. Firmly believing that a revolution in Europe would only occur after successful revolutions overseas, he criticized the PCF for its general indifference to colonial problems and offered it suggestions on how best to strengthen its anti-colonial recruitment, propaganda, and education. (4)

After having conceded that it had been "poisoned by the ideology of the old Socialist Party," the PCF then dramatically wished Abd-el-Krim success in his revolution in Morocco. In 1925, it called for fraternization between French soldiers and the people of the Rif, "not a man, not a penny" for the Moroccan War, refusals to manufacture or transport war matériel, and the total evacuation of French forces. The Communists also held demonstrations, distributed anti-war literature among the troops, and, on 12 October 1925, organized a twenty-four-hour general strike involving some 100,000 workers. It was the first Metropolitan political strike against a colonial war and cost some PCF leaders a spell in prison.

During most of the 1920's and into the 1930's, however, the PCF was in general decline at the polling booth, in membership, and in overseas support. Not until roused by the Vietnamese uprisings in 1930 did the PCF again take an active interest in colonial affairs. On Vietnam, it called for total independence, solidarity with the Vietnamese revolutionaries, amnesty for the rebel leaders (for which Parliament censured Maurice Thorez, the Party's Secretary-General), subversive work among the soldiers and sailors, and refusals by French workers to ship arms to Indochina. The PCF even sent a "workers' delegation" to investigate the situation in Indochina. (5)

Meanwhile, the old SFIO, which had gradually surpassed the PCF as the leading left-wing party, remained generally more moderate on the colonial question. Conservative Socialists, especially the representatives of overseas federations, argued that immediate emancipation was impractical and would only reinstitute a reactionary feudalism. Yet, some Socialists were even more radically anti-colonialist than the Communists (and maintained close ties with the Trotskyists). Such men as Paul Rivet, Yves Farge, André Philip, Marceau Pivert, and Daniel Guérin rejected any "civilizing mission" in favor of complete and immediate independence. Profoundly disturbed by the Indochinese insurrections, some even endorsed the necessity of social revolution in the colonies.

A majority of the SFIO, led by Léon Blum and Marius Moutet, firmly rejected violent insurrections and complete independence (except as a long-range goal). Believing that the colonies were indispensable to the world economy, they basically espoused "assimilationism," i.e., the extension overseas of French political and social institutions, education, and culture. While Blum denied any "right of conquest" over "peoples who had not had the opportunity to be part of the white race or the Christian religion," he did believe that the "superior races had a right and a duty to draw to themselves those which had not attained the same degree of culture" and scientific and industrial progress. (6)

In June 1936, the Socialists, Communists, and Radicals won the Popular Front elections in France -- an event which elicited great enthusiasm overseas. While not elaborating a common colonial program, the Popular Front parties did agree on the need to extend civil and political liberties, and the need for amnesty for political prisoners, some local autonomy, the right to unionize, and health and educational facilities in the colonies. Marius Moutet, the new Minister of Colonies, proclaimed that France would take its civilizing mission seriously.

However, colonial officials blocked many of the proposed reforms. Other measures were left stillborn, including independence for Syria, increased citizenship for the Arab-Berber population of Algeria (the famous Blum-Viollette Bill), a Colonial Fund for Economic Development, and even a special Colonial Commission. Moreover, the Popular Front was actually responsible for a fair amount of repression overseas and, despite some liberalization in Indochina, kept thousands of Vietnamese nationalists in jail. As Moutet put it, he did not intend to be the "gravedigger of the colonies."

The PCF, while not participating in the ministry, basically supported the Popular Front's colonial policies. With the increased threat of Fascism (of paramount concern to the Soviet Union), it now argued that the interests of French national defense mitigated against the liberation of the colonies, whose best interests also lay with being associated with France. Moreover, the Communists hoped that, by accepting the "colonial consensus," they would become better integrated with the rest of the French nation. It was a momentous volte face for the Communists, who never again really returned to their more radical days.

Hence, although the Communists never quite subscribed to assimilationism or a Socialist colonial policy, they now basically accepted France's civilizing mission and the idea of

a fraternal union between the colonial peoples and a
"democratic France." Yet, lest repressive colonial policies
drive the overseas peoples, particularly the North Africans,
into the Fascist camp, the Communists urged progressive
reforms, including a purge of the colonial administration and
limited overseas representation in the French parliament, in
order to tie the colonial peoples more closely to the
Metropole. (7)

Throughout the 1930's, the French Left remained seriously
concerned about developments in Indochina. In 1930, the mutiny
of the Vietnamese garrison at Yen Bay had been engineered by
the Vietnamese Nationalist Party (Viet Nam Quoc Dan Dang, or
VNQDD), which was modelled on the Chinese Kuomintang and
essentially represented the petty bourgeois intelligentsia but
lacked roots among the peasantry and urban proletariat. Soon
after Yen Bay, the Indochinese Communist Party (ICP), newly
formed from a variety of small Marxist groups by the future Ho
Chi Minh, organized a number of strikes and even established
peasant "soviets" in two provinces of north central Vietnam.

The French repression of Yen Bay and its sequels was
brutal. Vietnamese villages were bombed by airplanes;
thousands of people, overwhelmingly peasants and some workers,
were imprisoned or executed. The VNQDD was virtually
eliminated as a significant nationalist force, and the way was
cleared for the Communists, who were better capable to survive
underground and to mobilize mass support.

The French Communists (before the Popular Front) now
wanted to abandon Indochina entirely. The Socialists and
Radicals wanted to buttress a non-Communist Vietnamese elite
to prepare for gradual decolonization and to defuse the
Vietnamese Communist movement. Among their suggested reforms
was to make Vietnam an independent, "Associated State."
However, except for expanding agricultural production, the
pre-Popular Front governments generally ignored the warnings.
The Vietnamese Communists revived, expanded to urban areas,
and became active in local politics. Under the Popular Front,
they enjoyed a semi-legal status, for which they postponed the
ideas of violent insurrection and immediate independence.

The Popular Front itself did little to alter traditional
colonial policies in Indochina. Léon Blum's government did
release some 1,200 political prisoners (a small percentage),
promulgate a Labor Code, and slightly increase wages. Yet,
Paris also rejected any policy of industrialization, refused
to permit trade unions, and, fearing to support even
non-Communist nationalists, preferred to preserve the
traditional social and political elite in Vietnam. The French
Socialists feared Vietnamese Communism too much to favor
granting further civil and political liberties. Over none of
this did the French Communists seriously protest.

Thus, on the eve of World War II, France, unlike the
United Kingdom, was yet to entertain any decolonization
strategies. Both the Socialists and Communists shared the
colonial consensus. In Vietnam, most nationalists,
increasingly under the Communist aegis, now realized that
their only recourse was revolution. (8)

NOTES

Notes have been grouped according to topic.

1. Stuart Schram and Hélène Carrère d'Encausse, Marxism and Asia, London, 1969 (including texts), pp. 7-15, 115-125; Karl Marx and Friedrich Engels, On Colonialism, New York, 1972 (selected writings); Grégoire Madjarian, La Question coloniale et la politique du PCF, Paris, 1977, pp. 13-27.

2. Schram and Carrère d'Encausse, pp. 15-16, 125-133; Manuela Semidei, "Les Socialistes français et le problème colonial entre les deux guerres (1919-1939)," La Revue française de sciences politiques, December 1968, pp. 118-1125; Madeleine Rebérioux and Georges Haupt, "Le Socialisme et la question coloniale avant 1914," Le Mouvement social, October-December 1963.

3. Schram and Carrère d'Encausse, pp. 16-31, 134-167; V. I. Lenin, The Right of Nations to Self-Determination, 1916 and Imperialism: The Highest Stage of Capitalism, 1917; Jacob Moneta, Le PCF et la question coloniale, Paris, 1971, p. 17.

4. Moneta, pp. 18-29; Irwin M. Wall, French Communism in the Era of Stalin, Westport, Connecticut, 1983, p. 182; William J. Duiker, The Comintern and Vietnamese Communism, Athens, Ohio, 1975, pp. 3-6; and his The Communist Road to Power in Vietnam, Boulder, 1981, pp. 14-17.

Vietnamese specially trained in the Soviet Union, rather than French Communists, were responsible for the formation and early development of the Indochinese Communist Party.

5. Moneta, pp. 38-40, 44-47, 53-74; Irwin Wall, "The PCF, the Colonial Question, and the Popular Front," paper presented to the International Working Class Conference, Linz, Austria, September 1984, p. 4.

Gauchistes, extreme-left critics, always contrast the PCF's actions against the Rif War to its "opportunism" on colonial issues later on. Even Thorez considered the PCF's activities on Indochina in the early 1930's "scandalously insufficient" compared to those against the Rif War.

6. Semidei, pp. 1125-1152; William B. Cohen, "The Colonial Policy of the Popular Front," French Historical Studies, Spring 1972, pp. 371-374; J. Lagrosillière (SFIO, Martinique), Le Parti socialiste et la question coloniale, Paris, 1926; Daniel Guérin, Au Service des colonisés, 1930-1953, Paris, 1954; and his Front populaire, révolution manquée, témoignage militant, Paris, 1970; Léon Blum, Journal officiel, 10 June, 11 July 1927, pp. 1841, 2528.

On the Rif War, the SFIO, as part of the government, wanted peace but not complete independence or the evacuation of French forces. Significantly, the PCF retreated to the same position in 1926 when it sought an alliance with the

SFIO. See Moneta, pp.   39-40, 53-54, 72-74.

7. Cohen, pp. 375-390; Moneta, pp.   105-143; Maurice
Thorez, La France du Front populaire et les peuples coloniaux,
Paris, 1937; Thomas Adrian Schweitzer, "The French Communist
Party and the Colonial Question, 1928-1939," M.A. Thesis,
University of Wisconsin, 1968.

Wall, op. cit. (unpublished paper), demonstrates that
the PCF's colonial policies changed only gradually, albeit
dramatically, after 1934 and continued to evolve until 1939.

8.   Daniel Hémery, "Aux origines   des   guerres
d'indépendence vietnamiennes: Pouvoir colonial et phénomène
communiste en Indochine avant la Seconde Guerre mondiale," Le
Mouvement social, October-December 1977, pp.   3-35; Andrée
Viollis, Indochine, S.O.S., Paris, 1935 (profoundly influenced
French public -- and PCF -- thinking about Indochina).

PART ONE
THE LEFT IN POWER
1944–1947

I
Liberation
AUGUST 1944–SEPTEMBER 1945

At the time of the liberation of France in late 1944, most French people, including those in the government, were too absorbed by internal affairs and the end of World War II in Europe to pay much attention to far-off Indochina. They little noticed the Japanese take-over of March 1945 or the liberation of Vietnam in the "Revolution of August." French people still spoke easily of the "civilizing mission" of France and the "indefectible attachment of the native peoples." Few realized that the Empire was in jeopardy, and almost no one doubted that Indochina would return to the French fold once the Japanese were defeated.

On these issues the differences between the political Right and Left in France were not great. Even the Communists shared in the great colonial consensus. The main differences were that the Right wanted to subdue the Vietnamese partisans (as well as the Japanese) and re-establish the old colonial order, whereas the Left wanted to permit the Vietnamese some autonomy within a reformed imperial structure called the "French Union." The Provisional Government in Paris, headed by Charles De Gaulle, unable to send French troops to Indochina, reluctantly acknowledged a Vietnamese role in the "common fight" against the Japanese but never once thought of negotiating with a Vietnamese nationalist movement, much less recognizing a separate Vietnamese government. Nor did, initially, the French Communists or Socialists. (1)

The Communists, preoccupied with the struggle against Fascism, were particularly eager to join in the defeat of Japan. In the winter of 1944-1945, many members of the <u>Franc-Tireurs et partisans</u> (FTP, the armed wing of the Resistance) enthusiastically joined the newly formed French Expeditionary Corps to the Far East (a decision later regretted by many leftist soldiers).

The Communists had emerged from the Resistance in a highly patriotic and nationalist mood, determined to restore France as a first-rate power and loathe to see it lose its overseas dependencies. Although more powerful politically, socially, and economically than ever before, they were not

about to make a revolution in France or empathize with
revolutionary movements in the colonies. They only advocated
certain colonial reforms in order to satisfy partially the
aspirations of the overseas peoples and to tie them more
closely to the Metropole.

The PCF had gained enormous prestige and a sort of moral
pre-eminence for having spearheaded the Resistance. Except for
the period of the Nazi-Soviet Pact (1939-1941), its patriotic
credentials were unchallenged. Although it was the _aile
marchante_ of the Resistance and claimed to be the party of
"75,000 _fusillés_" (a gross exaggeration), the PCF, at the time
of the liberation, was revolutionary and Jacobin in
temperament only. Reintegrated into the life of the country,
it had earned the right to some important political positions
without a violent seizure of power. Although some of the
multitude of young and enthusiastic new recruits anticipated
something more adventurous, Stalin and the old PCF leadership
feared that an attempted insurrection would break the unity of
the Resistance, provoke a civil war, and relegate the PCF to
the dreaded political ghetto, if it was not simply crushed by
the American Army. The Soviet Union much preferred a friendly
France whose foreign policy might be shaped partially by a
large, governmental Communist party.

In November 1944, De Gaulle, having included two
Communists in his ministry, got them reluctantly to accept a
dissolution of the _milices patriotiques_ (Patriotic Guards) in
return for the amnesty of their Secretary-General, Maurice
Thorez (who had deserted the army in 1939) and a treaty of
alliance with the Soviet Union. This put an end to any ideas
of a forcible seizure of power. Upon his return to France
from the Soviet Union (where he had spent the war), Thorez
called for unity with Socialists, Catholics, and other
Resistance groups and urged French workers to produce more for
the reconstruction of France. The Communists had not given up
hopes of coming to power but sought it through legal and
democratic means. Had it not been for the Cold War _and_
Indochina, the PCF might very well have succeeded in becoming
a truly National Communist party, preserved left-wing unity,
realized the social and economic programs of the Resistance,
and, perhaps, initiated a peaceful and liberal process of
decolonization.

In the municipal elections in the spring of 1945, the PCF
became the "first party of France," with 30 percent of the
vote. The new _Mouvement républicain populaire_ (MRP) came in
second with 15 percent and the Socialists third with 11
percent. Although De Gaulle refused to reshuffle his cabinet
to reflect the election results, Stalin insisted that the PCF
remain in the government. Moreover, the end of the war
against Nazi Germany, in which the Red Army had played a
preponderant role, provided the PCF with enormous
psychological prestige. By the time of its Tenth Congress in
June 1945, the Party could claim almost 900,000 members and
was aiming at a million. Its daily newspaper, _L'Humanité_,
with a circulation of 456,000, was the most widely-read paper
in France; its evening counterpart, _Ce Soir_, counted 419,000
readers. (In contrast, _Le Figaro_ had 382,000 and _L'Aurore_
101,000.) The Communists also controlled the nation's largest

youth organizations,   particularly   the   Union des jeunesses
républicaines.

     The Communists basically wanted unity -- the unity of the
Resistance forces, unity with the Socialists, the unity of the
trade union movement, and the unity of the overseas   peoples
with the Metropole. Recalling the main tendue of the Popular
Front (1934-1936) and the front français of 1936-1938, they
appealed   to   all "bons français." Declining to attack the
entire bourgeoisie (only the "men of the trusts"), they hoped
to increase their   popularity   among the middle classes, reach
more   social   groups,   and   penetrate more easily into other
movements.   Although   the   unity   of   the   Resistance or the
formation of a single   "French Workers   Party" failed quickly
and completely,   the fusion of the CGT (Confédération générale
du travail), the principal trade union movement, was a lasting
success.   Although the Communists probably never wanted strict
organic unity with the   Socialists,   the   two parties, closely
allied, could   have dominated the government and possibly have
negotiated an early settlement of   the   Indochina   crisis.   A
divided Left,   on   the other hand, made it much easier for the
MRP   and   the   old-style colonialists   to   formulate   colonial
policy.

     The Communists' approach to the   colonial   question
reflected the rest of their political style.   Despite -- or
perhaps because of -- their theoretically powerful   position,
they did not advocate or endorse any radical measures for the
overseas territories. Desiring to remain integrated in the
mainstream of French political life, they also expected the
colonies to remain a part of a   "Greater France," possessing
one hundred million souls (sixty   million   overseas and forty
million in the Metropole), in which the   old   colonial   abuses
would be eradicated and the overseas peoples allowed to share
in all the benefits and reforms of a "progressive and
democratic" France. Such   was   the   enthusiasm and benevolence
many French leftists (and overseas representatives) exhibited
at this time. (2)

     The   Socialists   did not carry the   same   post-Liberation
momentum   as   the   Communists. Although   many   Socialists had
suffered under the   Occupation   and several had been prominent
in the Resistance, a large number of deputies   had   had   to be
expelled   for   having voted full powers   to   Marshal   Philippe
Pétain in 1940. With their party structure   shattered   and   no
longer   being   the   leading left-wing   party,   the   Socialists
developed an inferiority   complex   vis-à-vis   the   Communists.
Nevertheless, although hardly revolutionary,   they   wanted   to
create   a   truly   social   republic   and   use   their   power   to
implement a number of important reforms.

     To   rebuild   its   structure,   the   SFIO   established   a
forty-five-member   Comité   directeur   to   make   most   major
decisions   in   liaison   with   the   Socialist   parliamentarians.
Although   factionalism   (the   traditional   plague   of   the
non-Communist Left) diminished, the   annual   Party   congresses
were   permitted   little   substantial   debate   and   issued   only
general   resolutions   without the   authority   to   enforce   them.
For example, the Socialist   ministers,   parliamentarians,   and
the   Comité   directeur   made   all   the   important   decisions   on

Indochina, ignoring the many congressional resolutions (after 1947) for negotiations with Ho Chi Minh and a cessation of hostilities. Hence, party structure partially determined the SFIO's positions on Indochina.

So did party membership. Not really much of a proletarian party, the SFIO could claim only 20 percent of its members as workers or peasants, whereas the PCF could claim 60 percent. Most Socialist leaders came from the liberal professions, the civil service (especially education), white-collar occupations and bourgeois backgrounds, whereas a sizeable proportion of the PCF parliamentary delegation was proletarian. The Comité directeur contained mostly lawyers, professors, and journalists, and only three workers. Generally, the business and professional elements in the SFIO supported the government's actions in Indochina more than the workers or white-collar employees, and the provincial elements more so than the urbanites.

Finally, certain Socialist personalities strongly influenced policy, above all Léon Blum. Once the most hated man in France as a Jew and the leader of the Popular Front, Blum had defended himself eloquently under Vichy and, after returning from Buchenwald in May 1945, had become, for his Socialist admirers, "beatified in his lifetime." Although he did not stand for elections or continue as editor of Le Populaire, he remained the moral leader of the SFIO and exercised a particularly strong influence over Vincent Auriol, Paul Ramadier and Daniel Mayer. Blum also remained as anti-Communist and anti-Soviet as ever and firmly opposed any exclusive alliance with the PCF. On Indochina he was confused: he strongly opposed the reimposition of colonial rule but also the Communist character of the Vietnamese movement. (3)

During World War II, the Communists, Socialists, and the internal French Resistance in general were much less concerned about the fate of the colonies than were De Gaulle's Free French, for whom Africa was a prime base of support. The charter of the Conseil national de la résistance (CNR) advocated "political, social, and economic rights" for the overseas peoples but not independence. The Communists, who had briefly encouraged colonial revolts during the period of the Nazi-Soviet Pact, quickly reverted to the colonial consensus of the Popular Front once they became active in the Resistance. Indeed, they hoped that the overseas territories would raise an army of one million soldiers for the anti-Fascist struggle. "Greater France" was "one and indivisible."

Free French and Resistance elements first seriously examined the colonial question at the Conference of Brazzaville in early 1944. The delegates were mostly colonial administrators and members (including some Communists and Socialists) of De Gaulle's Consultative Assembly at Algiers. Taking account of the political evolution in the colonies which the war had accelerated, Brazzaville agreed to comprehensive programs of social and economic development and larger measures of political participation in the overseas territories. Cooperation would replace assimilation. However, the Conference emphatically ruled out "any idea of autonomy, any possibility of evolution outside the French bloc of Empire." "The eventual creation, even in the distant future, of <u>self-government</u> for the colonies is to be set aside."

Neither the Communists nor Socialists raised any objections at the time. Socialist Félix Gouin, President of the Algiers Assembly, perhaps best expressed the "spirit of Brazzaville" when he said that the Metropolitan Frenchmen were feeling increasingly responsible to "those creations of our own flesh and blood whom we owe it to ourselves to protect, aid, and assist more each day in order to bring them slowly toward a better future." (4)

A year later, as World War II ended and the colonial problem re-emerged, the Communists declared that times had changed "since one could consider certain races as incompetent and certain peoples as eternally minors." Moreover, "a large measure of international tranquility" depended on the fate of the overseas world. Clearly rejecting the old Empire, they were not too impressed with De Gaulle's idea of a reformed "French Union." "Too often 'new' formulas," wrote Henri Lozeray (the PCF's chief colonial expert) in March 1945, "seem to hide a policy whose basis has not changed."

At the same time, democracy could not come to the colonies until a true democracy was established in France. Explicitly, this meant that the colonial trusts would first have to be destroyed. Implicitly, the PCF would first have to come to power. In any event, the colonies, coveted by other powers, were not in a condition to guarantee their independence and, having been too closely tied to the Metropole by the <u>pacte</u> <u>colonial</u>, were "absolutely incapable of existing economically, and consequently politically, as independent nations." Only "Hitlerian and Trotskyist propaganda" could assert that the PCF was abandoning its traditional position on the colonial and national question and, for "opportunist reasons," was joining the imperialist camp.

At its 1945 Congress, the PCF paid scant attention to colonial problems and none at all to Indochina. Florimond Bonté warned of the "magnates of certain trusts" seeking to "profit from the legitimate dissatisfaction of peoples infatuated with freedom." Everywhere "sly maneuvers, intrigues, provocations" worked to exploit their resources. Thorez emphasized the need to help them industrialize and modernize their agriculture. (Even many non-Communists argued that overseas reforms were necessary to exploit resources more efficiently.) "Well before the proclamation of the Atlantic Charter," Thorez concluded, the Communists had supported the right of self-determination for all peoples. Yet, at the same time, they had always held that the right to divorce did not imply an obligation to divorce.

The PCF (and other liberals) basically proposed political "association" (i.e., participation in the French parliament), "autonomy" (i.e., participation in local administration), mutually beneficial economic exchanges, and a series of social reforms (the complete abolition of forced labor, increased wages, family allocations, social security, trade union rights and collective bargaining, medical care, sanitation, etc.). After all, as one PCF deputy put it, "a black baby is also a French baby, a future producer and a future soldier." (5)

An early test of the PCF's attitude was Algeria, where the Communists complained of "anti-French propaganda by pretended nationalists who chatter about 'independence.'" The feudal Muslim elite (and certain French colonial profiteers) would purposefully exploit racial tensions to keep the Algerians from joining with those Metropolitans fighting to create a new France. On 8 May 1945 (the day of the Nazi surrender), Algerians in several cities demonstrated for independence; in some places, the police fired upon the crowds; in others, riots led to the massacre of some French settlers. Whatever the exact sequence, the resulting repression was severe and included the bombing or shelling of whole towns. Perhaps as many as 40,000 Algerians died. Forty-eight were executed officially and another 2,000 imprisoned.

The PCF's reaction was that "agents of the trusts," "agents provocateurs" (in the service of the .French administration), and "Hitlerian agents" had inspired the demonstrations which, in turn, had caused "violent reprisals against a defenseless population." Both the French and Algerian Communists (largely settlers) called for a "rapid and pitiless punishment" of the organizers of the revolt. (Not until 1958 did the PCF publicly regret this interpretation of events.) (6)

The French Socialists tended to be more paternalistic and assimilationist than the Communists, and not as quick to attack the colonial trusts or the past history of French colonialism. (Younger Socialists were more willing than Third Republic veterans to tamper with the imperial structure.) Yet, most Socialists rejected the pacte colonial and strict assimilationism and accepted the "inevitable evolution" of the overseas territories, short of complete independence or substantial autonomy.

At the first post-war SFIO congress, in November 1944, Marius Moutet, former Minister of Colonies under the Popular Front, denounced the "intolerable oppression" endured by the colonial peoples, and called for "development" to replace exploitation. The Socialists had an "emancipating duty" to raise "the state of the economy and the intellectual, moral and social level of the natives" through improvements in sanitation, education, social security, public works, and the granting of "essential political rights" which would permit the overseas peoples "to associate more closely every day with the government and administration of their country." (7)

Such were the attitudes of the French Left on the eve of the Vietnamese thrust for independence in the summer of 1945. During World War II, the Vietminh ("League for the Independence of Vietnam"), formed by Ho Chi Minh in 1941, was the only nationalist group effectively operating on Vietnamese soil. Spearheaded by the old Indochinese Communist Party, the Vietminh was mostly a broad coalition of Vietnamese nationalists.   By the beginning of 1945, Admiral Jean Decoux's collaborationist regime had been discredited, and Japan's defeat, though not imminent, was inevitable. On 9 March 1945, however, the Japanese quickly struck, occupied all the major centers of Vietnam, easily overcame the French, and installed the young titular emperor, Bao Dai, who, in turn, immediately declared Vietnamese independence from France.

Two weeks later, on 24 March, De Gaulle's Provisional Government in Paris responded with a new statute for the "Indochinese Federation" which promised a "freedom commensurate with its degree of evolution" within the "French Union" (the first use of this term). The Indochinese would elect a "federal government" presided over by and responsible to the French Governor-General, but France would retain control of all foreign relations, and Vietnam would remain divided into three distinct "countries" (Tonkin, Annam, and Cochinchina.) (8)

The French Left received only confused information. The PCF press reported a "fierce and courageous" resistance by French soldiers and "an intense guerilla war" by the Indochinese people. It dismissed Bao Dai's "pro-Fascist clique" but all but ignored the Vietminh. Avoiding direct comment on the 24 March proclamation, the PCF wanted the "highly evolved" peoples of Indochina to be granted "substantial democratic liberties" in order to unite them in "a vast and unanimous fighting movement" alongside "the national and democratic forces of the great Chinese Republic" (referring no doubt to Chiang Kai-shek's government).

The Socialists recognized both a French and Vietnamese resistance but ignored Bao Dai. They fully endorsed De Gaulle's Proclamation, saying that the fidelity of the Indochina resistance required a "generous policy" and that Indochina should enjoy a "proper freedom" within the French Union. This was the only realistic way to protect French interests. Neither the PCF nor the SFIO press mentioned Indochina again until the end of August. (9)

Even the French parliament was little interested. A half-empty session in March 1945, the first devoted to colonial matters, revealed how insulated Paris was from overseas events and how much the deputies lived in the imperial past. A commission proposed to reorganize the Ministry of Colonies and to develop a comprehensive economic and social plan so that the overseas peoples could "evolve socially and morally" and be trained "to render us immense services." Gaston Monnerville (French Guiana), a centrist and the commission's chair, said that France had finally to "realize what is meant by the 'white man's burden.'" The Socialists and Communists were more liberal. Paul Valentino (SFIO, Guadeloupe) portrayed Brazzaville more as a beginning than a culmination. So did André Mercier (PCF), who feared that a serious overseas malaise could feed separatist movements with anti-French propaganda. (10)

Well before the end of World War II, the Communists, Socialists, and De Gaulle, well aware of a strong anti-colonial sentiment in Washington, worried about American

a real popular front and at that time enjoyed full support
from the people." The OSS team returned to its quarters that
evening to celebrate quietly the Vietnamese "Fourth of July."
(13)

NOTES

Notes have been grouped according to topic.

1. D. Bruce Marshall, <u>The French Colonial Myth and
Constitution-Making in the Fourth Republic</u>, New Haven, 1973,
pp. 190-194.

2. Stephane Courtois, <u>Le PCF dans la guerre</u>, Paris, 1980,
pp. 457-468; Jacques Fauvet, <u>Histoire du parti communiste
français de 1920 à 1976</u>, Paris, 1977, pp. 337-349; Alfred J.
Rieber, <u>Stalin and the French Communist Party, 1941-1947</u>, New
York, 1962, pp. 55-79, 108-109, 123-124, 152-154, 213-217;
Philippe Robrieux, <u>Histoire intérieure du Parti communiste
français</u>, Vol. II, <u>1945-1972</u>, Paris, 1981, pp. 19, 30-34,
41-42, 75-78, 83-85, 101-106; Unir (dissident Communists),
<u>Histoire du Parti communiste français</u>, Vol. III, <u>De 1945 à nos
jours</u>, Paris, n.d. (ca. 1960), pp. 7-11; Ronald Tiersky, <u>The
French Communist Party, 1920-1972</u>, New York, 1974; pp.
113-120; Irwin M. Wall, <u>French Communism in the Era of Stalin</u>,
<u>1945-1962</u>, Westport, Conn., 1983, pp. 29-35.

Most commentators agree that the PCF did not seriously
contemplate a violent seizure of power at the time of the
liberation, and Thorez's return effectively ended any
"adventurous" thinking. However, the Communists were prepared
to pursue a "<u>strategie de rupture</u>" if other groups would not
collaborate. The PCF later defended its post-liberation
posture and condemned Charles Tillon and André Marty for
having wanted to start an insurrection. See Courtois, <u>op.
cit.</u> and <u>L'Humanité</u>, 4 October 1952, and Roger Garaudy, "Le
Néo-Blanquisme," <u>Cahiers du communisme</u>, January 1953.

3. Roger Quilliot, <u>La SFIO et l'exercice du pouvoir</u>,
<u>1944-1958</u>, Paris, 1972, pp. 1-31; Owen Roberts, "The French
Socialist Party and Its Indochina Policy, 1946-1951," Ph.D.
Thesis, Columbia University, 1955, pp. 50-72, 130-134; Blum,
<u>Le Populaire</u>, 5, 11 July 1945.

4. Marshall, pp. 80-81, 93-98, 102-115 (Gouin); Forimond
Bonté (PCF), <u>Journal officiel, débats parlementaires,
Assemblée consultative provisoire</u> (JODPACON), 13, 18 January
1944.

5. Grégoire Madjarian, <u>La Question coloniale et la
politique de Parti communiste français, 1944-1947</u>, Paris,
1977, pp. 53-65; PCF, <u>Au Service de la renaissance française</u>,
Paris, (Fall) 1944, pp. 13-14, 82, 104-112, 127; Henri
Lozeray, "La Question coloniale," <u>Cahiers du communisme</u>, April
1945; Bonté, "La France et l'organisation de la paix," Report
to the Tenth PCF Congress, Paris, 1946, pp. 29-30; Thorez,
"Une Politique française: Renaissance, démocratie, unité,"
Report to the Tenth PCF Congress, Paris, 1946, p. 53,

Oeuvres, Vol. 21, p.   25.

6. Madjarian, pp.   93–117; Unir, September 1961; Joany
Berlioz, "L'Afrique du Nord, foyer d'activité pro–Hitlérienne
et antifrançaise," Cahiers du communisme, February 1945, pp.
47–53, August 1958, p.   16; L'Humanité,   12 May 1945, 21 June
1958; Alain Ruscio, Les Communistes français et la guerre
d'Indochine, 1944–1954, Paris, 1985, pp.   123–124 (denies that
Air Minister Tillon was responsible for the bombardments).

Similarly, the PCF condemned the uprisings in Syria in
May 1945 as "Doriotiste" (after Jacques Doriot, the former
Communist who, after leading the anti–colonial campaigns of
the 1920's, had turned Fascist in the 1930's) for putting "in
peril the traditional influence of France with the countries
of the Levant." The Soviet Union's recognition of Syrian and
Lebanese independence in 1946 was the only instance, in the
post–World–War–II period, when it conflicted sharply with PCF
colonial policy. See Madjarian, pp.   66–76; L'Humanité, 1, 2,
5, 20 June 1945; JODPACON, 16 June 1945.

7. SFIO, "Les Décisions du congrès national
extraordinaire, 9–12 Novembre 1944," Paris, n.d.

8. Journal officiel, décrets, 24 March 1945, pp.
1606–1607.

9. Ce Soir, 13, 27 March 1945; "Coup de force du Japon
militariste et fasciste contre les peuples d'Indochine,"
Cahiers du communisme, April 1945, pp. 93–94. Le Populaire,
11–12, 24, 26 March 1945.

10. JODPACON, 19 March 1945, pp.   556–571, 20 March 1945,
579–586, 596.

11. United States–Vietnam Relations, 1945–1967, (Pentagon
Papers), Washington, 1971, Vol. VII, Roosevelt, Teheran, 28
November 1943, p.   24; Roosevelt to the Secretary of State
(SOS), 24 January, 16 October 1944, pp.   30, 35–37; Roosevelt,
Yalta, 8 February 1945, p.   59; Foreign Relations of the
United States (FRUS), 1945, I, Charles Taussig, 15 March 1945,
p. 124; Walter LeFeber, "Roosevelt, Churchill and Indochina,
1942–1945," American Historical Review, December 1975, pp.
1277–1295; Edward R. Drachman, United States Policy Toward
Vietnam, 1940–1945, Rutherford, N. J., 1970.

An angry De Gaulle told Ambassador Jefferson Caffery that
American refusals to transport a French Expeditionary Corps to
Southeast Asia might drive France into the Soviet orbit. (The
French later reassured an American official that "colored
troops" in the planned expedition would be replaced by
"trained European volunteers.") See FRUS, 1945, VI, Far East
(FE), Caffery, 13, 24 March, pp.   300, 302; H. Freeman
Matthews, Europe (EUR), 23 May, pp.   309–311.

12. Pentagon Papers, VIII, Memorandum for the President
(Truman), "Suggested Re–examination of American Policy with
Respect to Indochina," pp.   4–21; Brassin de Saint Didier,
French Military Mission, to General Marshall, 29 May 1945,
pp.   34–35. United States, National Archives, Diplomatic

Series (USNADS) 851.00G, Dunn to Grew, 23 April 1945; Blakeslee, April 1945, in Gareth Porter, Vietnam: The Definitive Documentation of Human Decisions, Stanfordville, N. Y., 1979, pp. 23-27; FRUS, 1945, VI (FE), Grew to Caffery, 9 May, to Truman, 16 May, memorandum, 31 May, pp. 307-308, 311.

13. Archimedes L. A. Patti, Why Vietnam? Berkeley, 1980, pp. 125-133, 155, 178-181, 248-253; Philippe Devillers, Histoire du Vietnam, 1940-1952, Paris, 1952, pp. 132-143; Jean Sainteny, Histoire d'une paix manquée, 1945-1947, Paris, 1967, pp. 92-93; Charles B. McLane, Soviet Strategies in Southeast Asia, Princeton, 1966, pp. 249-250; J. Frankel, "Soviet Policy in Southeast Asia," in Max Beloff, Soviet Policy in the Far East, 1944-1951, London, 1953, p. 208.

II
The French Return
SEPTEMBER 1945–MARCH 1946

In the "Revolution of August," unlike most colonial revolutions, the Vietnamese did not directly liberate themselves from their colonial masters. What ensued was more a war of reconquest (or aggression) by the French.

The DRV tried to rule effectively and popularly right from the start. It launched a massive education and literacy campaign and suppressed the state-controlled monopolies on alcohol, salt, and opium (leaving customs as the only real source of revenue), but undertook no social-economic revolution, no widespread division of the land. Independence came first; socialism would come later. Reasonably maintaining public order and essential services, the DRV's control ran most smoothly in Tonkin and Annam. Even in Cochinchina, despite a number of competing Vietnamese factions and an angry and vindictive French population, it governed reasonably well. Had it not been for outside intervention, the DRV probably would not have been seriously challenged even in the south. (1)

The Allied Conference at Potsdam in July 1945, however, had decided to divide Vietnam into two zones (at the sixteenth parallel) for the purpose of accepting the Japanese rendition. In September, an inordinately large Chinese Nationalist army entered from the north, seized control of customs, and resorted to widespread pillaging. It also brought in its wake a number of anti-Vietminh groups but did little to disturb the DRV's existence. In Cochinchina, a British army (made up mostly of Indian troops) entered under General Douglas Gracey, a typical colonial officer who flatly refused to work with the DRV authorities in Saigon. When the Vietnamese responded with a series of strikes, he instituted martial law. Then, he released French colonial troops from Japanese prisons, enabling Colonel Jean Cédille, on 22–23 September, to conduct a fast and brutal coup d'état. Although "welcomed on arrival by the Vietminh," Gracey later said, "I promptly kicked them out." Thus began the First Indochinese War.

Intense fighting in and around Saigon continued for several weeks. Short of manpower, the British and the French resorted to re-arming the Japanese. "If there is anything that makes my blood boil," General Douglas MacArthur commented, "it is to see our Allies in Indochina and Java deploying Japanese troops to reconquer the little people we promised to liberate. It is the most ignoble kind of betrayal." In October, large detachments of French troops under the command of General Philippe Leclerc (the "liberator of Paris") began arriving in the Saigon area. So also did Admiral Thierry d'Argenlieu, the new French High Commissioner. The British pulled out in January. (2)

Although the United States was little likely to recognize the DRV, OSS agents had reported from the beginning that, despite being "composed strictly of left-wing elements," it was in "full control," "well organized," and enthusiastically supported by the majority of the people. Major General Philip E. Gallagher, head of the American military mission, found the Vietminh the "dominant force" and "definitely in the saddle." While not ready for self-government, the DRV's administration was "remarkably effective" and, despite the "earmarks of some Russian influence," was not a "full-fledged doctrinaire" Communist government. Yet, Gallagher believed the French could crush the Vietminh with a couple of divisions. (3)

In any event, American sympathies for the DRV never went any further. On 5 October, Washington declared firmly that

> the United States has no thought of opposing the re-establishment of French control in Indochina; and no official statement by the United States government has questioned, even by implication, French sovereignty over Indochina. However, it is not the policy of this government to assist the French to re-establish their control over Indochina by force; and the willingness of the United States to see French control re-established assumes that the French claim to have the support of the population is borne out by future events.

Seriously disappointed, Ho Chi Minh wrote directly to President Truman and Secretary of State James F. Byrnes, recalling how the Vietminh had collaborated with the Allies, asking for DRV representation in the United Nations, and imploring the United States to live up to its professed ideals. Washington never responded to any of his eight separate requests. (4)

Ho Chi Minh also appealed to the leaders of the three main French political parties (Thorez, Blum, and Bidault) to approach the Indochina question with the ideals of the French Revolution:

> I can assure you, gentlemen, that if France agrees to recognize the independence of Vietnam, the Vietnamese people will be very much in

accord with France. If not, the Vietnamese
people are determined to bleed until the last
drop of blood to protect their country.

In Vietnam, Major Patti talked with two French Socialist
professors (and a Popular Republican) who, after having
participated in the liberation of Paris, had gone to Vietnam
and had organized students during the August Revolution.
However, they did not accept complete Vietnamese independence
and wanted France once more to be a great power. They
believed that, with a left-wing government in Paris, Vietnam
would become a sister-nation within the Francophone community,
but they were disappointed that no one in France, except De
Gaulle, seemed much concerned about Indochina. To Patti, these
men did not sound much different than Sainteny. (5)

Although the French Communists were disappointed that the
French army itself could not have received the Japanese
surrender, they accepted the Potsdam arrangements and were
relieved that the United States had not contested French
sovereignty. On 20 September, the PCF's Political Bureau
noted the popularity of the "Vietminh's provisional
government" (even in Cochinchina), called Bao Dai a "traitor"
and "collaborator," found General Leclerc's reaffirmation of
De Gaulle's March Proclamation "a regrettable step backward,"
and endorsed the principles of the United Nations Charter
against "certain imperialist intrigues" aimed at both France
and Indochina.

When the fighting began, the PCF severely denounced
"British imperialism" and the "scandalous" use of Japanese
troops, reported that the Vietnamese in Saigon had "fiercely
defended themselves, fighting foot by foot, from house to
house," accused the French government of repeating the same
"pernicious" and "anti-democratic" policy which had led to the
"loss" of Syria and Lebanon, and insisted that France
negotiate with the Vietnamese on a new basis. The Communists
feared that continued bloodshed would "put between Annam and
us an unbridgeable gulf and alienate us forever from her
heart." In November, steel workers in Paris "vigorously
protested" against the use of force against the "Annamite
peoples" and the arrest of Indochinese leaders in France and
called for the "unity of the Metropolitan and colonial
peoples." Although a CGT leader assured the Indochinese of
the full support of his movement, there were no strikes or
demonstrations.

Harold Isaacs, an American correspondent, asked some
Vietnamese Communists if they expected any help from the
Russians or the French Communists. "The Russians are
nationalists for Russia first and above all," one said
bitterly. "They would be interested in us only if we served
some purpose of theirs." As for the French Communists,
another one snorted with disgust that they were "Frenchmen and
colonialists first and Communists after. In principle they
are for us, but in practice? Oho, that is quite another
thing!" Still another spoke contemptuously of Thorez's
talking of the Vietnamese "finally arriving at their
independence": "A fine rubber phrase, is it not? . . . No, I
am afraid we cannot depend on these fine gentlemen. They are

the dominant party in France. And look what Frenchmen are
doing now in Indochina."

In September 1945, French leftists in Saigon, mostly
Socialists   such   as Louis Caput, formed   a Marxist Cultural
Group (GCM). Never having more than thirty members, the GCM
interceded with d'Argenlieu and other French authorities on
behalf of the Vietminh, served as an effective liaison between
French progressives and the Vietminh, and provided the PCF and
SFIO with useful information.   Although it worked closely with
other   liberal   groups in Saigon, the GCM eventually became
oriented to the positions of the PCF. (Between October 1946
and February 1947, except during the Haiphong crisis, the GCM
published an influential newspaper, Lendemains.)

In the fall of 1945, however, Isaacs learned that only
one member of the GCM had rallied to the Vietnamese. Indeed,
the group had distributed a circular on 25 September urging
the Vietnamese not to act "too rashly," to do nothing to
embarrass the Franco-Soviet alliance, to await the election of
the Constituent Assembly in France, when increased left-wing
strength might assure them a better settlement, and to send
emissaries to Moscow and Paris to become better acquainted
with "the perspectives of coming events." To Isaacs, the
document "displayed with remarkable and unusual bluntness" the
PCF's notion of the relation between a revolutionary movement
and Soviet foreign policy. "Bitten deeply with the bitterness
of having been abandoned by their ideological comrades," the
Vietnamese Communists decided in November to dissolve the old
Indochinese Communist Party. Oppressed by a "fearful sense of
loneliness," expecting no help from the Chinese, Americans,
Russians, or French Communists, Isaacs concluded, they sought
refuge in their own nationalism.   (6)

Initially, Socialists in France denied the popularity of
the Vietminh, asserted that Vietnamese independence was
unrealistic, and adhered to the 24 March Declaration. Yet,
admiring the British and Dutch proposals for Burma and
Indonesia, they hinted that Indochina might evolve toward a
fuller democracy within a few years. Le Populaire doubted the
"Annamite elements which fight the Allied forces" had the
support of the Indochinese people, believed they were "only a
Fifth Column organized by the Japanese," and suggested the new
regime would end up in a dictatorship.   Marius Moutet wrote
that there was too much diversity in Indochina -- five
"countries" with distinct histories and ethnic groups at
various stages of development -- to permit the formation of a
viable nation-state. France had to remain also to protect
Cambodia and Laos from "Annam." The Vietminh were being misled
by Russian, Chinese and American ideologies and might succumb
to the domination of another power.   Their "intelligence,
will-power and high-mindedness" were inadequate without French
personnel and material resources.

So, at the beginning, only the French Trotskyists fully
endorsed the Vietnamese Revolution. They called for "total
solidarity with the Indochinese people in the struggle against
French imperialism," "not a man, not a penny for the purposes
of imperialistic pillage," and the complete withdrawal of the
French Army. Most immediately, they urged French workers and

dockers to refuse to transport arms destined for Indochina. (7)

Most French people, as we have said, were much more concerned about internal matters, such as the election of a Constituent Assembly. In the referenda and elections of 21 October, 66 percent of the electorate rejected the Communist proposal for a "sovereign Assembly" (and weak executive) but gave the PCF 26 percent of the vote and 160 seats in the Constituent Assembly. The Socialists came in second with 24 percent and 142 seats, which disappointed them. (The MRP got 23.6 percent and 152 seats.) Together the two left-wing parties had a bare majority. Yet, the new Communist electorate was neither revolutionary nor ideologically committed to Socialism. Drawn mostly from certain rural areas active in the Resistance, it supported the PCF basically as the leading "democratic" and "republican" party. This development reinforced the PCF's non-revolutionary ambitions to be a popular, respectable governmental party -- a posture which could not fail to affect its Indochina policy. (8)

Following the elections, the Communists proposed a "Popular Front" coalition with the Socialists and Radicals. The Socialists, however, refused to exclude the MRP. Moreover, De Gaulle became Premier and denied the Communists a key ministry, giving them, instead, four minor posts: Economy, Armaments (Charles Tillon), Industrial Production, and Labor, with Thorez named as a Minister of State. The PCF thus had no direct influence over foreign or colonial policies. Within a couple of months, the Socialists (pushed by their leftwing) -- significantly, not the Communists -- provoked a major crisis by proposing to limit the powers of the executive and to cut the military budget by 20 percent. When they eventually got Communist and Radical support, De Gaulle dramatically resigned on 20 January 1946. (9)

The PCF now proposed an essentially Communist-Socialist government headed by Thorez but met the determined opposition of the Socialists, the MRP and the military, all of whom realized, among other things, that the United States would not give economic aid to such a regime. So, instead, the three major parties agreed to a tripartite coalition. Félix Gouin (SFIO) became Premier, Thorez Vice Premier, Moutet Minister of Overseas France, Georges Bidault (MRP) remained Foreign Minister, and the PCF got two more minor ministries. American officials hoped the new arrangement (considered more satisfactory than De Gaulle's) would curb Communist radicalism and lead to a more "conciliatory and moderate" colonial policy. The Communists did, indeed, collaborate well with the other ministers and even supported Bidault's demands for the dismemberment of Germany, though this conflicted with Soviet policy. Thorez exhibited all the qualities of a good minister, with a taste for hard work, order, and authority. Indeed, some people quipped that he and Jacques Duclos were the only two Frenchmen not to read L'Humanité. (10)

In Vietnam, as d'Argenlieu proceeded to set up a separate Vietnamese Assembly for Cochinchina, the DRV, in January, held the first and only national elections in Vietnamese history until 1976. Although the pro-Chinese elements were guaranteed a certain number of seats and ministerial portfolios, the results were an overwhelming victory for the Vietminh. American observers said that the elections were held under reasonably free conditions and that 82 percent of the people had voted (even in Saigon) in "an efficient and orderly fashion."

Some commentators, however, have ascribed the results to the "enthusiasm of the moment" and the inexperience of an illiterate people. The choice of the voters was limited, and former "collaborators" and other "suspect" elements were not permitted to run. "But was this not the common lot of all liberated countries?" Devillers asks. "In France herself, at this time, was the choice so broad" that there could have been certain Munichois or pro-Vichy candidates? In the new Vietnamese government, Communists held four of twelve ministries, and non-Communists occupied the posts of Foreign Affairs and Defense. (The parliament voted a Constitution in November 1946 which followed a Western democratic style, similar to the French Constitution, and not at all like that of the Soviet Union or the "Popular Democracies" of Eastern Europe.) (11)

In Paris, the Communists wanted formally to recognize the DRV, while the MRP felt the best way to preserve the old colonial interests was through negotiations. Military leaders, although confident about the pacificiation of Cochinchina, did not believe that French forces could re-enter Tonkin without a heavy loss of life, much less reconquer the entire country.

General Leclerc, actually the Comte de Hautecloque, a conservative Catholic aristocrat and ardent Gaullist, keen to maintain a French presence in Indochina, appreciated that a guerilla war would consume more years and resources than France could sustain. He also believed that Ho Chi Minh, being less anti-French than the pro-Chinese Vietnamese, would probably accept a compromise. Leclerc thus gained the reputation of being a liberal; some people believe that had he been High Commissioner instead of d'Argenlieu (likewise a Catholic aristocrat and ardent Gaullist), full-scale war might have been avoided.

Commissioner Sainteny, whose wife was the daughter of Albert Sarraut, a former Governor-General of Indochina, came from a conservative family and had strong financial ties to the colonial regime. In some respects he was the Jacques Sadoul of the Vietnamese Revolution (Sadoul having been the French liaison with the Bolsheviks in 1917-1918.) Certainly he was the French official closest to the Vietminh leadership and well appreciated their hold over the Vietnamese people. Nevertheless, in 1946, Sainteny was a highly dedicated French colonialist who, except for an abiding personal admiration for Ho Chi Minh, was never seduced by the Vietnamese Revolution (as Sadoul had been by the Bolsheviks). Often lamenting that the Vietnamese failed to appreciate French accomplishments in Indochina, he at no time suggested that the French abandon their "legitimate interests." He believed the Vietnamese were a gullible people, "seriously misled" by the Japanese, Chinese and, above all, by the Americans. Yet, all this only further convinced him that the French could only return through negotiations.

Ho Chi Minh, totally isolated in the international arena and little prepared for full-scale war, also wanted to negotiate. He was prudent, calculating but not bloodthirsty, and extremely patient. Neither doctrinaire nor sectarian nor necessarily anti-French, he was willing to settle issues without recourse to violence. He also knew that France was his only source of economic and technical assistance and that its support might help him deal with the pro-Chinese opposition. Finally, as a cosmopolitan Communist, he may very well have hoped that peaceful progress in Vietnam would set an important precedent for the other colonies. (12)

Thus, with the full backing of the tripartite ministry in Paris, though not that of d'Argenlieu, Sainteny signed a "Preliminary Convention" with Ho Chi Minh on 6 March which recognized the "Republic of Vietnam as a free state having its government, parliament, army, and finances, comprising a part of the Indochinese Federation of the French Union." The French promised to settle the question of Cochinchina by referendum and, in a military annex, agreed to withdraw their troops progressively over the next five years.

France thus became the first white power (before the Netherlands, the United Kingdom, or the United States) to come to terms with Asian nationalism. Sainteny was pleased that war had been avoided, but Ho Chi Minh was more reserved: "In the final analysis you are the ones who have gained. You know very well that I wanted more than that, but I also understand that we cannot have everything in one day." Vietnamese General Vo Nguyen Giap compared the Accords to the necessary settlement the Bolsheviks had had to make with the Germans at Brest-Litovsk in 1918.

Indeed, both sides looked upon the Accords as a temporary compromise. The clauses were simply too ambiguous. Vietnam had her own government, finances, and army; but France controlled foreign relations, customs, and the overall military command. On both sides people were hoping to buy time in order to prepare better for war. Nevertheless, the Vietnamese probably benefitted more from the Accords than the French. Five years of peace would enable Ho Chi Minh to consolidate his regime and gradually replace the French -- a development the latter were not slow to grasp. Certainly the Vietnamese never wanted to return to the situation prior to the Accords, whereas many French leaders definitely did. To the Vietnamese, the March Accords were a basis for further negotiations; for the French they were, at best, a culmination.

In any event, as the only treaty between France and the DRV until the Geneva Accords of 1954, the March 1946 Accords constituted an important legal basis for the recognition of the DRV as the government of Vietnam. Opponents of the war always referred to these Accords in insisting that negotiations be undertaken with, and only with, Ho Chi Minh. (13)

Generally, the French Left supported the Accords. Only the Trotskyists criticized Ho Chi Minh for wanting to remain in the French Union, all because the Soviet Union feared American imperialism in Indochina. Similarly, Jean-Paul Sartre's journal, Les Temps modernes, argued that the Vietnamese had been quite capable of governing themselves before the arrival of the French and still were, and that only France threatened her independence.

The Socialists were proud that their own Premier and Overseas Minister had backed the negotiations. Although France could have easily scored a military victory, it would not have been worth the cost. "How many deaths, how much destruction and never-quenched hatred would have been engendered by a new and very long military campaign?" wrote Oreste Rosenfeld, a Socialist expert on colonial affairs. "The time is past for occupations maintained by brutal force." Yet, "we must proceed in stages." André Labrouquère observed: "We cannot be satisfied if, finally laying down the heavy white man's burden, we are not certain of leaving our proteges' future to a really democratic government."

The Communists saw the Accords in the best interests of both countries, reinforcing their ties in the "democratic family of the French Union," but warned that reactionary military elements and the colonialist trusts might undermine them. The March 1946 Accords became a cornerstone of PCF policy for several years. Although the PCF avoided trying to resolve the inherent ambiguities, it always insisted that the Accords had recognized the DRV as the sole, legitimate government of Vietnam, denied legitimacy to other Vietnamese representatives, and defended Vietnam's territorial integrity. (14)

Was the PCF responding primarily to its own national interests or to directives from the Soviet Union? Probably to both. The European Communist parties did not have a common approach to colonial issues. In terms of size and governmental influence, the Italian Communists most closely resembled the French, but Italy had no colonies. The British did have colonies, but their Communist Party was extremely small and without any governmental influence and, moreover, agreed with the ruling Labour Party's advocacy of independence for India and Burma. In Belgium, Communists held minor posts in the ministry, but none of their colonies were in revolt. The East Indies were in revolt, but the Dutch Communists were not part of the government. The Indonesian Communists, moreover, unlike the Vietnamese, were not the leaders of the revolution, and the Dutch Communists did not advocate Indonesian independence until both the Soviet Union and United States did in 1947.

The Soviet Union was too preoccupied with its own post-war reconstruction and too much in need of a rapprochement with France to promote revolution in any French colony. Even if the PCF had been a much smaller and less influential party, it might not have taken a more radical position on Indochina. As a large influential governmental party, it had less reason. The interests of the USSR and the PCF converged remarkably well on the colonial question in general and on the Vietnamese Revolution in particular.

NOTES

    Notes have been grouped according to topic.

    1. Jean Chesneaux, Contribution à l'histoire de la nation
vietnamienne, Paris, 1955, pp. 234-243; Philippe Devillers,
Histoire du Vietnam, 1940-1952, Paris, 1952, pp.   177-185;
Archimedes L. A. Patti, Why Vietnam? Berkeley,   1980, pp.
294-296;   Ellen J. Hammer, The Struggle for   Indochina,
1940-1955, Stanford, 1966, pp. 145-146.

    Vietnamese Catholics asked the Pope's blessing for the
new regime, and their bishops complained that their "dear
country" was "being invaded" and was "defending   its
independence." See Témoignage chrétien, 30 November 1945.

    2. Devillers, pp.   163-170, 191-202; George Rosie, The
British in Vietnam: How the Twenty-Five Year War Began,
London, 1971, and "Britain Re-Arms the Japanese," London
Sunday Times Magazine, 11 June 1972, pp.   30-33; Concerned
Asian Scholars, The Indochina Story, New York, 1970, p.   13
(MacArthur's statement).

    3. United States National Archives, Diplomatic Series
(USNADS) 851.00G, General William J. Donovan, OSS Director,
Memoranda for SOS James F. Byrnes, 5-6 September 1945, in
Gareth Porter, editor, Vietnam: The Definitive Documentation,
Stanfordville, N. Y., 1979, pp. 71-72; U.S. Senate, 92nd
Congress, 2nd Session, 1973, Committee on Foreign Relations,
Hearings on the Causes, Origins and Lessons of the Vietnam
War, pp.   251-262; Gallagher to McClure, Kunming, 20 September
1945, Memorandum (meeting with Ho Chi Minh), 29 September
1945, Gallagher Papers, Center for Military History, U.S.
Army, Washington, D.C., in Porter, pp.   77-78, 80-81; Foreign
Relations of the United States (FRUS), 1946, VIII, Far East
(FE), Sharp, Southeast Asia (SEA), Memorandum of Conversation
with General Gallagher et alii, 20 January, pp.   15-20.

    4. FRUS, 1945, Vol. VI (FE), Acting SOS Acheson to
Robertson (China), 5 October, p.   313; United States,
Department of Defense, United States-Vietnam Relations,
1940-1967 (Pentagon Papers), Washington, 1971, Book I, Ho Chi
Minh to Truman, 17 October 1945, pp.   73-74, to SOS Byrnes, 22
October 1945, pp.   80-81, to Byrnes, 1 November 1945, p.   90,
to Truman, 16 February 1946, pp.   95-97.

    In 1919, Ho Chi Minh, then known as Nguyen Ai Quoc, had
asked Presidènt Woodrow Wilson to apply the Fourteen Points to
Vietnam and the rest of the colonial world.   Wilson never
responded, but the authors of the Pentagon Papers did locate
the request in the National Archives.

    5. Ho Chi Minh, Appeals by Chairman Ho (1941-1949),
Hanoi, 1958, p.   55, in Porter, pp.   87-88; Patti, pp.
282-284.

6. Ce Soir, 29 September, 9, 11, 18, 23, 24, 30 October 1945; L'Humanité, 15, 21 September, 9, 10, 13 October, 14, 19 November 1945; Charles Fourniau and Alain Ruscio, "Le PCF face au déclenchement de la première guerre d'Indochine," Cahiers d'histoire de l'Institut Maurice Thorez, Nos. 19, 22, 1976-1977, p. 201; Ruscio, "Le Groupe culturel marxiste de Saigon, 1945-1950," ibid., No. 31, 1979, pp. 187-208; Ruscio, Les Communistes français et la guerre d'Indochine, Paris, 1985, pp. 89-95, 315-332; Grégoire Madjarian, La Question coloniale et la politique du PCF, 1944-1947, Paris, 1977, pp. 141-147; Harold Isaacs, No Peace for Asia, New York, 1947, pp. 172-175.

Until 1950 the ICP survived only as a Marxist study group. The PCF did not criticize its dissolution as it had that of the American Communist Party during World War II.

7. Le Populaire, 31 August, 2-3, 24, 29 September, 23 October, (Moutet) 22, 26, 27 December 1945. See also Moutet Papers, Ministry of Overseas France, Carton 8, Dossier 169. La Vérité (Trotskyist), 4, 13 October, 9, 19 November 1945.

8. Paul-Marie De la Gorce, L'Après-Guerre, Paris, 1978, pp. 104-112, 125-143; Georgette Elgey, Histoire de la IVe République, Vol. I, Paris, 1965, pp. 49-56, 60-62.

During the referenda campaign, the Délégation des Gauches (Communists, Socialists, Radicals, the CGT, and the League of the Rights of Man) called for "immediate talks with the most representative elements" of Vietnam in order to "prepare by a common accord an evolution of these peoples towards a very large autonomy."

9. De la Gorce, pp. 113-123, 143-145; Elgey, pp. 62-95.

10. Elgey, pp. 99-113; FRUS, 1946, V, Western Europe (WE), Caffery (Paris), 27 January, p. 407; FRUS, 1946, VIII (FE), Caffery, 6 February, pp. 24-25.

11. Hammer, pp. 123-124; Devillers, pp. 163-185, 200-201; Bernard Fall, Le Vietminh, Paris, 1960, pp. 45-54; George Sheldon, "Status of Vietnam," Far Eastern Survey, 18 December 1946, pp. 373-377 (American observers); R. E. M. Irving, The First Indochina War, London, 1975, pp. 16-17, n. 19, p. 35.

Irving and Donald Duncanson (Conflict Studies, October 1973, p. 5) surprisingly assert that the Vietminh held no elections in January 1946.

12. Hammer, pp. 150-154; Elgey, pp. 161-163; Jean Lacouture, Ho Chi Minh, Paris, 1967, pp. 98-99, and Un Sang d'encre, Paris, 1974, pp. 57-60, 69-72; "Rapport du général d'armée Leclerc faisant suite à sa mission en Indochine" (8 January 1947) in Vincent Auriol, Journal du septennat, 1947-1954, Paris, 1970-1978, Vol. I, 1947, pp. 661-664; Jean Sainteny, Histoire d'une paix manquée, Paris, 1953, and Face à Ho Chi Minh, Paris, 1970.

Leclerc later opposed further concessions in the summer
of 1946, developed an intense dislike for the Vietminh, and,
by the end of the year, endorsed a politique de force. Early
in 1947, he declined to become High Commissioner. That
November he died in a plane crash over Algeria.

Sainteny   became   persona   non   grata   with   the   Paris
government after negotiations broke down late in 1946. He
returned, however, to Indochina as an official representative
in 1955 and again in 1969 for Ho Chi Minh's funeral.   In the
late 1960's and early 1970's, he was highly instrumental in
arranging talks between the Americans and Vietnamese in Paris.
He died in 1978.

D'Argenlieu was a Catholic monk and head of the Carmelite
order in France. He has no biographer, and his memoirs deal
only with World War II. He died in 1964.

13. Devillers, pp. 205-226; Elgey, I, pp. 157-158.

14. Le Populaire, 23 February, 9 March 1946; Labrouquère,
"L'Indochine et la conscience française," La Revue socialiste,
June 1946, pp. 192-196; La Vérité, 16 March, 14 June, 12, 26
July 1946; Tran Duc Thao, Les Temps modernes, February 1946,
pp. 878-900; L'Humanité, 9 March 1946.

III
Negotiations
MARCH–OCTOBER 1946

The March 1946 Accords were to be followed by a definitive treaty negotiated in France in the summer of 1946. Before this, however, a colonialist reaction set in which sought to block further concessions to the DRV, to prevent the promised referendum in Cochinchina, and to create an alternative Vietnamese government. The general indifference of the French public (and many members of the political elite) to overseas affairs abetted this reaction.

In the spring of 1946, most attention focused on the drafting of a new Constitution. A final version completed in April, largely inspired by the Communists and Socialists, favored a strong legislature, dominated by the political parties, and a weak executive. It dealt with colonial issues only sporadically, saying nothing specifically about Indochina, Tunisia, or Morocco (whose status could only be settled by special accords). It also held that the overseas territories adhered to the "one and indivisible" French Republic by "free consent" (which implied a right of secession). Some people even proposed French citizenship for all overseas peoples and the direct election of overseas deputies. Since the latter would have a three-to-two advantage over the metropolitan deputies, the Assembly, by a special law of 19 March 1946, granted full French citizenship only to the inhabitants of the "old colonies" -- Guadeloupe, Martinique, Guiana, and Réunion -- which also became full French departments (although economically and socially they retained a colonial status). The other overseas peoples had only "equality under the law" and the right to elect local assemblies. The Communists (who favored greater overseas autonomy) generally liked the provisions more than the Socialists (who continued to stress overseas assimilation to the Metropole) or the MRP (who feared that increased autonomy would rapidly lead to total independence).

Overseas Minister Moutet argued that France could not remain a great power without satisfying the "legitimate aspirations" of the overseas peoples, treating them as equals, and instituting a number of important political, social and economic reforms, on a basis of "free collaboration." The

Communists made the sharpest attacks on the colonial system and proposed the strongest reforms, including the nationalization of the "colonial trusts" (including the Banque d'Indochine), a radical purging of all "Vichyite personnel" in the colonial service, and a bold program of industrial and technological development overseas. Yet, they cautioned the overseas peoples to await more "favorable developments" in the Metropole to satisfy their demands. Pierre Cot, a PCF ally, asked them not to use "inopportunely" their right to organize their national existence. In their march toward freedom, he held,

> France's role is no longer . . . that of a master for a slave or servant nor even that of a guardian for his ward. It is rather that of an older brother who accompanies his younger brother, holding his hand over the most difficult passages, the older brother who helps his younger brother benefit from his experience, being careful not to abuse that experience. (1)

Meanwhile, strained relations between the Communists and the Socialists made the possibility of a coherent left-wing colonial policy more remote. In the spring of 1946, Léon Blum went to Washington as a special emissary to negotiate a major loan, which, he hoped, would be politically useful to his party. So did many American officials who now found the Socialists more reliable than either the MRP or the Gaullists. (Ambassador Jefferson Caffery was particularly intimate with SFIO leaders.) The Communists later charged that, in return for the loan, Blum had agreed to help eliminate them from the ministry. Blum and his associates, however, categorically denied these assertions. Most probably Washington did not explicitly make the departure of the Communists a sine qua non condition for its aid, but it no doubt implied that their elimination would greatly simplify Franco-American relations. (2)

In May, the French electorate turned down the new Constitution by a 53 percent to 47 percent margin, with 21 percent of the voters abstaining. In the elections to a new Constituent Assembly in June, the spirit of anti-Communism (even among the Socialists) ran high. However, although the MRP came in first with 28 percent (a gain of 800,000 votes) and 160 seats, the Communists held their own with 26 percent (a gain of 200,000 votes) and 146 seats. The big losers, to the chagrin of Washington, were the Socialists, the loan to Blum notwithstanding, who got 21 percent (a loss of 400,000 votes) and 115 seats. The Left now no longer commanded a majority in the Assembly, and the SFIO was more reluctant than ever to unite exclusively with the Communists (though it also opposed any ministerial arrangement which excluded them). Bidault formed a new ministry, gave the PCF six minor posts, and named Thorez as Vice Premier. (3)

The SFIO's electoral defeat aggravated a serious internal crisis. For some time, many militants had felt uncomfortable about being no longer the leading left-wing party, about being a part of the government, and about being allied with the clerical and bourgeois MRP. Guy Mollet, the leader of the dissidents, favored unity with the Communists, possibly even "organic unity," certainly "unity of action," and ideally "unity of opposition." On the colonial question, the Molletistes proposed to "fight all forms of imperialist exploitation, aid the overseas peoples in their struggle for independence, and guide them on the road to social revolution." The Socialist crisis peaked at the annual party congress in August; and, in September, Mollet replaced Daniel Mayer, Blum's protegé, as Secretary-General. Overall, however, the Party blended Blum's "Socialist humanism" with Mollet's "Marxism," permitted its ministers to remain in the cabinet, and rejected "organic unity" with the PCF in favor of "unity of action." (4)

Meanwhile, in April 1946, the French and Vietnamese, led by d'Argenlieu and Giap, had resumed their talks at Dalat (the resort in southern Vietnam). Essentially, the Vietnamese proposed bilateral agreements between two sovereign and independent nations (the French Union would only be a loose and informal association). D'Argenlieu, on the other hand, wanted to retreat from the March 1946 Accords to the positions of De Gaulle's March 1945 Proclamation by which the French would maintain overall administrative control of Indochinese affairs and Vietnam would remain divided. Cochinchina was now rapidly becoming the Vietnamese Ulster, Alsace-Lorraine, or (in Ho Chi Minh's metaphor) Corsica. So, Dalat ended in a stalemate which the PCF found "particularly pessimistic." Further discussions were scheduled for the summer in France.

Ho Chi Minh was received as a head of state in Paris on 7 July. The next day negotiations began at Fontainebleau. The French delegation, heavily dominated by the MRP, included only one Socialist (Paul Rivet) and one Communist (Henri Lozeray). Even before the conference began, Premier Bidault told Max André, the MRP leader of the delegation (who was closely tied to the Banque d'Indochine and the Catholic missions), not to yield anything in the realm of foreign affairs, lest Vietnam move into the Soviet orbit. General Leclerc argued that France held the military advantage, although he believed that "some time" would still be necessary before order was "completely re-established." Later that summer, an "Estates General of French Colonization" in Paris, representing the settler interests and greatly fearing a referendum in Cochinchina, reinforced the government's intransigeance.

In 1949, Rivet revealed that the French delegation at Fontainebleau had determined, beforehand, to deadlock the negotiations, discredit Ho Chi Minh, and lay the basis for an alternative Vietnamese government under Bao Dai. (Rivet immediately resigned. Lozeray remained, mostly to keep his Party informed, but did not actively participate.)

Pham Van Dong, the head of the DRV delegation, sharply attacked the French efforts to detach Cochinchina. Although he stirred up a great deal of public interest, he was unable to make any headway during the next three weeks. The French delegation maintained that only its parliament was competent to settle the issue of Cochinchina (still officially a colony,

whereas Tonkin and Annam were protectorates), and it no longer
agreed to a referendum. Gradually the Vietnamese lost hope of
a substantial settlement and, on 1 August, dramatically walked
out when they learned that d'Argenlieu had invited the
"Cochinchina Council" to an alternative conference at Dalat.
Moutet now wanted to remove the Admiral; but Bidault, not
wanting to give in to the Socialists and Communists, stood by
him.

Disappointed by Fontainebleau, Ho Chi Minh feared to
return home with empty hands lest more radical Vietnamese
elements discredit his moderate approach. Perhaps also hoping
that the left-wing parties would improve their situation in
France, he concluded a _modus_ _vivendi_ with Moutet on 14
September. The two men agreed to establish "mixed commissions"
to study the questions of customs and a referendum in
Cochinchina and to resume more formal negotiations in January
1947. With this, Ho Chi Minh departed for Vietnam, leaving
behind an official delegation in Paris. (5)

During his stay in Paris, the Vietnamese leader had met
regularly with Thorez and other PCF leaders -- the first
direct contact between the French and Vietnamese Communists
since before World War II. In the summer of 1946, they
appeared very amiable; later testimonies indicate a great deal
of mutual confidence and friendship. Certainly, the PCF press
played up the Vietminh's role in the Resistance, its struggle
for   independence,   and   the   January   1946   elections.   It
portrayed the DRV leaders as essentially moderate types who
sincerely wanted friendship with France, as "men who have
lived in France," who knew "the strong democratic traditions
of our people," who called France their "second Fatherland."
Yet, the PCF did not promote a Vietnamese independence outside
the French Union and sometimes believed the Vietnamese lacked
faith in the "new France."

The PCF never suggested the terms of a reasonable
settlement at Fontainebleau but did fear that the conference's
failure would lead to a full-scale war and render unrealizable
the dream of the French Union. As Simone Téri very succinctly
and quite candidly wrote in L'Humanité:

> What would France be in the future, in effect
> reduced to her sole little Metropolitan terri-
> tory, if she roused up irremediably against
> her those peoples, like her infatuated with
> liberty, instead of gathering them in the great
> family which the French Union should be? Fail-
> ing to be faithful to the spirit of '89, after
> having lost Syria and Lebanon yesterday, we
> should lose Indochina tomorrow and after that
> North Africa.

Only on Cochinchina did the PCF take a hard and unequivocal
stand, categorically insisting on the territorial integrity of
Vietnam.

The PCF preferred to blame the problems on d'Argenlieu,
the "colonial trusts," and the "Saigon Vichyites," not on the

Paris government of which it was a member. Yet, the Communists had little responsibility for determining Indochina policy, most of which, in Paris, fell to a special Interministerial Committee, dominated by the MRP and including only one Communist (Tillon, a non-voting member) and two Socialists (Moutet and Jules Moch). The Communists were clearly in no position to grant total Vietnamese independence or even to force a settlement at Fontainebleau. Moreover, Ho Chi Minh, as a veteran Comintern agent, understood, and maybe partly agreed with, basic PCF strategy and probably did not expect special favors because of its presence in the government.

Apparently, former leaders of the Franc-Tireurs et partisans discussed techniques of urban guerilla warfare with members of the DRV delegation, who appeared "very interested." One wonders, however, how much any Resistance group in France had to teach the Vietnamese on guerilla warfare. There are also reports that certain Communist militants de base set up secret networks whereby, with the complicity of the Minister of Armaments (Tillon), sympathetic sailors, and international black marketeers, French arms passed into the hands of the Vietminh. No doubt the Vietminh did fight mostly with French (and American) weapons, not all of which were captured on the battlefield. There is also a certain "hidden history" of the French Left during these times, indications of which later surfaced during the miners' strikes of 1948 and the dockers' strikes of 1949. Moreover, General Georges Revers, the French Chief of Staff, alleged (in 1949) that large quantities of arms being sent to Indochina had been sabotaged. However, in 1946, arms trafficking was hardly compatible with the basic PCF posture, certainly not with the complicity of a Communist minister. (6)

The French Socialists in the summer of 1946 began to divide over Indochina. A few were not keenly interested in a settlement at Fontainebleau, not particularly irate over d'Argenlieu's actions, and even regretted the March Accords. The majority, led by Blum, still hoped for a negotiated settlement. The Populaire group criticized the government's policies, shared the Communists' sympathy for Ho Chi Minh, and vigorously denounced Cochinchinese separatism. Oreste Rosenfeld, the chief writer on colonial affairs, called the High Commissioner a "slave trader" who gave the impression that French policy was "full of hidden meanings, ulterior motives, and duplicity." Another Populaire writer declared that France risked "losing everything," both its "prestige" and its "economic resources" if the present policies continued and the Vietnamese turned elsewhere for aid. (7)

The failure of Fontainebleau disappointed American officials. In a lengthy assessment on 9 August, Abbot Low Moffat accused the French of "double-dealing," violating the March Accords, avoiding a referendum in Cochinchina, and suppressing all pro-DRV or anti-French opinion. Vietnam, Moffat held, could not be pacified "except through a long and bitter military operation," and France should "abide by the spirit" of the March Accords. French officials now countered that the prominence of Communists in the Vietnamese government (and Chinese Communist operations in Indochina) made them reluctant to negotiate more thoroughly. Most American officials remained skeptical. (8)

Meanwhile, in the French Constituent Assembly, a newly formed "Intergroup" of overseas deputies (partly inspired by Ho Chi Minh's presence in Paris) proposed that France renounce "all unilateral sovereignty over the colonial peoples" and recognize "their freedom to govern themselves and manage their own affairs democratically." Within a period not to exceed twenty years, the overseas peoples should exercise the right of self-determination. The Constitutional Commission endorsed these proposals. However, Edouard Herriot, a Radical-Socialist, under strong pressure from colonial interests, attacked the draft, rejected the right of secession, and praised the benevolence of the colonial regime. De Gaulle held that the Constitution could not be permitted to lead the overseas peoples to "agitation, dislocation," and foreign domination. Bidault also objected, and Moutet, on 11 September, proposed a number of revisions, declaring that the French Republic was "indivisible." The Assembly of the French Union, with a disproportionate settler representation, would only be advisory. The overseas peoples, although "equal under the law" with French nationals, could normally only become "citizens of the French Union."

Aimé Césaire and other overseas representatives protested directly to Bidault, asking if they were "as French as the others," to which the Premier replied that they knew that France was not a racist country. Some Communist and Socialist deputies spoke in defense of the Intergroup, but their leaders seconded Bidault and Moutet. In the Assembly, Yves Angeletti (PCF) tried to blend a "French presence everywhere" with "free and voluntary adhesion" to the French Union. However, Thorez preferred to gain Bidault's endorsement of his Civil Service Statute. De Gaulle commented dryly on this deal: "You give me the French Union, and I will give you the civil servants."

As finally devised, Article VIII on the French Union, the largest section of the Constitution, held that France rejected "any arbitrary system of colonization" and guaranteed to all "the individual or collective exercise of rights and liberties." France promised "never to employ its forces against the freedom of any people" and "to lead the peoples of whom it has taken charge to the freedom of governing themselves and of managing their own affairs democratically." The French Union was to consist of nations and peoples who "combine or coordinate their resources and their efforts." (Absent were the phrases "agree to combine" or "free consent.") Generally vague, confused, and even contradictory, some clauses affirmed equality between the overseas peoples and the Metropole, while others sanctioned Metropolitan pre-eminence.

Moutet defended the formula, arguing that "banditry and anarchy" could not replace order, peace, and "true civilization." Duclos held that the "French presence" was a "factor for progress and freedom" whose "absence would be exploited against the associated peoples themselves." The politicians were satisfied, but in October the French electorate only narrowly accepted the new Constitution. The

enthusiasm of the liberation had yielded to a deep political
malaise, and the Communists and Socialists were clearly on the
defensive. (9)

NOTES

Notes have been grouped according to topic.

1. D. Bruce Marshall, The French Colonial Myth, New
Haven, 1973, pp. 215-219, 227-228; Alain Ruscio, Les
Communistes français et la guerre d'Indochine, Paris, 1985,
pp. 40-44; Journal officiel, débats parlementaires, Assemblée
constituante (JODPAC), 20 March 1946, pp. 908-912 (Henri
Lozeray), 23 March, pp. 1036-1043 (Moutet), pp. 1043-1045
(Cot); Henri Lozeray, "La Lutte du peuple français pour la
démocratie et l'émancipation des peuples coloniaux," Cahiers
du communisme, April 1946, pp. 368-378.

2. Foreign Relations of the United States (FRUS), 1946, V
(WE), Caffery, 4 April, pp. 421-422; National Advisory
Council, Washington, 6 May, pp. 440-447; Joyce and Gabriel
Kolko, The Limits of Power: The World and United States
Foreign Policy, 1945-1954, New York, 1972, pp. 154-156;
Georgette Elgey, Histoire de la IVé République, Vol. I, Paris,
1965, pp. 140-141; Alexander Werth, France, 1940-1955,
Boston, 1966, pp. 314-316; Jean Davidson, Correspondent à
Washington: Ce que je n'ai jamais cablé, Paris, 1954, pp.
15-16.

3. Elgey, I, pp. 202-204, 209-212; Paul-Marie De la
Gorce, L'Après-Guerre, Paris, 1978, pp. 152-153; E.
Rice-Maximin, "The United States and the French Left,
1945-1949," Journal of Contemporary History, October 1984,
pp. 732-733 (on American contingency plans to intervene
militarily if the PCF resorted to illegal actions once the
first Constitution failed).

4. Elgey, I, pp. 217-219; Roger Quilliot, La SFIO et
l'exercice du pouvoir, 1944-1958, Paris, 1972, pp. 170-184.

5. Philippe Devillers, Histoire du Vietnam, 1940-1952,
Paris, 1952, pp. 31-37 (Cochinchina in history), 227-232,
256-270 (Dalat), 289-310 (Fontainebleau); Ellen J. Hammer, The
Struggle for Indochina, 1940-1955, Stanford, 1966 pp.
168-172; Elgey, I, pp. 163-164 (Leclerc); Grégoire Madjarian,
La Question coloniale et la politique du PCF, 1944-1947,
Paris, 1977, pp. 155-156, 177-178 (the colonialist reaction);
L'Humanité, 28 April 1946; FRUS, 1946, VIII, O'Sullivan
(Hanoi), 5 June, p. 46 (a referendum in Cochinchina); Paul
Rivet, "Le Drame franco-vietnamien," Cahiers internationaux,
June 1949, pp. 45-66; Ruscio, pp. 116-118 (Lozeray).

Rivet was a distinguished anthropologist and Director of
the Musée de l'homme and was strongly humanitarian, if also
quite paternalistic. (A former American mistress called him a
"racist.") Rivet revealed full details of the Fontainebleau
episode to the National Assembly in 1949, after he had quit
the SFIO over its Indochina policies. In January 1950, he

somewhat qualified his remarks.

6. Ruscio, pp. 108-116, 120-122; William Duiker, The Comintern and Vietnamese Communism, Athens, Ohio, 1975, pp. 5-6; Joseph Buttinger, Vietnam: A Dragon Embattled, Vol. I, New York, 1967, p. 618; Charles Tillon, On chantait rouge, Paris, 1977, pp. 449-452; Jacques Doyon, Les Soldats blancs de Ho Chi Minh, Paris, 1973, pp. 109-116; Philippe Robrieux, Maurice Thorez, Paris, 1975, pp. 301-304; Léo Figuères, Ho Chi Minh: Notre camarade: Souvenirs de militants français, Paris, 1970; Edgar Snow, Saturday Evening Post, 2 February 1946; Bernard Fall, "Tribulations of a Party Line: The French Communists and Indochina," Foreign Affairs, April 1955; France nouvelle, 8, 15 June, 7 September 1946; L'Humanité, 18 June, 6, 24 (Téri), 30 July 1946; Ce Soir, 23-24 June, 7 August 1946.

In a recent interview with Tillon, Ruscio learned that the FTP did pass documentation on guerilla warfare to Giap's staff. Ruscio also effectively challenges the credibility of certain statements often attributed to Thorez, such as not wanting to be "the eventual liquidator of the French position in Indochina" (e.g., Devillers, p. 269).

The Vietnamese have been reticent about publicly commenting on the PCF's colonial policies most probably because of the support they later received. Phan Van Ban's "Les Rapports entre le Parti communiste français et la révolution vietnamienne," Nghien cuu lich, Hanoi, 1961, portrays the PCF as very sympathetic to the Vietnamese Revolution, especially after 1949, but says very little about the 1945-1947 period. Ruscio's recent interviews with Vietnamese leaders confirm their appreciation for the PCF's approach.

7. Le Populaire, 18 June, 6, 11 August, 7-9 September; B. D. Graham, The French Socialists and Tripartism, 1944-1947, London, 1965, pp. 246-253; R. E. M. Irving, First Indochina War, London, 1975, pp. 22-26.

8. FRUS, 1946, VIII, Moffat (Chief SEA) to John Carter Vincent (Director FE), 9 August, pp. 52-54; Reed (Saigon), 17 August, 17 September, p. 59; Caffery, 11 September, 29 November, pp. 58, 63; Acheson to Hanoi, 9 October, p. 61; O'Sullivan, 1 November, 3 December, pp. 62-65.

Acheson wanted to know why the DRV flag had a red field. Ho Chi Minh told Caffery he was not a Communist.

9. Marshall, pp. 228-231, 252-255, 261-262, 276-283, 295-305; Elgey, I, 221-229; JODPAC, 18-19 September, Angeletti, pp. 3787-3788; Herriot, pp. 3814-3818; Lozeray, pp. 3843-3845; Sportisse (PCA), pp. 3852-3854. For the principal overseas speakers, see JODPAC, 18 September 1946, Senghor, pp. 3790-3792; Césaire, pp. 3795-3797; Lamine-Guèye, pp. 3797-3801; Abbas, pp. 3803-3804; Monnerville, pp. 3808-3812; and Gaston Monnerville, Témoignage: De la France équinoxiale au Palais de Luxembourg, Paris, 1975, pp. 369-405.

IV
War

Although the modus vivendi agreed to by Ho Chi Minh and Marius Moutet was a face-saving device which failed to resolve fundamental differences, the French Communists and Socialists still hoped for a comprehensive settlement, especially if they increased their strength in the parliamentary elections. However, certain other policy makers in Paris and Saigon had already determined to block further negotiations.

In October, French authorities in Vietnam unilaterally seized control of customs, ignoring the promise of the March Accords that the DRV have "its own finances" and the provision of the modus vivendi that the customs question be resolved through mixed commissions. Deprived of their major source of revenue, DRV leaders stepped up military preparations. Sporadic fighting increased considerably. The French were now ready to provoke a major incident, believing their military situation had improved; they were also concerned to keep the political situation in Cochinchina from further deteriorating. Frustrated by a lack of popular support and real power, the head of the Cochinchina government (Dr. Nguyen Van Thinh) committed suicide on 10 November. On the same day in France, the PCF once again emerged as the leading party in the parliamentary elections. Determined to force a showdown, High Commissioner d'Argenlieu left for Paris. (1)

The PCF had won almost 29 percent of the vote (their highest total ever), while the MRP (having campaigned for the exclusion of the Communists) declined slightly, and the Socialists lost over 800,000 supporters. Although the combined Left now had only 46.5 percent, the Communists still fantasized about "Thorez au pouvoir," a thought mildly acceptable to only half the Socialists and thoroughly distasteful to almost everyone else. Thus, a political stalemate developed, while a lame-duck Bidault ministry carried on for another eighteen days. During this interval D'Argenlieu and the MRP-dominated Interministerial Committee decided to force the issue in Vietnam. Although the Vietnamese had not retaliated for the French seizure of customs in October, Bidault told the National Defense Committee that war was inevitable and that "il faut tirer le canon."

On 20 November, Vietnamese militia (Tu Ve) clashed at Haiphong with French sailors who had seized a Chinese junk suspected of carrying contraband. Colonel Debès, the commander on the spot, wanted to take strong action but was restrained by General Louis Morlière, who arranged for a cease-fire. However, General Jean Valluy, with full approval from Paris, instructed Debès:

> to give a stern lesson to those who have
> treacherously attacked us. By every means
> at your disposal, you are to take complete
> control of Haiphong and to force the Viet-
> namese government and army to recognize
> their errors.

Accordingly, on 23 November, while French troops moved in, the fleet shelled the city, killing at least 6,000 Vietnamese and injuring several thousand more. The French public was kept mostly ignorant of the events for several critical weeks. Not until 10 January 1947 did General Morlière provide Paris with a version different than Valluy's. Full details of the episode were not generally known until three years later.

In Paris, the Interministerial Committee on Indochina, including Bidault, Moutet, d'Argenlieu, and Tillon, meeting at the very moment of the shelling, approved Valluy's initiative. So did General Leclerc. Bidault told the Committee that, while France would continue to pursue a policy of negotiations, it was determined to remain in Indochina and would defend its rights by "every means including force." When Moutet presented the matter to the entire cabinet on 27 November, there was little discussion. All the ministers tacitly approved all the actions taken, but the Communists did obtain agreement that the modus vivendi was still in force. The Interministerial Committee met once again on 29 November, with Tillon absent, and affirmed a politique de fermeté in Indochina. (2)

L'Humanité called Haiphong a "deplorable incident" but did not elaborate. Ce Soir mentioned the shelling but not the heavy casualties. The PCF press quickly exonerated the Vietnamese, blamed the matter on a generally confusing situation, and, only after several days, on French authorities. The Communist press called for further negotiations and a strict application of the March Accords but did not demand the restoration of the status quo ante 20 November, at least not until "the French government judges it possible."

The Socialists blamed both sides, the Vietnamese for having challenged French control of customs, and the French authorities in Saigon, particularly d'Argenlieu, for having created an explosive situation. "A veritable state of war existed," and an agreement with Ho Chi Minh was now possible only if the French colonialists could be restrained. (3)

Much depended, also, on the new French government. Thorez was denied investiture by fifty-one votes (the closest any Communist has ever had of becoming Premier in France). Only a few Socialists, fearing to alienate the workers, supported him; most adamantly objected. After Bidault likewise failed (by seventy votes), Vincent Auriol, the President of the National Assembly, proposed a temporary, all-Socialist cabinet under Léon Blum, and the PCF agreed. (Another tripartite ministry was not possible because the MRP would not agree to the PCF having a key post.)

Blum's stand on Indochina was important to his selection. On 10 December, he had written that France had to maintain a "presence" in Indochina but also might negotiate a settlement that included "independence." (He did not mention Ho Chi Minh.) France could not win a war but had to deal with the Vietnamese absolutely clearly and without equivocation. Most importantly, the cabinet alone, not the military nor the colonialists nor even interministerial committees, had to make the necessary decisions. Having satisfied all sides, Blum was elected almost unanimously as Premier on 13 December. Although not anxious for the assignment, he felt that the Socialists had to fill the gap. Yet, they would also be weak and divided arbiters in a time of crisis. (4)

Shortly before Blum's appointment, American Far Eastern specialist Abbot Low Moffat went on a special mission to Indochina where he met with a variety of French officials and also with Ho Chi Minh and other DRV leaders. Moffat concluded that the French were chiefly to blame for Haiphong, that by seizing customs, they had tried "to strangle Vietnam economically." Officials in Washington now suggested that both sides needed "new faces." Certain French officials, like d'Argenlieu, had lost their "usefulness" because of their colonialist outlook and open dislike of any Vietnamese; the latter needed "more reasonable, moderate" leaders. Consul Charles Reed II (Saigon) suggested Bao Dai. Some other Americans officials favored third power or United Nations mediation, an idea the French flatly rejected.

The State Department was ambivalent about French charges of Communism in Vietnam. "French concern over Communism," Consul James O'Sullivan (Hanoi) wired, "may well be devised to divert Department attention from French policy in Indochina," that is, "preparing to force the Vietnamese government to collaborate on French terms or to establish a puppet government in its place." In Washington, Assistant Secretary of State Dean Acheson, however, held that "the least desirable eventuality would be the establishment of a Communist-dominated, Moscow-oriented state in Indochina." Moffat believed that the Vietnamese were in "direct" contact with the Chinese Communists and possibly in "indirect" contact with Moscow. (5)

After Haiphong, certain French officials in Vietnam wanted to press their advantage. Sainteny told Consul O'Sullivan that they were ready to undertake "a police action" to eliminate certain Vietnamese leaders; General Valluy requested major reinforcements. The Vietnamese discovered a Valluy memorandum (written in October) which indicated an intention to topple the DRV and execute its leaders. People began to panic. Refugees from Haiphong poured into Hanoi,

threw up barricades, and prepared to flee the city.
Ambassador Caffery reported that Vietnamese officials
bombarded the French Communists with telegrams asking the CGT
to order the dockers to stop loading troop and supply ships
bound for Indochina. (He believed this embarrassed the PCF
leadership, which was trying to portray itself as a "safe
custodian of France's international interests.")

On the Vietnamese side, General Giap wanted to strike
back, but Ho Chi Minh told Sainteny (and wired Blum) that he
still wanted to avoid a rupture if the French would return to
the situation that existed prior to 20 November. The telegram,
held up by French authorities in Saigon, did not arrive in
Paris until nine days later, five days too late. With no
response from Blum, Ho Chi Minh gave Giap the signal to go
ahead. On 19 December, the Vietnamese attacked the French at
several points, killing forty civilians in Hanoi, wounding a
number of others (including Sainteny), and kidnapping another
two hundred. Although the casualties were small compared to
Haiphong, French newspapers made the most out of Hanoi.

The Communists and Socialists, clearly annoyed by the
sensationalism of the right-wing papers, tried to play down
the Hanoi incidents. The Communists blamed the "Vichyites,"
financial trusts, d'Argenlieu, and the Gaullists and feared
Chinese or American intervention. Although urging an
immediate resumption of negotiations with Ho Chi Minh, they
did not, however, insist on a restoration of the status quo
ante 19 December. They also endorsed Blum's declaration to
"make respected our rights as recognized by the Franco-
Vietnamese Accords."

Addressing the National Assembly on 22 December, the
Premier completely ignored Haiphong and interpreted Hanoi as
the causus belli. Violence had been imposed on France, which
now had the duty to re-establish order. Nevertheless, he
refused to invalidate the March Accords or exclude Ho Chi Minh
from further negotiations. Later at the Populaire offices,
Blum broke into tears: "Again it has to be me," reflecting on
his inability to save the Spanish Republic in 1936, "I have
not merited this." Yet the adoption of a politique de force
was not just one man's doing. All the Socialist ministers
approved and, by general consent, so did the Communists and
Popular Republicans. (6)

Having appeased the Left (but not the Right), Blum next
sent Moutet, Leclerc, and d'Argenlieu (to appease the MRP) on
a mission of inspection. Ho Chi Minh wired the Premier of his
willingness to meet with the Overseas Minister in Hanoi in
order to establish a cease-fire and return to the positions of
17 December (significantly no longer those of 20 November).
Whatever his initial intentions, Moutet dramatically changed
his opinions after meeting with French officials in Saigon and
after viewing the destruction in Hanoi. He toasted the
propserity of the Cochinchinese government and refused to meet
with any DRV representatives, accusing them of premeditated
criminality. "Before any negotiations, we first need a
military decision." Moutet hoped, not for an interminable
guerilla war, but only for "a reversal of climate" which would
"abruptly thrust the native masses back toward the French

authorities and bring forth personalities with whom these authorities would be able to speak." (7)

Greatly embarrassed, the French Communists accused Moutet of deliberately contradicting the official policies of the Blum government. Or was it, L'Humanité wondered, that the government itself had changed? PCF correspondent René L'Hermitte went to Indochina and managed to contact several members of the maquis. The DRV, he concluded, had the "total and impassioned" support of "an entire people," and a war would render impossible any harmonious association between Vietnam and France.

Even certain Socialists, including André Fontaine and Léon Boutbien, a member of the Comité directeur, refused to blame the Vietminh totally and insisted that negotiations with Ho Chi Minh were still possible. Fontaine cited the shelling of Haiphong as the major cause of the war and declared that the Vietminh was the best organized party in the country. Boutbien agreed on Haiphong but felt that the French had acted in legitimate self-defense after Hanoi. He proposed a policy of "neither surrender nor reconquest." France had to avoid a full-scale war and logically had to negotiate with its adversaries rather than with its friends. Such dissenting opinions notwithstanding, Blum's all-Socialist cabinet accepted the essence of Moutet's report. (8)

The French public, even after Hanoi, remained largely indifferent to events in Indochina. Even most of the intelligentsia was little concerned. To Raymond Aron, the Vietnamese responsibility for the bloody tragedy was "indisputable" and French soldiers were "making the same sacrifices by which the independence and greatness of fatherlands have been preserved throughout the centuries." Yet, he did not endorse military reconquest nor sympathize with the Cochinchina experiment. To Jean-Paul Sartre, the French were to the Vietnamese what the Nazis had been to the French during the Occupation, though without a Gestapo and without concentration camps, or "so at least we hope." To François Mauriac, this ignored seventy-five years of French accomplishments in Indochina. Sartre replied that had the Germans remained for that long in France, they undoubtedly would have made a few contributions to French civilization. Indeed, he found it quite scandalous that Mauriac, as a Christian, could not, for one moment, step outside of himself and view himself with the eyes of another. (9)

Blum's all-Socialist government terminated in January 1947 with Vincent Auriol's election as President of the Fourth Republic. Formerly President of the Constituent Assembly, Auriol was an able mediator but distinctly conservative on the colonial question and jealous of his role as President of the French Union. He immediately asked Socialist Paul Ramadier to form a new tripartite cabinet. The PCF gained a key ministry -- Defense -- only after separate ministries of War, Air, and Marine were distributed to other parties, and Thorez again became Vice Premier.

On Indochina, Ramadier insisted that order had to be re-established but also that the government did not want a

war. He said nothing about negotiations. When he rendered
homage to the French troops, even the Communists rose and
applauded. Ramadier, however, did want to replace Admiral
d'Argenlieu as High Commissioner with General Leclerc in order
to placate both the Left and the Right. The General believed
that Communism was less important than nationalism in Vietnam
and that any negotiations had to include the Vietminh. Yet, he
also wanted France to negotiate from a position of strength
and locate "more representative" Vietnamese spokesmen. In any
event, after conferring with De Gaulle, Leclerc declined the
offer because the government could not clearly define its
policies nor give him full powers. Nevertheless, d'Argenlieu
resigned when Ramadier chose, for a special mission, Emile
Bollaert, a Radical with a good Resistance record and a
capable administrator. On 5 March the cabinet unanimously
endorsed him as High Commissioner. (10)

     The United States, although continuing to charge the
French with a "lack of understanding" and a "dangerously
outmoded colonial outlook," now began to view Indochina
through the prism of the Cold War. The crisis threatened to
undermine French "civil and economic objectives" and
ultimately threaten "all Western interests in Southeast Asia."
While calling for an "equitable solution," Washington accepted
the thesis that the Vietminh had started the war on 19
December, supported the search for alternatives to Ho Chi
Minh, and even hinted at possible military assistance.
Secretary of State George C. Marshall, arguing that Ho Chi
Minh had "direct Communist connections," would not allow the
French regime to be supplanted by a "philosophy and political
organizations emanating from and controlled by the Kremlin."
Yet, none of his lieutenants in Southeast Asia could find any
evidence of direct Soviet involvement. Reed felt that
"Annamite Communism" was perhaps being "over-emphasized as a
present danger, although it is definitely a potential one."
(11)

     Cold War clouds also began to settle over France.
American newspapers fanned rumors of a Communist insurrection
and the possibility of a civil war. To one American official,
the PCF was the "principal lever" of the "the long hand of the
Kremlin" in Europe and was "undermining French authority in
the colonies." In Washington, Dean Acheson argued that, with
French Communists in the ministry, the nationalized
industries, and the military, and a worsening economic
situation, "the Russians have only to shake the branch at any
moment they choose to collect the fruit. . . . France is ripe
to fall into the hands of Moscow." Other officials, however,
felt the French Communists were "for the moment behaving
themselves" and probably would not precipitate a serious
political crisis on the eve of the Moscow Foreign Ministers
Conference (called to settle the German question). Indeed, it
was the French Right which sought to disrupt tripartism over
Indochina. (12)

     At an important cabinet meeting on 5 March, Moutet and
Bidault clearly opposed any entente with the Vietminh. Thorez
tried to switch the blame to the Cochinchinese separatists but
did agree on the need to preserve French sovereignty in
Indochina. For this he was allowed to help draw up the

instructions for the new High Commissioner -- a major concession to a Communist minister. Thorez even prevailed on most of the principal points: negotiations would be resumed as soon as possible, Ho Chi Minh would not be excluded, the "royal dynasty" would not be restored, and there would be no attempt to reconquer Vietnam militarily. In exchange, he promised to support military credits.

Six days later, the Cold War erupted in the French National Assembly, where the Right tried to force the PCF out of the government over the Indochina issue. (On the same day, in Washington, President Truman announced his famous "Doctrine" to stop Communist expansionism. Although immediately concerned about Greece and Turkey, he no doubt also had France and China in mind.) In Paris, right-wing deputies discredited Ho Chi Minh, hoping to block further negotiations, and accused the PCF of distributing Vietminh propaganda in France. At one point, Paul Reynaud denounced Duong Bach Mai, a DRV leader, who was sitting in the gallery, as a murderer, and the guards forcibly ejected him. At this, Thorez led the Communists out of the Chamber in protest.

When the session resumed, the Socialist Daniel Mayer tried to pacify both sides by arguing for "neither surrender nor reconquest." A total French withdrawal would only engender a Vietnamese civil war, and a continuation of the war would be disastrous to both the French and Vietnamese. Mayer favored increased powers for the Cochinchinese government and negotiations with Bao Dai. He did not want to exclude Ho Chi Minh but was not sure if he effectively represented the Vietnamese people. (Ramadier said he was not sure the Vietnamese leader was still alive.)

Pierre Cot replied for the Communists five days later, agreeing with the need to maintain a French "presence" but blaming French authorities for Haiphong and for trying to undermine the DRV. Since to continue the war would be too long, too costly and too unpopular, France had to negotiate with the DRV even if it was dominated by Communists. Cot told the deputies:

> You do not have the right to object to a govern-
> ment because you do not like it. The only
> question is what is the real government of Viet-
> nam. . . . According to all responsible men --
> I clearly say, all -- Ho Chi Minh possesses the
> greatest political influence over there, even in
> Cochinchina.

Moutet responded, two days later, that the Vietminh had completely violated the March Accords and that France could not negotiate with those who practiced "systematic terrorism." Duclos then charged the government with violating the Constitution by pursuing a military solution, one which could only end, moreover, with France being chased completely from Indochina. Nor could France maintain its influence in the Orient by negotiating with "house spokesmen" (repeating Napoléon's mistake with Toussaint L'Ouverture in Haiti). Hence, the Communists were forced to abstain on the vote for military credits. (The Central Committee confirmed this position that evening.) Never since the Liberation had the PCF taken such a strong stand against the government.

When Ramadier rendered homage to the French troops, the Communists refused to rise, including François Billoux, the Minister of Defense. An MRP deputy proclaimed: "France has stood up!" But Billoux never moved. Ramadier wondered how someone could be both Defense Minister and an anti-militarist, both a part of the government and in the opposition, at the same time. He asked the Communists if they wanted to destroy the Republic and split France radically into Communist and anti-Communist blocs. Trying conciliation, he praised Thorez's governmental abilities and spirit of cooperation, but Duclos would only concede not to vote against the military credits.

When Ramadier attached a vote of confidence to the issue, the PCF's Political Bureau permitted the PCF ministers (not the deputies) to vote for the credits. (Following the debate, Thorez and the other ministers would sign Bollaert's instructions, as agreed to on 5 March.) However, when Ramadier again rendered homage to the troops, the implacable Communists still refused to rise despite cries of "Stand up! Stand up! Are you not Frenchmen?" At the end of the debate, Saravane Lambert, one of several overseas deputies who had also abstained, warned the Assembly against treating the Vietnamese people -- and, "in consequence, all the overseas peoples -- as vassals." (13)

In the seventeen days following the ministerial compromise of 5 March, the positions of the tripartite parties had hardened considerably. Truman's speech and the ouster of Communist ministers from the Belgian and Italian governments contributed to the crisis, as did De Gaulle's re-entry into the political arena. The MRP feared losing supporters to the Gaullists, and the Socialists felt compelled to stretch to the Right in order to preserve the Republic. Yet, the government still wanted an entente on the German question with the Soviet Union, and most Socialists did not believe that they could remain in the government without the Communists. However, after the Communists refused to support military credits for Indochina, tripartism could not long survive. Neither the MRP nor the Socialists were willing to compromise any longer; both hoped to force the Communists to make further concessions. The PCF, for its part, did not think that disagreement over Indochina warranted a breakup of the ministry; but many of its supporters were dissatisfied about the government's wage policies. Hence, the PCF drew the line, not over a colonial issue, but over one more intimately affecting the interests of the French working class. (14)

NOTES

Notes have been grouped according to topic.

1. Philippe Devillers, Histoire du Vietnam, 1940-1952, Paris, 1952, pp. 314-327.

V
Cold War
MARCH–DECEMBER 1947

In 1947, the Cold War, combined with colonial crises, a Gaullist revival, and major domestic strikes, forced the French Communists out of the cabinet and, eight months later, cost the Socialists control of colonial policy -- a serious displacement of the French Left which significantly altered the politics of the Indochina War.

Within two weeks of the Indochina debate, a rebellion broke out in Madagascar. (In the ensuing repression, some 80,000 people lost their lives.) Moutet wanted to lift the parliamentary immunity of the three Madagascan deputies allegedly behind the insurrection, who were closely associated to the PCF and some Socialists. At a heated cabinet meeting on 17 April, Thorez denounced Moutet, threatened to leave the government, and stormed out of the session. The next day, he warned that the PCF deputies would be free to vote against the government on Madagascar or any other question. The non-Communist ministers, however, replied with tougher stands on Indochina. On 25 April, the Overseas Ministry explicitly rejected further negotiations with Ho Chi Minh. Then, when the Moscow Foreign Ministers Conference failed, Ramadier deliberately sought pretexts to remove the PCF ministers. (1)

Tripartism's coup de grâce came not, as expected, from a foreign or colonial dispute but from a strike at the main Renault plant which the PCF and CGT belatedly supported lest they alienate the working class and be out-maneuvered on their left. Some PCF leaders hoped to use the strike as leverage against Ramadier and perhaps even force the formation of a more congenial government. After a three-day debate at the beginning of May, the Communist deputies and ministers voted against Ramadier's freeze on wages, though Thorez still hoped to support the cabinet on other issues. At the urging of the Socialist parliamentarians, Ramadier decided not to resign, although many within the SFIO did not want to remain in the government without the Communists. Instead, on 4 May, when Thorez refused to resign, Ramadier revoked the Communists' portfolios.

The astonished PCF ministers accepted their ouster stoically, believing it only temporary. "Those who speak of a general strike," Duclos declared, "are imbeciles." (For over thirty years the PCF was not to return to that council chamber.) The SFIO's National Council, after a bitter session, that pitted the Molletistes against Blum and the majority of the Socialist parliamentarians, voted to remain in the government, fearing that De Gaulle would profit from an interminable governmental crisis. (2)

General Revers, the French Chief of Staff, later reported that the American government had urged Ramadier to remove the PCF ministers. Ramadier always denied this. Former Premier Gouin said the Americans were usually more subtle and discreet. Bidault said there was no reason for being more explicit, for the other ministers implicitly shared the American viewpoint. Certainly, the Socialists discussed the matter beforehand with Ambassador Caffery. Moreover, the American officials in Paris wanted the Communists removed from all government agencies and the labor movement split or neutralized. For this, they needed the support of "substantial Socialist elements" with "substantial roots in the working class" and a prestigious leader. However, they would not consider De Gaulle, and they feared that Blum's heading an anti-Communist crusade might split the Socialist Party. Hence, "the best that could be hoped for," Caffery said afterwards, was the expulsion of the PCF ministers. (3)

Throughout the summer of 1947, the Communists were not certain to remain in the opposition. At their Congress of Strasbourg in June, some PCF delegates still cried "Thorez au pouvoir." However, Soviet analyses of the Marshall Plan (European Recovery Program) as an aggressive instrument of American foreign policy, with political as well as humanitarian overtones, soon compelled the Western European Communists to oppose vigorously all their governments' policies. Nevertheless, the United States continued to worry about a possible PCF return to power. Not wanting to interfere vigorously or directly lest "large sections of French public opinion" turn against the United States, Secretary Marshall preferred to secretly fund existing anti-Communist organizations. Other officials warned the non-Communist parties that a PCF return would greatly diminish the prospect of American aid. (4)

With the Communists gone, the other ministers started to formulate new Indochina policies, although Bollaert's initial instructions were still technically in effect. When, in May, Ho Chi Minh rejected a demand (conveyed through Paul Mus) to turn over French deserters and permit the free passage of French troops, Paris said he no longer wanted seriously to negotiate.

However, the Socialist leadership hesitated to endorse any alternative Vietnamese government. Auriol learned from some observers that, even by conservative estimates, Ho Chi Minh had the support of 80 to 85 percent of the population but was told by others that the Vietminh was collapsing and that the Baodaists were "strong, coherent, and centralized." Some

Socialists preferred General Nguyen Van Xuan, but Blum, in August 1947, still held to Ho Chi Minh as "the authentic and qualified" representative of the Vietnamese people. After having produced a minor sensation, he said he had expressed "nothing more nor less" than his own feelings. (Ho Chi Minh had just sent him a touching personal message.)

In September, in a major speech at Hadong, High Commissioner Bollaert spelled out a new policy. Addressing all Vietnamese "parties and groups," he was willing to grant Vietnamese "autonomy" (not independence) and "unity" (if the Cochinchinese agreed) but wanted France to retain control of the army, diplomacy, customs, currency, and the budget. He also implied that France did not favor a settlement with those responsible for the December 1946 uprising. Both the DRV and Bao Dai were disappointed. Consul Reed felt the Hadong proposals offered no solutions, sounded threatening, definitely retreated from the March 1946 Accords, and had been made deliberately unacceptable to the DRV. (5)

Meanwhile, the United States debated its own Indochina policy. State Department officials had little doubt about Ho Chi Minh's popularity. To Consul Reed:

> Unfortunately, the majority of the natives stoutly maintain that Ho Chi Minh is the man, and the only one, who represents them; and they will oppose the putting forward of any other candidate as the creation of but another puppet and the erecting of a smoke screen for France's real intentions.

Caffery and several other officials concurred, but Secretary Marshall was more concerned about Vietnamese Communism. O'Sullivan replied that Vietnamese intellectuals found Communism a lesser evil than French colonialism but that there was no "direct connection between Vietnam and Moscow." Moreover, he found it "curious that the French discovered no Communist menace in Ho Chi Minh's government until after September 1946 when it became apparent that the Vietnamese government would not bow to French wishes." Reed basically concurred, but Caffery did not find it at all curious.

As for the French, Marshall was "increasingly concerned by the slow progress toward a settlement" and confessed that the United States had been "dangerously one-sided" in ignoring Haiphong. Although he wanted neither a puppet government nor a restored monarchy nor an agreement with the DRV, he did look for some sort of reasonable arrangement to stem anti-Western, pan-Asiatic, and Communist tendencies. Any setbacks to the long-range interests of France would be "setbacks of our own." Yet, Reed, while unwilling "to let the natives run wild," cautioned that the United States would lose much prestige in Asia if it associated too closely with France. (6)

In the summer and autumn of 1947, President Truman sent William C. Bullitt as a special emissary to France and Southeast Asia. Bullitt suggested detaching the Vietnamese nationalists from the Communist nucleus surrounding Ho Chi

Minh by giving them independence; but, under no circumstances, he told Auriol, should France negotiate with Ho Chi Minh. In an article for _Life_, Bullitt said that the "black tragedy" in Indochina was that the Communists had "captured" the Vietnamese Resistance. Yet, to surrender to Ho Chi Minh would be the "worst disaster which could befall the French, the Annamites and the civilized world." (It would also tighten the Soviet noose around China.)

The French Communists (and others) complained that the Bullitt mission indicated American interference in the Indochina conflict. Actually, Bullitt was probably acting more on behalf of certain French personalities with whom he had long been intimate, trying to sell their Indochina policies to the American government and people, not _vice versa_. Truman had to push hard for congressional and popular support of a vigorous foreign policy in which Indochina was a secondary concern. The Bao Dai solution was made in France, not Washington. (7)

By the end of the summer of 1947, the French Socialists were not faring well, and they remained divided on Indochina. In one year, their membership had dropped from 350,000 to 280,000. Socialist dissidents, unable to blame the growing number of strikes entirely on Communist agitation, opposed the wage freeze, favored a more directed economy, and wanted their ministers to resign. Some Socialist deputies even threatened to vote no confidence in their own government. The SFIO Congress in August adopted Mollet's "moral report," calling for "_dirigisme_ total," closer supervision of parliamentarians, and a return to being a "class party." (Ramadier was so distressed that he almost resigned at this point.)

On Indochina, the Socialist ministers and most deputies moved cautiously in the direction of Bao Dai, but important segments of the Party remained attached to Ho Chi Minh. In October, the _Comité directeur_ called for negotiations with Ho Chi Minh _and_ "the most representative elements of the Vietnamese people." _Le Populaire's_ positions were likewise ambiguous. While "personally convinced" that Ho Chi Minh was "the most authorized spokesman" of the Vietnamese "spiritual family," Henri Noguères did not believe he represented all the people of Vietnam. Yet, the Bao Dai solution would also be unrepresentative if it excluded the Vietminh.

Ho Chi Minh's staunchest supporters in the SFIO were Paul Rivet, Léon Boutbien, Jeanne Cuisinier, Yves Dechezelle, Jean Rous, and the Young Socialists. Rous, a companion of Trotsky in the 1930's and former _résistant_, edited _La Pensée socialiste_, a short-lived proletarian newspaper and dissident forum, which insisted, with repeated reference to the January 1946 elections, that the DRV was neither dictatorial nor dominated by Communists, and condemned negotiations with "straw men." Rous soon quit the SFIO but continued his anti-colonial campaigns in _Franc-Tireur_ and _Esprit_. In 1948 he helped found the Congress of Peoples against Imperialism (both French and British). Sartre, Claude Bourdet, and Jean-Marie Domenach (_Esprit_) have said Rous was one who saw "earliest and clearest" in colonial matters. In 1949, Auriol alleged (without elaborating) that Rous was an unwitting accomplice of the Soviet Union and involved in a "paid plot" to subvert the French Empire. (8)

As Rous' itinerary suggests, by the middle of 1947, a number of independent left-wing views had emerged on Indochina which not only put the options of the Communists and Socialists into better perspective but also considered a wider variety of questions. First of all, the Trotskyists, not surprisingly, criticized the Vietnamese "Stalinists" for playing the Soviet game (i.e., keeping Vietnam in the French orbit to block American penetration of Southeast Asia) and for not carrying out a real social revolution.

Also, on the extreme left, Pierre Monatte's Révolution prolétarienne opposed French, American, and Soviet imperialism but cautiously supported the Vietnamese Revolution, albeit headed by Stalinists. Refusing to identify with "bourgeois anti-Communism," the "anarcho-syndicalist" paper supported Ho Chi Minh because he had the majority of the peasants and workers behind him. Even a Stalinist revolution, it conceded, could be popular. Too internationalist to accept complete independence for Vietnam, Monatte's group believed the French Union might still be viable if the French workers could surmount their national chauvinism and effectively stop the war. Hence, the refusal of dockers to resupply the Ile de France on its way to Indochina in April 1947 was a prime example of international working-class solidarity.

On the moderate left, the Ligue des droits de l'homme, generally paralleling the liberal Socialists, called for a parliamentary commission of inquiry. Combat considered Bao Dai a "Quisling" and called for negotiations primarily, if not exclusively, with Ho Chi Minh. Esprit called the Bao Dai solution "stupid" and insisted on an accord with Ho Chi Minh, although he was "far from being without sin" and was turning Vietnam into a Communist country. Highlighting the moral dilemmas of the war, the Catholic personalist journal published distressing stories. One soldier wrote that

> Our campaign in Tonkin has certainly been victo-
> rious. There is no longer a man, a woman, an
> old man, a baby, a water buffalo, a donkey, a
> cat or a bird where our liberating troops have
> passed. . . . We will have to kill everything
> if we hope to get out of this.

To Esprit this was "an atrocious war." (9)

The PCF, even after its expulsion from the cabinet, did not dramatically change over Indochina. Until 1949, it organized no mass demonstrations or strikes against the war. Indochina was not yet a key ingredient in the Cold War, and the PCF's opposition remained essentially verbal. Although it still blamed the war on private French interests, it now increasingly accused the United States of wanting to penetrate economically Indochina and other French colonies. At the same time, the PCF remained committed to the French Union, did not endorse complete Vietnamese independence nor demand the return of the Expeditionary Corps, and even argued that Ho Chi Minh

could be better counted on to protect French interests than
Bao Dai, who wanted to put Vietnam into the American orbit.
An article in <u>France nouvelle</u> lamented, at some length, the
loss of Indochinese rice, rubber, and tea and described the
"loyal and fruitful economic cooperation" that might ensue if
Vietnam remained attached to France. (10)

A further reason for the PCF's attitude was that the
Soviet Union was still little interested in Indochinese
affairs. For example, the Russians had published only four
brochures on Indochina since 1945, compared to twenty-seven
for the 1935-1940 period, seven between 1940 and 1945, five in
1948, and sixteen in 1949-1950. In 1946 and 1947, they had
published only one press article on Vietnam, compared to
eleven on Japan, ten on China, nine on Korea, and four on the
Philippines. In 1948, they did not publish a single article on
Vietnam, although eleven were to appear in 1949 and 1950.
Before 1947, the Soviet Union held a moderate position on the
colonial question, endorsing only trusteeships and gradual
independence, not armed insurrections, criticizing only
"colonialist elements," not the colonial powers themselves.
It insisted that the Vietnamese sought peaceful ties with
France but did not blame the war on France until after the
March 1947 parliamentary debate. (11)

Then, at the founding of the Cominform in September,
Andrei Zhdanov divided the world into an anti-democratic,
imperialist, and bellicose camp headed by the United States
and an opposite one headed by the Soviet Union. He
specifically criticized the PCF for wanting to return to the
government through some new arrangement with the Socialists.
Soon afterwards in Paris, Thorez confessed that the PCF had
been unable to influence substantially the government's
policies, for example, on Indochina. Now, the Party had to
organize a strong popular movement to champion French economic
and political independence <u>and</u> oppose the Vietnam War. Most
Party militants were relieved and enthusiastic about being in
the opposition; for, as a part of a governmental party, they
had found it difficult to condemn the Indochina War, for
example, or the repression in Madagascar. Although the
Cominform Conference paid scant attention to colonial issues
and apparently none at all to Indochina, Zhdanov had urged the
European Communists to identify more closely with overseas
movements. So did a Soviet article in December. (12)

The series of severe political and working class crises
which shook France in the autumn of 1947 deeply divided the
Left, cost the Socialists their key governmental positions,
and left the Communists stunned and isolated. In the
municipal elections of October, the spirit of anti-Communism
united the Socialists and inspired the Gaullists, who captured
40 percent of the vote, even though the PCF held its own with
30 percent. The Socialists declined slightly to 18 percent.
Ramadier was forced to reshuffle his cabinet, notably
replacing Moutet as Overseas Minister with the MRP's Paul
Coste-Floret to reflect the victory of the traditional
colonialists.

The United States was generally pleased with the election
results but hoped the Gaullists would make overtures to the

Socialists and the working class and soften their positions on Germany and Indochina. As Acting Secretary of State Robert Lovett put it:

> It has been clear since the Liberation that the isolation and ostracism of the French Communists was essential if France was to remain in the Western orbit. It was equally clear that politically speaking the break must come to the left of, or at the very least, in the middle of the Socialist Party. Translated into labor terms, the healthy elements of organized labor must be kept in the non-Communist camp.

Yet, Ambassador Caffery felt they could no longer rely on the Socialists:

> I think we have all shared the view that . . . a coalition government made up of middle of the road parties, such as we have had under Ramadier, guaranteed the best hope. . . . It is now inescapable that this experiment has failed. (13)

Lovett was right to focus on the labor problem. With living conditions harsher than at any time under the Occupation, a wave of strikes had developed, which even Caffery considered "fully justified" (i.e., from an economic point of view). A "great fear" spread over the land -- the Communists feared being outlawed, and their opponents feared a Communist insurrection or civil war. In November, with major rioting in Marseille, "an immense working class revolt" spread over the country, eventually involving over three million strikers. Although the Communists, initially, were no more responsible than they had been in 1936, they pushed the strikes to their limits. When the situation got completely out of hand, Ramadier resigned. Auriol then wanted Blum to form an anti-Communist _and_ anti-Gaullist coalition of Socialists and centrist parties. To attack only the Communists, Blum told Caffery, would alienate most of the workers. He also favored negotiations in Indochina, as soon as possible, even with Ho Chi Minh, in order to free French troops to quell a possible Communist uprising in France. However, the MRP's Robert Schuman became the new Premier, with the Socialists relegated to "junior partners," concerned chiefly with social affairs.

Then, Jules Moch, the SFIO Interior Minister, turned to repress the strikes, while, for six days and nights, the National Assembly was in turmoil and strikers and scabs fought bitterly. As support for the strikes diminished, CIA agents and American union leaders (whose intervention Blum told Caffery had been "very helpful") aided Léon Jouhaux and the _Force ouvrière_ faction to split the CGT. Caffery called the split "the most important event" in France since the liberation. Indeed, the CGT was critically weakened, the French labor movement generally demoralized, and even _Force ouvrière_ discredited by its American connections. The PCF had suffered a stunning defeat and was totally isolated

politically.   Although oppositional tactics hardened many
militants, defections increased dramatically.

    Neither Indochina nor the Marshall Plan had been issues
in the strikes, which, except for the activities of American
agents, were purely domestic in character. (No one has found
evidence of Soviet intrigue.)   Nevertheless, the strikes (and
their repression) plunged France fully into the Cold War and
permitted an MRP-dominated government uninhibitedly to pursue
the Bao Dai solution in Vietnam. (14)

NOTES

    Notes have been grouped according to topic.

    1. Georgette Elgey, <u>Histoire de la IVe République</u>, Vol.
I, Paris, 1965, pp.   272, 276-277; Alexander Werth, <u>France</u>,
<u>1940-1955</u>, Boston, 1966, pp. 352-353; Paul-Marie De la Gorce,
<u>L'Après-Guerre</u>, Paris, 1978, pp. 272-278; Grégoire Madjarian,
<u>La Question coloniale et la politique du PCF, 1944-1947</u>,
Paris, 1977, pp.   214-236; Vincent Auriol, <u>Journal du
septennat</u>, Vol. I, <u>1947</u>, Paris, 1970, 9, 17 April, pp. 183;
Moutet Papers, Archives, Ministry of Overseas France, Carton
7, Dossier 158, Sous-Dossier 5.

    2. Elgey, I, pp. 263-293; De la Gorce, I, pp. 233-236,
284-293; George Ross, <u>Workers and Communists in France</u>,
Berkeley, 1982, pp. 45-47; United States National Archives,
Diplomatic Series (USNADS) 851.00, Caffery, 14 May 1947;
Auriol, I, 1947, 1-7 May, pp. 204-217.

    3. Elgey, I, pp.   277-279; Jacques Fauvet, <u>Histoire du</u>
<u>PCF</u>, Paris, 1977, pp.   386-387; Irwin Wall, <u>French Communism</u>
<u>in the Era of Stalin</u>, Westport, Conn., 1983, pp. 53-56;
USNADS 851.00B, Douglas MacArthur II (a nephew of the General)
to Woodruff Wallner, (T/S) Personal, 26 March 1947; <u>Foreign</u>
<u>Relations of the United States</u> (FRUS), 1947, III, Caffery, 31
March, 3 April, 12 May (T/S), pp. 695-696, 709-713.

    For the "Trojan Horse" idea and the SFIO fear of
Communist penetration of the nationalized industries, see
Auriol, I, 1947, 4 February, p.   54, and Irwin Wall, "The
Failure of Left-Wing Unity in France: 1947 and 1977," paper
ppresented to the annual meeting of the American Historical
Association, New York, December 1979.

    4. USNADS 851.00, Matthews, 25 June, Marshall (T/S), 28
June 1947; Fauvet, pp. 388-390; Joyce and Gabriel Kolko, <u>The</u>
<u>Limits of Power: The World and United States Foreign Policy</u>,
<u>1945-1954</u>, New York, 1972, pp. 361-365.

    5. Auriol, I, 1947, 22 March, pp. 163-165; De la Gorce,
I, pp. 345-349; Philippe Devillers, <u>Histoire du Vietnam</u>,
<u>1940-1952</u>, Paris, 1952, pp. 389-390, 405-410; Léon Blum, <u>Le</u>
<u>Populaire</u>, 6, 16 August; FRUS, 1947, VI, Reed, 15 September,
pp. 137-138.

6. FRUS, 1947, VI (FE), Reed, 14, 24 June, 24 July, 15 September, pp. 104, 123-126, 137-138; O'Sullivan, 3, 19, 21 July, 15 September, pp. 108, 120-123, 136-138; Caffery, 31 July, pp. 127-128; Marshall, 13, May, 17 July, pp. 95-97, 117-118; Stuart (China), 18 October, pp. 143-144. See, also, Philip F. Dur (a close associate of Caffery), "The American Ambassador's Views of French Policies in Indochina, 1946-1949," paper presented to the annual meeting of the French Colonial Historical Society, Lafayette, La., March 1981.

When General Raoul Salan argued that the Vietminh were really a wartime creation of imperial Japan, fighting with former Japanese soldiers, O'Sullivan sharply retorted that France was not an Axis creation simply because many former German soldiers fought with the Foreign Legion.

7. Ellen J. Hammer, The Struggle for Indochina, 1940-1955, Stanford, 1955, n. 21, p. 216; Auriol, I, 1947, 26 September, p. 450, 13 October, pp. 469-471; Life, 29 December 1947, cited in Allan B. Cole, editor, Conflict in Indochina and International Repercussions: A Documentary History, Ithaca, N. Y., 1956, pp. 83-84; FRUS, 1947, VI (FE), Reed, 11 July, pp. 110-116; author's interviews with Claude Bourdet and Jean Chesneaux, Paris, May-June 1973.

8. Auriol, I, 1947, 17-18, 26 August, pp. 397-398, 405-407, 433, n. 46 (August), pp. 791-792; Auriol, III, 1949, 12, 20 July, pp. 290, 303, n. 62, p. 653; Daniel Ligou, Histoire du socialisme en France, 1871-1961, Paris, 1962, pp. 551-553; Roger Quilliot, La SFIO et l'exercice du pouvoir, 1944-1958, Paris, 1972, pp. 239-243, 287-293; SFIO, Bulletin intérieur, May-June 1947, p. 7, September-October 1947, p. 4; La Pensée socialiste, August 1946, pp. 21-23, February 1947, pp. 4-7, October 1947, pp. 20-22; Le Populaire, 11, 19 September 1947.

See, also, Paul Alduy, "Le Probleme colonial à la lumière du socialisme," La Revue socialiste, October 1947, pp. 298-302; E. Cohen-Hadria, "Réflexions sur l'Union française," ibid., pp. 303-312, 452-463; Jean Rous, Chronique de la colonisation, Paris, 1965; Rous, Le Congrès des peuples s'adresse aux démocrates de France, Paris, 1950; Paul Clay Sorum, Intellectuals and Decolonization in France, Chapel Hill, 1977, pp. 17-18, 48, 98-99.

9. La Vérité, 9, 30 January, 5 March 1948; Henry Babert, "Le Drame vietnamien," Révolution prolétarienne, April 1947; J. Péra, "De Madagascar à l'Union française," ibid., May 1947; "Où en est la guerre d'Indochine," ibid., August 1948; Les Cahiers de la Ligue des droits de l'homme, January 1947, pp. 118-122, November 1947, pp. 251-255; Combat, 1, 22 August, 12, 19 September, 11 October 1947; Esprit, July 1947, pp. 64-65, December 1947, pp. 956-957, February 1948, pp. 289-292.

10. L'Humanité, 5, 27 June, 4 July 1947; Jean Guillon, "Le Vietnam et la politique nationale et coloniale," Les Cahiers du communisme, March-April 1947, pp. 217-245; Léon

Rivière, ibid., August 1947, pp.   768-786; France nouvelle, 23 August, 11 October 1947.

11. J. Frankel, "Soviet Policy in Southeast Asia," in Max Beloff, Soviet Policy in the Far East, 1944-1951, London, 1953, p.   208; Charles B. McLane, Soviet Strategies in Southeast Asia, Princeton, 1966, pp.   249-254,   266-275; Bernard Fall, Le Vietminh, Paris, 1960, p.   118.

12. Elgey, I, pp.   334-335; Fauvet, pp.   390-395; De la Gorce, I, pp.   301-307; McLane, pp.   354-356.

13. Werth, pp.   373-375; Elgey, I, pp.   337-339; De la Gorce, I, pp.   296-301; FRUS, 1947, III, Lovett to Paris, 25 October (T/S), pp.   790-792; Caffery, 29 October (T/S), pp. 794-795.

14. FRUS, 1947, III, Caffery, 29 November, 20 December, pp.   803-804, 819-820; Auriol, I, 1947, November-December, pp.   533-534, nn.   64, 74, pp.   820-821; USNADS 800.00, Report 9935 (on the strikes), 24 November 1947; Werth, pp.   380-386; De la Gorce, I, pp.   307-322; Elgey, I, pp.   344-377; Fauvet, pp.   395-400; Dominique Desanti, 1947: L'Année où le monde a tremblé, Paris, 1975, pp.   177ff.

See, also, Maurice Agulhon, CRS à Marseille, Paris, 1970; René Gallisot, "L'Illusion républicaine: Socialistes et communistes en 1947," Le Mouvement social, July-September 1975; Darryl Holter, "Miners Against the State, 1944-1949," Ph.D. Thesis, University of Wisconsin, 1980, pp.   253-266.

PART TWO
THE LEFT DIVIDED
1948–1950

VI
Bao Dai
DECEMBER 1947–MARCH 1949

Paris now embarked on the great gamble -- to oppose an admittedly highly popular Vietnamese movement (and government) led by Communists with a non-Communist nationalist regime lacking popular roots but willing to adhere to the French Union. The French Communists were in a poor position to protest, and the Soviet Union remained aloof. The Socialists and the Americans were skeptical but forced to go along by the dictates of the Cold War.

Meanwhile, the classical Right, the Gaullists and the colonial lobby objected to the very concept of the French Union (still only a theoretical concept) and denounced as "unconstitutional" and "criminal" any further concessions to the overseas peoples. Indeed, by 1948, a colonialist reaction had set in everywhere in the French Empire. In Algeria, a Socialist High Commissioner, Marcel-Edmond Naegelen arrested opposition leaders, stuffed ballot boxes, and in other ways rendered the liberal 1947 statute a dead letter. In Madagascar, the trial of the rebel leaders and the three deputies was a travesty which disgusted President Auriol.

The "Bao Dai solution" required over fourteen months to be formalized and another eleven to be ratified. The MRP, the main promoters, hoped Bao Dai's installation would cause the Vietminh Resistance quickly to disintegrate; yet, they were reluctant to give him full independence lest this cause adverse reactions in North Africa. Most Socialists and Radicals, opposed to monarchies of any kind, looked to General Nguyen Van Xuan to develop a bourgeois-democratic, "third-force" style of government. Some Socialists would only accept Bao Dai as a mediator, to persuade Ho Chi Minh to join a government of "national union." Only a few Socialists still remained exclusively attached to the DRV.

In December 1947, Bao Dai signed a protocol with High Commissioner Bollaert which contained the word "independence" but left most Vietnamese leaders dissatisfied. Bao Dai then backed off for several months. Despite being satirized as a "night-club emperor" who preferred the pleasures of Hong Kong or the Riviera, he was actually less a French puppet than a

cautious and calculating politician, hoping to eliminate the
French with American support and, possibly, even with the
cooperation of Ho Chi Minh (for whom he had a sneaking
admiration). Bao Dai certainly knew that without adequate
guarantees of independence and unity, he did not stand a
chance against the DRV leader.

In June 1948, General Xuan, as the head of a new "central
government," stepped in to sign new accords with the French at
the Bay of Along, with Bao Dai as witness. While France
recognized Vietnamese "independence" and "unity" (in theory),
and Xuan promised to accept the French Union and severe
restrictions on his military and diplomatic authority, very
few people in Vietnam or France were pleased. The DRV
condemned Xuan as a "Quisling." The MRP feared that he might
increase his demands and perhaps even make a deal with Ho Chi
Minh. The Gaullists claimed that the Bay of Along Accords,
negotiated by an unrepresentative, minority government in
Paris, had alienated French territory. (The Right generally
preferred military pacification and a complete restoration of
French sovereignty.) U.S. Consul George Abbott (Saigon)
thought that Xuan had "only a dubious chance of success."
Even Secretary Marshall, finding "no evidence of a direct
link" between Moscow and Ho Chi Minh, admitted that the DRV
leader seemed "quite capable of retaining and even
strengthening his grip . . . with no outside assistance other
than the continuing procession of French puppet governments."

On the military front, General Valluy's major offensive
of the fall of 1947 had failed to find and destroy the main
Vietminh units. French casualties mounted, especially among
the officer corps, and morale sank. French troops found
themselves facing a new and bewildering type of war, whose
aims remained obscure, and much public apathy at home. (The
war did not "hit home" as much as the later Algerian or Second
Indochinese Wars because France had a volunteer army, less
than half of which was Metropolitan.)

The Vietminh, for their part, were unable to launch major
operations but controlled about two-thirds of the territory
and more than one-half of the population. They maintained a
sort of dual sovereignty in the Tonkin Delta, collected taxes
even in Hanoi and Saigon, and had achieved much success with
their massive literacy campaign. Although the DRV enjoyed the
diplomatic recognition of no nation, Communist or otherwise,
its delegation in Paris regularly published information
bulletins and collaborated with various left-wing and anti-war
groups. When, in January 1948, Vietnamese workers went on
hunger strikes to protest the arrest of Tran Ngoc Danh, the
head of the DRV delegation, and the internment of one hundred
Vietnamese leaders, French workers and Communists supported
them. (Danh was released in March, but several hundred
Vietnamese immigrants remained in camps.) (1)

The French Socialists were not pleased with the Bay of
Along Accords. Le Populaire considered them an attempt to
impose "a government which did not issue from the freely
expressed will of the people." The SFIO congress in July 1948
once again called for negotiations with Ho Chi Minh and the
"authentic representatives of the Vietnamese people," but the

Party never repudiated the agreements with General Xuan. Meanwhile, a Socialist minority extolled the Vietminh's campaigns against famine and illiteracy and blamed the French for starting the war at Haiphong and for a number of atrocities. Ho Chi Minh, having rallied the "disinterested nationalists" and "a large number of patriotic Catholics," wrote Jeanne Cuisinier, had against him only some of the former mandarins, some of the former bureaucrats, a few elements of the wealthy bourgeoisie, and certain individuals who, under the Japanese regime as under the French, were seeking personal advantages. To Cuisinier the war was both absurd and criminal. (2)

The Communists chided the Socialist ministers for betraying the resolutions of their congresses. For its part, the PCF supported the DRV's right to admission to the United Nations but not to independence outside the French Union. Nor did the PCF demand the immediate repatriation of the Expeditionary Corps nor organize any mass anti-war demonstrations. While not forgetting the French colonialists, the Communists, with repeated reference to the Bullitt mission, blamed the United States for trying to penetrate Indochina economically and to use it as a base whence to aid Chiang Kai-shek. (In all this, they accused the Paris government of complicity.) Finally, the Communists noted that the war inhibited the reconstruction of France, contributed heavily to the misery of the working class, and was rent with atrocities. In a phrase initiated by Le Monde but popularized by the Communists, it was la sale guerre (the filthy war). (3)

Communist criticism notwithstanding, the Socialists had lost much of their influence over Indochinese affairs. Although their presence in the ministry helped to save the Republic, they had to yield on most issues not related to social-economic policies. Their remaining in the government (tied to the clerical MRP) and helping to shatter the unity of the working class had cost the them much popularity. Party membership dropped by 50 percent in two years, especially in the north. Several SFIO publications ceased, and Le Populaire reduced its spread to only two pages until revived by American trade union funds (at the end of 1948).

To stem this decline, and to ward off the Gaullists and Communists, Léon Blum proposed, in January 1948, a "third force." However, this essentially heterogeneous parliamentary arrangement lacked a class basis, and the SFIO and MRP, around whom the concept hinged, disagreed over religious education, social-economic policies, and Indochina. While both parties supported some variation of the Bao Dai solution, the Socialists were probably more sincere about having a democratic, non-Communist and independent Vietnam, whereas the MRP was reluctant to grant substantial concessions to any Vietnamese government. Whether with Ho Chi Minh, Xuan, or Bao Dai, the Socialists wanted a negotiated settlement, whereas the MRP first wanted a military solution.

Disillusioned with the third force, some Socialists turned to Sartre's Rassemblement démocratique révolution- naire. More radical than the Communists on a number of

issues, including the colonial question, the RDR appealed to
those Socialists, such as Rous and Boutbien, who refused the
hegemonies of both Washington and Moscow and who could not
remain ("co-exist") in a party so heavily responsible for the
Indochina War. However, heavily made up of Parisian
intellectuals, the RDR had no working-class following.
Incessantly attacked by the PCF, it moved to the right,
causing Sartre to pull out in 1949. By 1950 it was defunct.
Many left-wing Socialists, including Marceau Pivert, the
leading SFIO dissident of the 1930's, suspected the RDR of
"Trotskyist sentiments." In July, the SFIO congress
overwhelmingly condemned (by a vote of 3675 to 733)
association with the RDR and deprived Rous and Boutbien of
their seats on the Comité directeur. (The latter returned to
the SFIO only after the RDR broke up.)

Although encouraged by the third force, American
officials became increasingly disillusioned with the
Socialists. Caffery told Blum that SFIO opposition to cuts in
the civil service was "completely incomprehensible" unless the
Socialists were more interested in Socialist doctrines and
partisan politics than in the survival of the third force.
Expressing "pained surprise," Blum replied that the Socialists
could "not alone be expected to bear all the sacrifices."
"Increasingly concerned" by the SFIO's attitude, Secretary
Marshall told Caffery not to hesitate "to approach Blum again
or other leaders whose parties show signs of bolting."
American officials also felt that Force ouvrière's tendency
"to seek government favor rather than struggle to gain the
confidence of the working class" was producing "a bad effect
at the intermediary and lower levels." (4)

On the other hand, American officials felt that the
Communist movement still hung "like a Damocles sword over the
head of any government in France," despite its
"anti-nationalist attitude" on the colonial question and
"demagogic" demands for higher wages. (They did not seem to
worry specifically about the PCF's stance on Indochina.) The
Communists did, indeed, exhibit amazing resiliency.
L'Humanité's readership sharply declined, but the PCF's loss
in membership was not as drastic as the Socialists'. The CGT
even persuaded the non-Communist unions to join in demanding
wage increases, thus mitigating the labor split. By
pressuring the Socialists on the questions of laïcité and
military credits, the PCF helped to strain the third force.
Indeed, the Communists still called for a "government of
democratic union" to include itself and just about anyone
except the Gaullists. (5)

In July 1948, the French National Assembly heatedly
debated the military budget (32 percent of national
expenses). Indochina itself, which had cost 3.2 billion
francs in 1945, 27 billion in 1946, and 53.3 billion in 1947,
was now consuming 89.7 billion francs. Although the
government was willing to concede a 5 billion franc reduction
in military spending, the Socialists demanded an additional 3
billion -- not a very large sum. It was, as the Communist
claimed, only a "household quarrel" (and not one over
Indochina) -- but very important symbolically, because the
government had just cut back on 150,000 civil service jobs, a

prime Socialist constituency.   The Communists, on the other
hand, proposed that the ending of the Vietnam War and the
preservation of the French Union would provide more jobs and
raw materials. However, when a Communist deputy declared that
the Vietnamese had a right to handle their own affairs, a
right-wing deputy ironically interjected, "like Tito!" Duclos
then countered that former German SS had been recruited to
fight in Indochina. In the end, the Communists supported the
SFIO amendment, which passed by a vote of 297 to 214 and
forced Schuman to resign. (6)

The new cabinet, under André Marie (a Radical), lasted
less than a month but was distinguished for a new statement on
Indochina. Because of a serious clash between civilian and
military authorities, most Socialists (led by Auriol and
Mayer) wanted a parliamentary debate to "restore order to the
house." By a two-vote margin, the Assembly agreed. However,
in the cabinet, Ramadier suggested that a "solemn declaration"
might postpone a debate. Blum argued against a politique de
force (advocated by Coste-Floret) and suggested that "the best
partner" for negotiations remained Ho Chi Minh. Paul Reynaud,
however, said that the American Embassy wanted only Bao Dai.
In the end, on 19 August, the government's declaration
(drafted by Blum) pledged "solemn adherence" to the
"principles" of the Bay of Along Accords and appealed to "all
the spiritual and political families" of Vietnam to cooperate
in creating, through popular consultations, a "democratic and
free" government, as soon as circumstances permitted.
However, Marie stipulated that Ho Chi Minh remained excluded
and that France had not conceded anything essential.   The
Declaration was approved by a vote of 347 to 183, a full
debate was postponed, and the Bay of Along Accords were never
ratified. (7)

Washington clarified its position one month later.
Despite the "unpleasant fact" that Ho Chi Minh was "the
strongest and perhaps ablest figure in Indochina" and
"supported by a considerable majority of the Vietnamese
people," acknowledging that any solution which excluded him
was "an expedient of uncertain outcome," and finding "no known
communication between the USSR and Vietnam," the State
Department, nevertheless, recommended that the French not
negotiate with him "because of his record as a Communist." In
another report, the Department found evidence of
Kremlin-directed conspiracies "in virtually all countries" of
Southeast Asia "except Vietnam." (8)

In Paris, Henri Queuille, a Radical, formed another third
force ministry (with Ramadier as Defense Minister). Having
taken the wind out of the Gaullist sails by postponing the
cantonal elections, Queuille then faced the Communists and
several serious strikes. Even the CFTC and Force ouvrière had
joined the CGT's demands for higher wages, the Socialists had
gone along, and Blum had even asked Caffery for American
support. However, when Robert Lacoste, the Socialist Minister
of Industry and Commerce, introduced some tough measures in
the coal industry, the miners replied with a massive strike.
Caffery called it the lowest point in national morale since
the war:

There is real evidence that the trend which
resulted in the split between Communist and
non-Communist labor unions (the capital event
of post-war France) has come to a stop and may
be reversed and replaced by a trend toward
unity in which the superior organization of
the Communists would prevail.

To both Washington and the Socialists, the miners'
strikes were strategic and political. Despite some very
bitter resistance, the miners never aimed at an insurrection,
and the CGT had only limited success in organizing sympathy
strikes. At the end of October, Jules Moch, as Interior
Minister, began a systematic and militarized reconquest of the
mines. (John L. Lewis accused him of using American funds to
break the strike.) Although Moch was unable to prove that the
Cominform had been involved, the ensuing repression was
severe, the number of unionized miners sharply declined, and
the CGT lost all key union positions.

The miners' strikes only indirectly affected the
Indochina War, which the Socialists now increasingly
interpreted as an essentially anti-Communist struggle. The
Communists, realizing that the defeated and demoralized
working class itself could not end the war, now appreciated
that liberal anti-war campaigns, across class lines, could
help to move them out of their isolation. (9)

The Indochina War now moved into the international arena,
and the imminence of a Communist victory in China inspired a
new settlement with non-Communists in Vietnam. Léon Pignon
(MRP) replaced Bollaert as High Commissioner, and Paris turned
once more to Bao Dai. Although the French government was ready
to yield on the colonial status of Cochinchina, Bao Dai, at
the urging of the Gaullists, insisted that the National
Assembly ratify the issue.

American officials, however, were not too confident about
the Bao Dai solution. Abbott reported a "real danger" of
defections to the Vietminh rather than to Bao Dai. Officials
in Washington were generally reluctant to support a "puppet
government" which lacked "popular appeal." Secretary Acheson
did not believe the French had shown an "impressively sincere
intention or desire to make concessions." Caffery, fearing,
among other things, that American intervention in Indochina
might strengthen the PCF's political position in France, urged
"a wait-and-see attitude." (10)

In France, Socialist dissidents (with some encouragement
from the DRV mission in Paris, Caffery reported) now made one
last effort to block the Bao Dai solution. Paul Alduy, SFIO
leader in the Assembly of the French Union and author of
L'Union française, mission de France (a sharp critique of
European colonialism) and Oreste Rosenfeld of the Populaire
group led the attack. Both urged talks with Ho Chi Minh.
Auriol angrily replied:

> You are going to ruin everything. . . . Only
> the Socialists and Communists will be together.
> . . . You will be beaten, and you will not
> have resolved the Indochina problem. . . .

Not to accept Bao Dai, the President added, would be to lose
Indochina and the Fourth Republic. Communism would sweep over
Southeast Asia, and, ultimately, "you will hand over Europe to
Russia!" Somewhat shaken, Rosenfeld still proposed to meet
personally with Ho Chi Minh. Mollet agreed, but Auriol said he
could only go to Vietnam as a journalist.

In January, the SFIO's Comité directeur, at Alduy's
behest, asked Mollet to protest directly to Premier Queuille.
In his letter, the Socialist leader recalled his Party's
traditional opposition to a military solution or to exclusive
negotiations with Bao Dai or General Xuan. France could not
have peace without treating with Ho Chi Minh on the basis of
the 1946 and 1948 Accords, for most Vietnamese patriots
considered him the "authentic representative of their
aspirations." Moreover, with the changeover in China, time
was running out, Mollet noted. France risked losing Indochina
entirely and under the most humiliating conditions, with
severe repercussions for the rest of the French Union. He
concluded with a veiled threat to pull out of the government
if the other ministers could not change their policies. Le
Populaire printed the letter on 10 March (over Auriol's
objection), two days after the Auriol-Bao Dai Accords and only
because Franc-Tireur had published it a day earlier. In the
meantime, the SFIO National Council, late in February,
endorsed an entente with all Vietnamese leaders, including Ho
Cho Minh, and insisted that Bao Dai be considered only a
mediator, not a sovereign. (11)

On 8 March, Auriol and Bao Dai formally exchanged letters
at the Elysée Palace. France formally recognized the
independence of Vietnam as an "Associated State" within the
French Union and promised to accept Vietnamese unity as soon
as the "interested populations" had been consulted. Bao Dai
agreed to French control of foreign and military affairs,
joint control of customs (the bugaboo of 1946), and, among
other items, allowed the piastre to remain tied to the French
franc.

The new Vietnamese status was considerably less than that
enjoyed by British Commonwealth nations, and the Communist and
near-Communist press unreservedly condemned the Elysée
Accords. Even newspapers favorable to the third force
exhibited little enthusiasm, and Le Populaire hoped that
fuller negotiations would follow. Rosenfeld told the Assembly
of the French Union that "we are not in Indochina to establish
a regime which pleases us." Bao Dai should be considered only
if Ho Chi Minh refused French proposals. (12)

Both the Right and the Left attacked the Accords in the
National Assembly. Edouard Frédéric-Dupont accused the
Socialists of fundamentally disagreeing with the rest of the
ministry. (He also called for the outlawing of traitors,

presumably the Communists, "who dared insult our soldiers!")
The Communists, for their part, interpreted Mollet's letter as
an attempt to "mask in the eyes of public opinion the war
policy followed by the Socialist ministers," to regain a
little bit of popularity for the SFIO. The Socialists replied,
through Gaston Defferre, that, although Ho Chi Minh was a
brutal, authoritarian, Stalinist Communist, he nevertheless
headed a de facto government with which France realistically
had to negotiate.

During the debate, Paul Rivet, now an independent deputy,
made his famous revelations about the sabotaging of the
Conference of Fontainebleau in 1946. There was also a fair
amount of witty and caustic repartee. When a right-wing
deputy referred to Bao Dai's royalty, Duclos sardonically
interjected: "The Government of the Republic behind His
Majesty! That's charming!" Yet, when Duclos called Bao Dai a
former Japanese valet, a deputy from the other side replied,
"You have never reproached Stalin for having negotiated with
Hitler!" When Lambert Saravane compared Ho Chi Minh to Gandhi,
as a man of the people, Maurice Schumann (MRP) countered, "If
only Ho Chi Minh had practiced the same non-violence!"

Ultimately, the government was unable to bring the entire
Elysée Accords to a vote and succeeded only in obtaining the
passage, 348 to 202, of a special law on the status of
Cochinchina. The Gaullists, supported by the PCF, entered a
motion of censure. The Socialists voted with the government,
and Caffery was pleased that they had been brought "to heel."
(13)

NOTES

Notes have been grouped according to topic.

1. Vincent Auriol, Journal du septennat, Vol. II, 1948,
Paris, 1974, pp. xxi-xxvi (colonialist reaction), n. 79
(June), p. 655; Philippe Devillers, Histoire du Vietnam,
1940-1952, Paris, 1952, pp. 397, 416-438; Alexander Werth,
France, 1940-1955, Boston, 1966, pp. 445-446, 450-452 (Bao
Dai); Ellen J. Hammer, The Struggle for Indochina, 1940-1955,
Stanford, 1955, pp. 223-224 (the DRV); Jean Chesneaux,
Contribution à l'histoire de la nation vietnamienne, Paris,
1955, pp. 275-293 (the DRV); Paul-Marie De la Gorce,
L'Après-Guerre, Paris, 1978, pp. 351-356 (the Expeditionary
Corps); Foreign Relations of the United States (FRUS), 1948,
VI (FE), Stanton (Bangkok), 24 February, pp. 21-23; Caffery,
9 June, pp. 24-25; SOS Marshall to China, 2 July, to Paris,
T/S, 3 July, pp. 28-30.

2. Le Populaire, 10 January (André Fontaine), 4 February
(Colonel F. Bernard, a non-Socialist overseas authority), 14
February, 6-7 June 1948, (Oreste Rosenfeld) 20 August, 29
October 1948; Jeanne Cuisinier, La Revue Socialiste, June-July
1948, pp. 157-174.

3. L'Humanité, 20 January, 1-3 February, 4 June, 18
August, 25 November, 9 December 1948; France nouvelle, 5 June,

14, 21 August, 23 October 1948; Raymond Barbé, "Les peuples d'outre-mer dans la lutte anti-impérialiste," Les Cahiers du communisme, March 1948, pp. 271-286.

4. Georgette Elgey, Histoire de la IVe République, Vol. I, Paris, 1965, pp. 313-315; Werth, pp. 411-413 (American funding); Auriol, II, 1948, pp. xi-xvii; 26 January, p. 48; Roger Quilliot, La SFIO et l'exercice du pouvoir, 1944-1958, Paris, 1972, pp. 281-297, 363-364; Joel Colton, Léon Blum, Paris, 1967, p. 476; Jean Lacouture, Léon Blum, Paris, 1977, pp. 540-543, 549-552; De la Gorce, pp. 435-441; Michel Fabre, The Unfinished Quest of Richard Wright, New York, 1973, pp. 326-327, 330, 335, 375 (the RDR); FRUS, 1948, III (WE), Caffery, 29 January, pp. 613-614; SOS Marshall to Paris, 30 January, p. 622.

5. Auriol, II, 1948, pp. xi-xii; United States National Archives, Diplomatic Series (USNADS) 851.00B, Caffery, 6 February 1948; Norris B. Chipman (Paris), "Report to the Third European Intelligence Conference," Frankfurt, Germany, 2-7 June 1948, relayed by Caffery, 10 June.

6. De la Gorce, I, pp. 342-344; Auriol, II, 1948, pp. 302-303; Journal officiel, débats parlementaires, Assemblée nationale (JODPAN), 15-19 July 1948, Jean Capdeville (SFIO), pp. 4742, André Philip, pp. 4750-4751, Charles Lussy (SFIO), pp. 4852-4853; Jean Guillon (PCF), pp. 4255-4257, 4714, 4734-4737; Pierre Villon (PCF), 15, 19 July, pp. 4605ff., 4854-4855.

7. Auriol, II, 1948, pp. 314-315, 361-363; 19 August, p. 369, n. 43 (July), p. 661; Devillers, pp. 436-440; L'Année politique, 1948, p. 341 (Marie Declaration).

In the spring of 1948, Bollaert sent Louis Caput, the SFIO representative in Indochina, on an unsuccessful mission to contact DRV emissaries in Hong Kong. Caput, one of the founders of the Marxist Cultural Group of Saigon and quite sympathetic to the Vietminh, had played a key role in the March 1946 Accords. Although Bollaert may have been using Caput to bluff the Baodaists, Paris was scarcely pleased with the initiative. When, later in August, the DRV invited Caput to meet with their representatives in Tonkin, Paris blocked the move.

8. FRUS, 1948, VI (FE), DOS Policy Statement: French Indochina, 27 September, pp. 43-49; U.S. Defense Department, United States-Vietnam Relations, 1945-1967 (Pentagon Papers), Washington, 1971, Book I, Part II, pp. A42, A49-A50.

9. Elgey, I, pp. 396-404; Werth, pp. 402-405; Irwin Wall, French Communism in the Era of Stalin, Westport, Conn., 1983, 78-81, 85-88; Auriol, II, 1948, 1-3 September, pp. 409, 411, 416; 1, 20, 29 October, pp. 453, 491, 504-505; nn. 79, 83, (November), pp. 698; nn. 88, 89 (December), p. 706; De la Gorce, I, pp. 328; Darryl Holter, "Miners Against the State, 1944-1949," Ph.D. Dissertation, University of Wisconsin, 1980, pp. 399-466; Jules Moch, Un si longue vie, Paris, 1976, pp. 327-329.

FRUS, 1948, III (WE), Caffery, 5 October, pp. 662-664; Lovett (Acting SOS) to Paris, 27 October, pp. 672-673; Marshall (Paris) to Lovett, 28 October, pp. 673-674, Memorandum of Conversation with Queuille, Caffery et alii, T/S, 18 November, pp. 677-682; Caffery, no. 5593, 28 October (not printed); USNADS 851.00, Caffery, "The Political Foundation of the Queuille Government at the End of 1948," 22 December 1948.

Although Caffery felt De Gaulle might emerge as a new Bonaparte to break the "Communist hold" over the working class, most American officials found the General's policy toward labor disturbing ("he talks about economics as a woman talks about carburetors") and feared he might provoke a civil war.

10. Hammer, pp. 230-231; Devillers, pp. 439-443; Buttinger, II, pp. 720-723; Auriol, II, 1948, 18 October, pp. 484-487; Auriol, III, 1949 (Paris, 1977), 13, 17, 19 January, pp. 14-16, 23, 33-34; n. 7 bis (February), p. 546; Francis Borella, L'Evolution politique et juridique de l'Union française depuis 1946, Paris, 1958, pp. 166-168; FRUS, 1948, VI (FE), Abbott, 28 August, 5 November, pp. 39, 54-55 (found no evidence of Soviet or Chinese Communist involvement in Indochina); FRUS, 1949, VII (FE), Lovett to Paris, 17 January, pp. 4-5; SOS Acheson, 25 February, pp. 8-9.

11. Auriol, II, 1948, nn. 2, 7 (August), p. 667; Auriol, III, 1949, 12, 21, 27 January, pp. 12-13, 38-40, 68; 21 February, pp. 125-126; Quilliot, pp. 324-326; SFIO, Bulletin intérieur, January 1949 (Alduy's report).

12. Hammer, pp. 233-238; Devillers, p. 443; L'Année politique, pp. 311-323 (for complete text of Elysée Accords). Libération, 9 March 1949; Le Populaire, 9 March 1949; Auriol, III, 1949, n. 37 (March), p. 560.

13. Auriol, III, 1949, nn. 64, 102 (March), pp. 562, 565; JODPAN, 10 March 1949, Frédéric-Dupont, pp. 1507-1513; Rivet, pp. 1513-1518; Guillon (PCF), pp. 1521-1526; 11 March 1949, Tillon, p. 1566; Defferre, pp. 1557-1562; Mutter-Duclos, pp. 1562-1565; Saravane-Schumann, pp. 1581-1583; conclusion, pp. 1590-1592; FRUS, 1949, VII, Caffery, 18 March, pp. 14-15.

When Rivet again brought up the subject of Fontainebleau during the January 1950 debate, Jean Letourneau, the MRP Minister of Overseas France, retorted that Rivet had already settled his grievances through correspondence with Max André and Moutet and that Rivet knew full well that the French delegation had not played any double game. Rivet meekly replied that he had not intended to criticize André or Moutet and that he had been speaking only of the general spirit which had animated the French delegation. See JODPAN, 28 January 1950, pp. 660-663.

VII
The Peace Offensive
1949–1950

The year 1949 was a time of "happy illusions" in the French colonial world, while Paris held firm against the overseas separatists. For a brief period, a pre-1939 mentality re-emerged. However, as the Socialists continued to yield ground on the colonial question, the Communists did make Indochina a peripheral issue in their massive Peace Offensive. (1)

The failure of the 1947 and 1948 strikes, the coup de Prague, the Berlin blockade, Tito's schism, and a 1949 Vatican ban on even the reading of Communist literature left the PCF more politically isolated than ever. L'Humanité's circulation had dropped to 270,000, a number of party publications had ceased entirely, and membership cards issued had fallen by 250,000. Nevertheless, still maintaining a large electorate (23 percent in the cantonal elections of March 1949), the PCF sought to break out of its ghetto through "unity of action" with potential allies and, above all, through a vast, popular movement for peace. Clearly the massive strikes had not changed the orientation of the government nor alleviated the misery of the workers. Only by moving across class lines could the Communists hope to defeat the Marshall Plan and the Western military alliance.

Anti-Communists dismissed the Peace Offensive as a "Communist front," accusing the PCF of subordinating the movement to its own (and the Soviet Union's) political purposes, of not sincerely wanting peace. Extreme leftists (gauchistes), on the other hand, blamed the Communists for seizing on an easy issue, one devoid of radical content (in a revolutionary Socialist sense), and for being more concerned about a threat of war against the Soviet Union than an actual one in Indochina. Actually, the Peace Movement had a number of non-Communist sources and ultimately greatly increased public distaste for the Indochina War.

By 1948 "neutralist" sentiment and a desire for peace and national independence were widespread in France. Although public opinion was generally pro-West, it was also anti-war. Even the most die-hard anti-Communists did not want a violent showdown with the Soviet Union. Conscious of these popular feelings, Paris often played a "double game" with Washington. Some non-Communists even believed that the Soviet Union was a lesser threat to peace than the United States. Left-wing intellectuals such as Claude Bourdet and Sartre reflected a popular "plague-on-both-your-houses" attitude and refused to consider the USSR as the incarnation of evil to be eradicated by war. Etienne Gilson, the Thomist philosopher, argued frequently in Le Monde against the "inevitability" of war and particularly the idea of a "preventive war." (American officials accused the paper of "poisoning the mind of France.") The neutralist movement, however, lacked organization, received no Communist endorsement, and, ultimately, was unable to remain neutral.

Meanwhile, in the spring of 1948, Yves Farge, aided by Charles Tillon, started a distinctive peace movement, the Combattants de la liberté. In August, Polish Communists organized a World Council of Intellectuals for Peace, whose headquarters moved to Paris. In October, Stalin called for political action against American and British leaders wanting to unleash a new world war. In November, the PCF, despite its long-standing distrust of liberal pacifism, joined with Farge's group to organize a National Congress for the Defense of Peace and Freedom, which attracted some 12,000 sympathizers. Duclos foresaw a formidable movement sweeping the country, and Georges Cogniot thought it would be much broader than the Popular Front. Accordingly, L'Humanité appealed to "all democratic organizations" -- trade unionists, women, youth organizations, peasants, religious groups, cultural organizations, scholars, writers, journalists, artists and democratic political figures. (2)

In January 1949, Marcel Cachin, doyen d'age in the National Assembly, opened the parliamentary year with a plea for peace. A few days later, in a spectacular interview with an American journalist, Stalin called for joint Soviet-American renunciations of war and pledges to disarm progressively. Discussions soon began about lifting the Berlin blockade. Meanwhile, in France, Thorez dramatically declared that "the French people will not, will never wage war on the Soviet Union." He explicitly told the Central Committee that "the glorious defenders of Stalingrad" could not be "aggressors toward any country whatsoever." However, if the Soviet Union was "forced to pursue aggressors onto French soil, could the French people do anything other than what had been done by the peoples of Poland, Rumania, and Yugoslavia?"

Although Gaullist deputies denounced Thorez as another Laval and demanded that the PCF be outlawed, the government hesitated to make him into a martyr (and could not prove that he had absolutely refused to fight the Red Army). Moch did not want to have to prosecute every PCF deputy who might repeat their Secretary-General's remarks, and Ramadier did not want to appear to oppose those wishing peace. (3)

After a campaign to register several hundred thousand petitions against the proposed NATO Pact, the PCF co-sponsored, in April 1949, the First World Congress of the Partisans of Peace at the Salle Pleyel, where over fifty

countries, chiefly France, Russia and Italy, were
represented. Picasso's La Colombe (The "Dove of Peace")
adorned the city. Frédéric Joliot-Curie, head of the French
Atomic Energy Commission, presided. Yves Farge and Pietro
Nenni were among the principal speakers, and Paul Robeson sang
poignantly as if with "the voice of all the colored peoples in
revolt against imperialism and colonialism."

The delegates spoke for five days about American
imperialism, the atomic bomb, colonialism, violations of the
United Nations Charter, and the re-arming of Germany and
Japan, but little about Indochina. The Congress attracted a
large number of non-Communists and closed with a huge
demonstration at the Stade Buffalo. For the PCF, it had been a
great success. Following the meeting, the French delegation
organized the Mouvement de la Paix, bringing together
religious and political leaders of various persuasions. (The
movement and its journal, Combat pour la paix, remained quite
active during the American war in Indochina.) (4)

The American Embassy took the Peace Movement quite
seriously and urged Premier Queuille, as early as March, to
undertake "energetic" measures "to counteract its effects and
put the Communist Party on the defensive." Otherwise, the
Peace Campaign would have "far-reaching and highly unsettling
effects" on French opinion and also on NATO, the Military
Defense Assistance Pact (MDAP) and American foreign policy in
general. French officials complained that, because of a lack
of facilities and organization, Secretary of Information
François Mitterrand "could not be counted on to organize and
carry out such a campaign effectively." The State Department
did not prevent American citizens from attending the World
Peace Congress, but Secretary Acheson denounced such "rigged"
events for vilifying democratic nations, confusing true
liberals, and destroying third-force movements. (5)

Caffery believed that the PCF, through the Peace
Movement, was returning to classe contre classe politics,
waging civil war against "bourgeois democracy," encouraging
"military defeatism," and staunchly opposing colonial
policies, particularly in Indochina. However, the Communists
were making no sharp "turn to the left" as in the 1928-1934
period. Indeed, the PCF was about to demote some of the
elements most often susceptible to "left-wing deviationism" --
"Titists," "Trotskyists," veterans of the International
Brigades, and "adventurist" leaders of the miners' unions.
Only the PCF's vigorous denunciation of the SFIO leadership
was reminiscent of classe contre classe.

The correct parallel to 1949 was the Popular Front or,
better yet, the Front français of 1936. The French Communists
were trying to break out of their isolation, not to confirm it
or to resign themselves to it. The Peace Movement promoted a
certain front national appeal across class lines and an
alliance with the pacifist bourgeoisie. The PCF was not being
revolutionary but conciliatory and (as an American official
pointed out) was actually afraid of isolating itself in the
Peace Movement by insisting on unequivocal support for the
Soviet Union or other Party policies. (6)

When the French parliament again debated the military budget early in June 1949, the Communists argued that the government could not fight a colonial war abroad without waging war on the working class at home. Consequently, Alfred Malleret-Joinville warned, the dockers and the railway workers would lead the resistance to the Indochina War as Charles Tillon and André Marty had resisted Allied intervention into Soviet Russia. The Communists also continued to charge that former German SS and French miliciens were fighting in the ranks of the Expeditionary Corps, including two who had participated in the massacre at Oradour-sur-Glane in 1944. When they were unable to furnish any names, a right-wing deputy asked where Tillon had been at that time. The former FTP leader called him an "imbecile." (7)

In July, the Peace Movement demonstrated against General Omar Bradley's arrival in Paris and the introduction of nuclear weapons in France. In September, the PCF conducted a "peace ballot" on the questions of German rearmament, the Vietnam War, nuclear weapons, and the French military budget. Communist youth organizations set up "action committees" in various neighborhoods and work places. A group of mothers whose sons had been killed in the war marched to the Ministry of Defense but were not received by Ramadier. In November, the Communists sponsored a "National Day of Peace" for which dozens of "peace caravans" travelled to Paris. Jeannette Vermeersch, fresh from the Congress of Asian women in Peking, vigorously denounced the Vietnam War. On 25 November, the CGT made peace an issue in a twenty-four-hour general strike. Two months later, just before the National Assembly debate on Indochina, 30,000 women rallied at the Vel' d'Hiv' against the Vietnam War. (The Chinese Communists cited this as a prime example of a broad and popular anti-imperialist front.)

Nevertheless, in an interesting piece of autocritique, Jean Guillon confessed that the PCF's fight against the Vietnam War was not yet comparable to its previous struggle against the Rif War of the 1920's, especially in terms of mass action. The anti-colonialist struggle was the business of all Communists, not just a few specialists, and an essential component of the entire working-class struggle. Only with more strikes and anti-war propaganda in the army could the French workers gain the confidence of the colonial peoples -- their necessary allies in the struggle against imperialism. In December, the Central Committee complained of too much "débrouillage individuel" ("undirected individual initiatives") and not enough "mass action" against the "fabrication, transport and storage of war matériel destined for the unjust Vietnam War." (8)

The most radical anti-war actions were the refusals of dockers to load or unload ships bound for Indochina. The main wave began in June 1949, when Algerian dockers refused to load two French naval vessels on their way to Southeast Asia. Approximately 800 Algerian soldiers demonstrated in their support and called for an armistice in Vietnam. (A considerable amount of anti-war agitation developed in Algeria and often spread to France via Algerian workers, particularly in Marseille.) From November 1949 through April 1950, the Marseille dockers, in a more or less continuous manner, refused to load war matériel destined for Indochina or to unload ships coming in with American weapons. Severals times the government sent in the CRS (riot police) and the army to break up the strikes and arrest the leaders, resulting in some bloody clashes. Eventually every major French port, except Cherbourg (where non-Communist unions were in control), was involved, especially Toulon, Sète, Port-de-Bouc, St. Louis, Bordeaux, La Rochelle, St. Nazaire, Lorient, Brest, Le Havre, Boulogne, Dunkerque, Bastia in Corsica, and Algiers and Oran in Algeria.

On 13 December, CGT head Benoît Frachon told the workers that, if they really wanted peace, they would have to emulate the dockers of Algiers and Marseille -- that, whether as railway workers, sailors, munition workers, or steel workers, they would have to make their actions conform to their words. (American officials called this "unpatriotic" and "subversive.")

The dockers' strikes reached a high point in the first months of 1950, coinciding with the Chinese and Soviet recognition of the DRV. On 17 February, the government threatened to send in troops to replace the dockers and to fire any munitions workers not performing their jobs properly. At Toulon several hundred dockers fought with the CRS, which was brought in to ensure the unloading of American ships. At Nice some 2,000 demonstrators broke through police lines to push what they thought was a rocket launcher into the sea. In most ports "action committees" supported the dockers. Sometimes railway workers, building workers, and munitions workers stopped work, often for several hours, to express their sympathy. Several times sailors joined the dockers, as when in January 1950 those manning the _Pasteur_ prevented 3,000 troops from boarding for forty-eight hours. So did soldiers such as the 700 at Fréjus who refused to board a troop train, saying, "No to the dirty war!" There were also reports of sabotage. General Revers estimated that some 40 percent of the equipment going to Indochina had been seriously tampered with and rendered useless in one way or another.

La Vie ouvrière (the CGT newspaper) published lists of anti-war actions undertaken each week, and various PCF publications reminisced about earlier anti-imperialist campaigns, from the days of Jules Guesdes and Jaurès to the Rif War, celebrating particularly the Black Sea Mutiny. Most dramatically, a young Communist _militante_, Raymonde Dien, threw herself on the railway tracks at Tours in February to stop a train loaded with arms for Indochina, defying the engineer to run her over. Second to Henri Martin, Dien, who got ten months in prison, became the most celebrated hero of the French Communist resistance to the Indochina War. (9)

The dockers, however, elicited little public support outside working-class circles. Even the liberal press was hostile, with _Le Monde_ warning that the strikes would "disarm our soldiers, starve them, and force France to submit to foreign dictates." The paper called upon the government to impose the necessary sanctions to keep the strikes from spreading. The Communists needed a more poignantly liberal cause -- Henri Martin's imprisonment for distributing anti-war literature -- to generate widespread popular support for the anti-war movement.

It is also not clear how much the Communists were actually orchestrating all these radical activities, though they no doubt welcomed and encouraged them. It may well have been that many disgruntled workers were acting on their own initiative, engaging in what the PCF called "débrouillage individuel," and were only belatedly supported and encouraged by the CGT. The frequently noted radical, anarcho-syndicalist spirit of the dockers, railway workers, and building workers who worked outdoors and in conditions less regimented than in heavy industry, could have been a contributing factor.

Furthermore, the Communists may not have been entirely pleased with all this "individual initiative" and consequently stressed "mass action," which was less radical and easier to control and to keep within legal bounds. They were particularly sensitive to charges of sabotage; Communists and former Communists interviewed by this author have either categorically denied being involved in this or have protested that they were unaware of such goings-on. Yet, we know little about the "hidden history" of the French Left during these times.

On 8 March 1950, over the PCF's vigorous protests, the National Assembly passed laws against sabotage, refusals to transport arms, and attempts to demoralize the army. Within a couple of months the dockers' strikes declined appreciably. Other incidences of anti-war activities continued. For example, about a year later, a group of people from the fourteenth arrondissement in Paris went to the Gare Montparnasse and, with the complicity of the railroad workers, disabled a train carrying American gun-carriers and unloaded the cargo. Recently written memoirs, by both Communists and non-Communists, testify that similar "heroic gestures" were taking place "everywhere in France" during these times.

The workers, of course, could never hope to stop American arms deliveries entirely. Theirs were mostly symbolic actions which, at best, temporarily delayed a shipment or caused it to be rerouted. The dockers had also acted at great economic sacrifice to themselves; even under normal conditions, they handled only a few ships a month, and an extra American ship or two would have made a great difference in their paychecks. For this reason the refusals to load or unload ships were particularly hard on the Algerian dockers. Clearly the dockers' strikes could not continue indefinitely.

Nevertheless, these and other anti-war activities added to public dissatisfaction with the Indochina War. They also became rapidly inscribed in the "heroic legends" of Communist literature. André Stil's account, Le Premier choc (a novel), merited the Stalin Prize. Even the conservative L'Année politique appreciated that by advocating a "defense of peace against American imperialism," the Communists had found an issue on which they could "see eye-to-eye with a much wider public" than their usual clientele. "Their campaign deeply affected wide sections of the population" who were otherwise "impervious to the other themes of Communist propaganda."

They were also "particularly shrewd . . . to exploit the growing distaste and weariness" that the interminable war in Vietnam was causing to "ever-growing sections of the French people." (10)

In March 1950, the Communists greatly amplified the Peace Movement when the Permanent Committee of World Peace Congresses, meeting in Stockholm, dramatically called for a worldwide signature campaign to outlaw the atomic bomb. (This came six months after the Soviet Union exploded its first atomic bomb and one month after President Truman ordered the construction of a hydrogen bomb.) By the end of the year, the "Stockholm Appeal" claimed some 500 million signatures, mostly from Communist countries, but also 15 million in France, 17 million in Italy, and even 2.5 million in the United States. Many non-Communists were involved, and the signature-collectors went literally everywhere, into the most remote villages, hamlets, and farms.

Gérard Belloir, a former Communist, has recently recalled that, while everyone was afraid of war, the Communists were chiefly responsible for mobilizing popular opinion. Non-Communists agreed to "godfather" (parrainer) certain aspects of the campaign so as to reach a wider audience, but the Communists did most of the hard work. Although the struggle for Socialism had been put on the back burner, Belloir felt that the Peace Movement and the campaigns against colonial wars gave the Communists a "progressive" image, allowing them to appear as the enemies of violence and national oppression.

The Catholic priest Jean Boulier, a Dominican, who, along with Yves Farge, was one of the original founders of the Peace Movement, argued that his support of the Stockholm Appeal was only an attempt to "turn around a situation which had become intolerable for a Christian." To say that he had been "duped" by the Communists was "villainous," for there were also Quakers in the movement, and the Church had said nothing about Catholic workers associating with Communists in strike actions. Any use of the atomic bomb, Boulier declared, was "criminal." It was simple idiocy to believe that a "good" bomb could be dropped on Moscow and only a "bad" one on New York. (11)

The Peace Offensive preoccupied American officials, who, despite certain disclaimers, appreciated its real successes. Ambassador David K. Bruce (who had replaced Caffery in May 1949) noted that, despite some "treasonable overtones," the Peace Movement was "gaining strength, especially among war veterans, deportée and Resistance groups" (who feared a revival of Nazism in Germany). For the first few months of 1950, the American embassies in Paris, Rome, Brussels, and The Hague reported extensively on a "general and intense" campaign against American military equipment, including dockers' strikes, throughout Western Europe, especially in France and Italy. The embassy in London urged all appropriate Washington agencies, including Labor, to work with the embassies "to minimize its effectiveness."

Accordingly, Washington actively enlisted American labor leaders, provided more funds for the "Voice of America," and denied visas to a delegation of "Peace Partisans" that included Pablo Picasso. On 22-24 March, American officials met in Rome to plan a "vigorous" counter-propaganda offensive to deprive the Soviet Union of its peace initiative.   The State Department also urged certain political, economic and military measures, and President Truman endorsed an   "intensified program to promote the cause of freedom against the propaganda of slavery." (12)

The Communists' Peace Offensive essentially protected the interests of the Soviet Union and only peripherally touched on colonial issues. Although the dockers' strikes focused on the Vietnam War, they skirted the limits of legality and did not gain much support outside of proletarian circles.   The Stockholm Appeal, completely unrelated to Indochina or to Socialist goals, was more congenial to the PCF's temperament and brought it its greatest amount of popularity (though no alliance with the SFIO) in a period of severe political isolation and social ostracism.   Then, as the Stockholm movement crested at the end of 1950, the Communists launched a massive and popular campaign, focusing primarily on French national interests, to free Henri Martin.

NOTES

Notes have been grouped according to topic.

1. Vincent Auriol, <u>Journal du septennat</u>, Vol. III, <u>1949</u>, Paris, 1977, pp. xvi-xx.

2. Marshall D. Shulman, <u>Stalin's Foreign Policy Reappraised</u>, Cambridge, 1963, pp.   80-92; Alexander Werth, <u>France, 1940-1955</u>, Boston, 1966, pp.   392-395, 427-428; Paul-Marie De la Gorce, <u>L'Après-Guerre</u>, Paris, 1978, pp. 395-396, 423-442; Irwin Wall, <u>French Communism in the Era of Stalin</u>, Westport, Conn., 1983, pp.   77-78, 110; Auriol, II, 1948, n. 53 (November), p. 696; <u>Foreign Relations of the United States</u> (FRUS), 1948, III (WE), Caffery, T/S, 2 October, pp. 661-662; United States National Archives, Diplomatic Series (USNADS) 851.00B, Caffery, 3 October 1948; <u>Cominform Bulletin</u>, 1 April, p.   3; 15 December (Georges Cogniot); Duclos, <u>Cahiers du communisme</u>, December 1948, p.   1335; <u>L'Humanité</u>, 25 February 1949.

Caffery reported that the Peace Movement ceased to be a purely French nationalist movement (as Tillon hoped) when the Soviet Union intervened in September 1948. Wall says further that Farge, Pierre Cot, and Emmanuel d'Astier de la Vigerie were secret PCF members, permitted to disguise their party identities in order to work with and attract non-Communists.

3. De la Gorce, p. 396; Auriol, III, 1949, 7, 12 January, pp. 6, 8; 2 March, p. 136; n. 1 (February), p. 546; Werth, pp. 438-439; USNADS 851.00B, Caffery, 3 October 1948.

4. Auriol, III, 1949, p.   220; Werth, pp.   439-441; Wall, pp.   97-98; Shulman, pp.   92-99;   Ce Soir, 13, 21 April 1949; France nouvelle, 30   April,   21 May 1949; Témoignage chrétien, 29 July, 12 August, 2 September 1949.

Left-wing Socialists, such as Marceau   Pivert,   and supporters of Sartre's RDR countered the World Peace Congress with a "Day of Resistance to Dictatorship and War."

5. USNADS 851.00B, Caffery, 3, 18 March; USNADS 800.00B, 7 June (121-page report on World Peace Congress); FRUS,   1949, V (USSR), SOS Acheson to Paris,   29 March, pp.   822-824, 826; 9, 16 December, pp.   839-851 (for a lengthy   DOS assessment of the Peace Offensive).

A DOS official said it was "practically impossible for governments -- particularly with constitutional structures such as ours -- responsive to the people, to wage wars of aggression."

6. FRUS, 1949, IV, Caffery, 3, 23   March,   pp.   633-637; USNADS, Caffery, 28 February, 21 March, 11, 13, 30 April 1949; Chipman, 23 March, 28 June 1949; Ambassador David K. Bruce (Paris), 28 June 1949.

Wall's dichotomy between "front populaire" and "front national" is not entirely convincing.   Both permitted broad alliances, and both served French national interests as well as those of the Soviet Union.

7. Journal officiel, débats parlementaires, Assemblée Nationale (JODPAN), 9-10 June 1949, pp.   3239-3243, 3303-3307; Werth, pp.   456-458; Auriol, III,   1949,   n.   43 (May),   pp. 577-578. Auriol was disturbed enough to have the charges about the SS investigated.

8. Alain Ruscio, Les Communistes français et la guerre d'Indochine, Paris,   1985,   pp.   236-240; Jean Guillon, "La Lutte contre la guerre du Vietnam," Les Cahiers du communisme, September 1949, pp.   111-1121; Central Committee (PCF), 10 December 1949, ibid., January 1950, p.   123; Meng Hsien-chang, cited in Stuart Schram and Hélène Carrère d'Encausse, Marxism and Asia, London, 1969, p.   280.

9. Ruscio, pp.   240-247, 251-258; Frachon, L'Humanité, 13 December 1949; Le Monde, 11, 12 December 1949, 11 January 1950; La Vie ouvrière, 22-28 December, 2 January-1 February 1950; Benoit Frachon, Au Rythme des jours, I (1944-1954), Paris, 1967, pp.   364-365; Francis Joucelain, Le PCF et la première guerre d'Indochine, Paris,   1973, pp.   30-34; Jacques Duclos, Mémoires (1945-1952), Paris, 1971, pp.   299-300.

The French Trotskyists first called for dockers' strikes against the Vietnam War in 1945; so did the Vietnamese after Haiphong in 1946. Révolution prolétarienne reported an incident in 1947 and Ambassador Caffery another one in 1948. Ruscio's doctoral dissertation (University of Paris-I, 1984) contains dozens of interviews with participants in the dockers' strikes and associated anti-war activities.

10. Ruscio, pp.   258-265; L'Année politique, 1950, pp.
8-9, trans. by Werth, p.   442; Gérard Belloir, Nos rêves,
camarades, Paris, 1979, pp.   80-86; Robert Francotte, Une Vie
du militant communiste, Paris, 1973, p.   261; Interviews with
Louis Odru, Jean Pronteau, and Jean Chesneaux, May-June 1973.

Ruscio vigorously defends the PCF's anti-war activities
against its left-wing critics, as well as this author's
earlier writings, noting, for example, that the Party had much
difficulty overcoming a colonialist mentality which had
"poisoned" the working class.   See Léon Feix, "Contre le
poison colonialiste," L'Humanité, 24 March 1952. One wonders,
however, how the party leadership could be so immune if the
workers were so afflicted.

11. Shulman, pp.   131-138; Belloir, op. cit.; Abbé Jean
Boulier, "Pourquoi j'ai signé 1'Appel de Stockholm,"
(unpublished brochure, 1950, located in the Bibliothèque
nationale, Paris); Francotte, op. cit.; Frédéric Joliot-Curie,
Cinq années de lutte pour la paix, Paris, 1954.

Charges that the Communists were involved in sabotage
appeared in the National Assembly as early as June 1948. See,
Auriol, III, 1949, n. 12, p. 569.

12. FRUS, 1949, IV (WE), Bruce, 7 October, p. 669; FRUS,
1950, V (USSR), Holmes (London), 23 January, 16 February, pp.
264-265, 269-270, SOS Acheson to Paris, 24 February, pp.
270-271; DOS Paper, 14 April, pp. 296-302, Editorial Notes,
pp. 273, 382, 305; FRUS, 1950, III (WE), Tyler (Paris), 3
February, pp. 1357-1359, Bruce, 17, 31 March, 9-10 June, pp.
1363-1364, 1368-1369, 1374-1378.

VIII
The Generals' Affair
1949–1950

In the spring of 1949, few people in the French government believed that the Elysée Accords had either satisfactorily or definitively settled the Indochina problem. High Commissioner Pignon worried about the fact that overall command was divided among the military staff, the Defense Ministry, and the Overseas Ministry; the military was not unified, civilians authorities clashed with the military, and officials in Vietnam resented those in Paris. Defense Minister Ramadier, for his part, with Pignon and Coste-Floret's approval, sent General Georges Revers, the Chief of Staff, to Indochina on a mission of inspection. Accompanying Revers was a parliamentary commission (three Popular Republicans and two Socialists) and a certain Roger Peyré. Ramadier secretly hoped that Revers' assessment would contradict the MRP's policies, silence anti-war opposition within the SFIO, and provide the basis for an honorable withdrawal. As a staunch laic and republican, he disliked the MRP's promotion of Christianity and monarchy in Vietnam and, despite his title, had little taste for war or the military. (1)

Although ignorant of Asian affairs, General Revers went everywhere in Indochina, worked day and night for over a month, and returned in the middle of June to Paris, where he drafted both a military and a political report. In the former, he recommended the abandonment of the increasingly indefensible frontier posts in northern Tonkin, where the French had suffered half their casualties. (His opponents countered that this would lead to the loss of all of Tonkin.) Revers also proposed an "enclave" strategy by which French forces would concentrate on the defense of the Tonkin Delta and gradually asphyxiate the Vietminh by cutting off their sources of rice, coal, and iron, while a reserve Baodaist army would liberate French units for more offensive operations. He thus rejected Leclerc's "oil spot" strategy, which, despite some success in Cochinchina, required enormous quantities of manpower, as well as Valluy's "search and destroy" operations which had never succeeded in engaging major Vietminh units or in securing much territory.

        In his even more controversial political report, Revers
recommended real independence for Vietnam, a constitutional
monarchy under Bao Dai (with General Xuan, the Socialist
favorite, as Premier), and the combination of civilian and
military affairs under a single, powerful French High
Commissioner (ideally, his friend General Charles Mast,
another Socialist favorite). Privately, Revers fantasized
about persuading Ho Chi Minh to accept a disguised French
protectorate (against Chinese domination) and, through Louis
Caput, the SFIO representative in Saigon, met with two
Vietminh emissaries. His report thus contradicted Paris'
official optimism, directly challenged tne MRP's policies, and
promoted Socialist alternatives. The Bao Dai solution was a
failure, the Expeditionary Corps could not hold out alone
against both the Chinese and the Vietminh, and France was on
the threshold of a complete catastrophe. The report
infuriated Pignon, who threatened to resign if it were
published. (He would have preferred simply to legitimize Bao
Dai as a monarch.) Generals Valluy and Jean Alessandri also
vigorously dissented. (2)

        The real scandal erupted when the report was leaked.
Although it had been reproduced, in mid-July, under the
strictest security, Revers gave a copy to his friend Mast, who
passed it on to a mutual friend, Roger Peyré, who passed it on
to associates of Bao Dai and Xuan, whence it passed into the
hands of the Vietminh, who broadcast parts of it at the end of
August. Coste-Floret, who learned about this during a trip to
Indochina, protested directly to Premier Queuille, who turned
over the matter (as a question of military law) to Ramadier,
who sat on it. Three weeks later (on 18 September) French
police arrested two Vietnamese for fighting with a French
soldier on a bus near the Gare de Lyon. At the home of one of
the Vietnamese, a well-known Vietminh sympathizer, the police
found a copy of the Revers Report. A tip from within the
Overseas Ministry next led them to the home of Van Co, an
associate of Bao Dai, where they found eighty more copies.
Van Co said he had gotten them from Peyré, who said he had
gotten them from Mast. At Peyré's place police found evidence
that he had given both Revers and Mast substantial sums of
money as part of a campaign to have the latter named as High
Commissioner. Soon afterwards police found dozens of copies of
the report throughout the city.

        Initially, the Generals' Affair focused on three people
-- Revers, Peyré, and Mast. The central figure, General
Revers, was not a classic military type, being neither an
aristocrat, nor a rightist, nor a graduate of the military
academies but rather a former postal clerk and reserve army
officer who had established an excellent Resistance record and
succeeded Jean de Lattre de Tassigny as Chief of Staff in
March 1947. Revers moved easily in Socialist, Radical, and
Freemason circles and naturally disliked the clerical MRP and
the idea of a Vietnamese monarchy. Although he probably made
his report in what he considered the best interests of France,
he was vain and naive and let himself be manipulated.

        Peyré, the key to the scandal, was "any man's agent" and
had worked for the French milice, the Gestapo, and maybe also

for the Resistance. (In any event, in January 1948 Revers recommended him for the Legion of Honor. Two months later, a Paris court acquitted him of the charge of collaboration.) After the war he engaged in the "import-export business" (apparently profiting from the exchange of Vietnamese piastres), and, on the side, worked for the French Secret Services. He also cultivated a number of Vietnamese and French politicians, especially Radicals and Socialists, and had accompanied Revers on a trip to the United States in February 1949 and on the infamous mission to Indochina in May. As for Indochinese politics, Peyré favored Xuan over Bao Dai, negotiations with Ho Chi Minh, Mast as High Commissioner, and, for himself, control of the Indochina Exchange Office.

Mast was Director of the Institut des hautes études de la défense nationale and former Resident-General in Tunisia. He had close Socialist and Kuomintang contacts and, having acquired a vast knowledge of the Indochina situation, considered himself very well qualified to direct the Bao Dai operation (or a Xuan equivalent). He became intimately involved with Revers and Peyré in 1947, and the three men formulated their plans for over a year before Revers's trip to Indochina.

On 22 September 1949, French police reported on their investigations to Interior Minister Moch, who passed the matter on to Queuille and Ramadier. The Premier then convened an interministerial meeting to which Coste-Floret was not invited. Although the ministers feared that the Affair would cause embarrassment with the United States (already suspicious about French intelligence leaks), Ramadier turned the case over to a military judge after carefully explaining that only a resumé and the political sections of the report, none of the military secrets, had been leaked. Thereupon, the judge dismissed the case, freed all those arrested, and restored all documents to their owners.

The press was astonished. So also were sections of the Secret Services. The latter quickly revealed how the Report had gotten into the hands of the Vietminh and how Queuille, Ramadier and Moch had interfered with their investigations. Cries of treason arose from several quarters. Asked by Ramadier to resign, Revers refused, insisted that he was innocent of any serious wrongdoing, and accused the MRP and the Secret Services of plotting against him. Meanwhile, Coste-Floret protested directly to Queuille that Revers was guilty of leaking the report and of having plotted with Mast, Peyré, and their Socialist friends to get Pignon replaced by Mast. However, before Queuille could do anything, his government fell (over another issue), and Coste-Floret's charges remained unanswered. For the next three months the Generals' Affair smouldered. With the apparent complicity of the Interior Ministry, Peyré fled in November with his family to Brazil; Revers quietly resigned as Chief of Staff in December. (3)

Although Bidault, the new Premier, tried to keep the Affair under wraps (to save embarrassment with the United States), the press brought it to the fore once again at the end of the year. On 26 December, Time magazine, over the objections of the French Ambassador, published some sensational revelations which directly implicated Revers. A couple of weeks later the Gaullist _Carrefour_ followed suit. When, on 13 January, _Le Monde_ implied that the Affair was far-reaching, Bidault was compelled to go before the National Assembly and, in a brief statement, conceded that Van Co had bribed Peyré to promote Mast as High Commissioner but denied that Revers had touched any money. Otherwise, he said nothing not already published and asked the Assembly to trust in his government. However, the Communists, surprisingly supported by the Socialists who wanted to clear themselves, called for an immediate debate. After much heated discussion, Bidault agreed to a parliamentary commission to investigate the Affair.

The "Delahoutre Commission" began its hearings in February and published a preliminary report in April and a final one in July. Its Communist member, Maurice Kriegel-Valrimont, conveniently leaked most of its testimony to _L'Humanité_. The results of the investigation showed that Revers and Mast, had evolved a mysterious patronage system through Peyré. Revers seriously disagreed with Pignon's war policies and wanted him replaced by Mast who may have had contacts with the Vietminh. The Commission severely denounced Peyré as a "traitor" and "denunciator" who had escaped just punishment due to Revers' influence, and as a "double or triple agent" who had indulged in lucrative traffics. Accordingly, Revers and Mast were chastized for having shared with such a character national defense secrets which the Vietminh eventually used to demoralize the army.

Such revelations chiefly benefitted the Gaullists, the MRP, and the Communists. The Gaullists hoped the Affair would undermine the moral authority of the Fourth Republic; the MRP was able to discredit the Socialists and maintain its control over Indochinese affairs, both in Paris and Saigon; and Pignon remained High Commissioner for a longer time than otherwise expected. At a more sordid level, it was alleged some Popular Republicans (and even some Gaullists and Socialists) kept their hands in the vast rackets in import-export licenses, opium, and, above all, in the exchange of Vietnamese piastres for French francs. Hence, the MRP probably deliberately leaked the Revers Report to discredit the Socialists and keep them out of the top posts (and the rackets). Finally, the Communists benefitted because the Affair clearly showed up all the dirt and corruption of the "filthy war." It helped justify the dockers' strikes and deflect charges of sabotage, and, above all, it made the public aware of the Indochina War and contributed greatly to the success of the Stockholm and Henri Martin campaigns.

The Delahoutre Commission's preliminary report exonerated Revers and Mast of having taken bribes but concluded that the former had lacked discretion in his choice of friends. (The two generals later went before a military disciplinary tribunal and were quietly pensioned off. Mast went into private business, but Revers waited twelve years before President De Gaulle rehabilitated him.) The Commission also, rather unconvincingly, concluded that Peyré alone had been responsible for the leaks. (Today, the most probable hypothesis is that the Revers Report had been leaked from several different sources.)

When the Assembly debated the Commission's report in May, the Communists wanted Ramadier tried for high treason, whereas the MRP and SFIO wanted him cleared in order not to provoke a governmental crisis. By a vote of 335 to 201, the Assembly excused Ramadier and Queuille for having dropped the case in September because they had acted in the "national interest," i.e., to protect the Chief of Staff from American charges of "French unreliability."

The Delahoutre Commission's second report in July concerned the "irregularities" of the police, e.g., the restitution of documents to Peyré and Van Co and the destruction of important evidence after the initial investigation. When the Assembly finally debated this matter in November, the Communists moved to have the former Interior Minister impeached and sent before the High Court. Although Moch escaped by a narrow 235 to 203 vote, the whole matter was a serious blow to his honor. The Socialists in general were bitter, for, even in the secret ballotting, it was clear that many non-Communists and non-Rightists had also voted against him.

In many ways the Generals' Affair resembled the Third Republic's Stavisky Affair of 1934 in that it involved corrupt politicians and police "irregularities." However, the Fourth Republic's scandal failed to provoke a governmental crisis or to sustain public interest. Nevertheless, its more sordid aspects provided the general populace with a great distaste for the Indochina War. More seriously, the Affair widened the divorce between military and civilian authorities and ultimately contributed to the collapse of the Fourth Republic eight years later. The Generals' Affair also did not end the leakage of military secrets. More were to occur in 1953 and 1954 and directly involved some cabinet ministers.

Nor did the Generals' Affair end all the corruption associated with the Vietnam War. Indeed, many people, including some big businessmen and some of Bao Dai's associates, had by now established a vested interest in the continuation of the war (and the rackets). In the summer of 1950, two men, one a journalist and the other a government official, died in mysterious air crashes over the Persian Gulf on their way to investigate the rackets in Indochina. Only in 1953, after numerous revelations in the left-wing press, did the National Assembly investigate the traffic in piastres and finally establish a new exchange rate. The parliamentary report, however, did not appear until after the Geneva Accords and was never debated. By then, the Franco-Vietnamese War was over, and most people had lost interest in the Generals' Affair. (4)

NOTES

Notes have been grouped according to topic.

1. Lucien Bodard, La Guerre d'Indochine, Vol. II, L'Humiliation, Paris, 1963, pp. 333-339; Vincent Auriol, Journal du septennat, Vol. III, 1949, Paris, 1977, p. 244, nn. 13, 65 (May), pp. 575, 579; Pignon to Coste Floret (7 April 1949), Annex III, No. 2, pp. 477-480.

2. Auriol, III, 1949, pp. xix-xx, 271-272, 296-298, 308-310, n. 17 (March), p. 558; Pignon to Coste-Floret (7 July 1949), Annex III, No. 4, pp. 482-489; R. E. M. Irving, The First Indochina War, London, 1975, pp. 68-69.

3. Auriol, III, 1949, 23 September, pp. 333-334, n. 73 (July), pp. 593-594; Irving, pp. 67-71; Alexander Werth, France, 1940-1954, Boston, 1966, pp. 458-463; Bodard, II, pp. 334-336, 339-343; Georgette Elgey, Histoire de la IVe République, Vol. I, Paris, 1965, pp. 476-485.

The terms "police" and "Secret Services" actually refer to different agencies which, for our purposes, need not be specified.

For a complete chronology of the Generals' Affair, first compiled by Le Monde, see L'Année politique, 1950, Annex II, pp. 277-280.

4. L'Année politique, 1950, January debate, pp. 6-8, February hearings, pp. 32-34, March hearings, pp. 48-50, April hearings, p. 77; May debate, pp. 96-98 and Annex VII (complete report), pp. 281-283; November debate, pp. 229-233, and Annex VIII (complete report), pp. 284-285; Werth, op. cit.; Elgey, I, pp. 487-496; Irving, pp. 71-77; Alain Ruscio, Les Communistes français et la guerre d'Indochine, Paris, 1985, pp. 380-385 (the PCF's reaction); Jacques Despuech, Le Trafic des piastres, Paris, 1953.

For more on the investigation of the piastre scandal, see Chapter Fourteen, pp. 136, 140-141n.4.

IX
Internationalization
MARCH 1949–FEBRUARY 1950

Until the winter of 1949-1950, the Indochina War was basically a Franco-Vietnamese conflict. The chief issues were whether, with whom, and what to negotiate. A number of options still remained. At the beginning of 1950, however, the major powers formally took up sides, and the scope of policies narrowed considerably.

American policy on Indochina markedly evolved in the course of 1949, primarily because of the outcome of the Chinese civil war. Washington had been only mildly pleased with the Elysée Accords of March 1949. Ambassador Caffery recommended moral and economic support but no direct military aid to Bao Dai lest his failure be a further blow to American prestige in Asia. The Western European desk held that the Accords were "too little, too late," and that Bao Dai's chances of success were barely fifty-fifty. The Southeast Asian desk doubted that many Vietnamese nationalists would rally, or that the French soon would make further concessions, or that the United States could do much "to alter the very discouraging prospects." Other officials wanted to withhold "public approbation" until the French National Assembly had ratified the Accords. Secretary Acheson, while believing Bao Dai was the only "alternative to the establishment of a Commie pattern in Vietnam," did not want to act without the support of "non-Commie" Asian governments.

No one in the State Department thought of dealing with Ho Chi Minh. To Acheson he was an "outright Commie" who refused to repudiate his "Moscow connections and Commie doctrine." While Vietnam was remote from the Soviet Union, it was not out of the reach of "Chi Commie hatchet men." Whether Ho Chi Minh was as much a nationalist as a "Commie" was irrelevant. "All Stalinists in colonialist areas" were "nationalists," but would subordinate the state to "Commie purposes" as soon as they got independence. He would treat Ho Chi Minh as a "Tito" "only if every other avenue" was closed.

Yet, Acheson was not enthusiastic about Bao Dai: "As our experience in China has shown, no amount of U.S. military and economic aid can save a government" if it does not represent "all important national groups" and loses the will to fight. Ambassador Bruce (Caffery's successor) concurred, noting that as the recent American experience in China had shown, "no amount of moral and material aid" could save a government "isolated from contact with its people and enjoying little popular support." (1)

Support from non-Communist Asian nations was not readily forthcoming. To Nehru, Ho Chi Minh was basically a nationalist, and Asian Communism was less important than European imperialism and racism. French promises of "progressive steps in the direction of self-government" were similar to what the British had, for over thirty years, promised regarding India -- "a rather worn device for doing nothing." The State Department, citing one Soviet press article and two broadcasts in over two years, tried to convince Nehru of a "Moscow connection" in Indochina, arguing inter alia that Russian imperialism of the twentieth century was qualitatively different than British and French in the nineteenth. Nehru listened but then, in October, sharply rebuked the Western powers, insisting on negotiations with the "real leader of the Vietnamese people." Neutrality, an American official warned, was the best that could be expected from India.

Thailand, although strongly opposed to a Communist-dominated Indochina, agreed to recognize Bao Dai only if the French granted him real independence and authority and if he gained substantial popular support, both of which prospects the Thai government seriously doubted. When a furious Dean Acheson suggested suspending all American aid to Thailand, Ambassador Edwin Stanton replied that "veiled threats" would have "little influence" on Thai thinking. Although Bangkok did give in several months later, Burma, Indonesia, and the Philippines still held off. (2)

The British, at first, also balked, insisting that "by no stretch of the imagination" could the Bao Dai regime, "as now constituted, be construed as being in de facto control" and that premature recognition might have an "unfavorable effect" on Commonwealth countries. When Washington countered that there simply was "no practical alternative," London did agree to help persuade the French to ratify the Elysée Accords and transfer more powers to Bao Dai.

In November, the United States asked High Commissioner Pignon to declare publicly that the Elysée Accords were "only one step in an evolutionary process." Acheson wanted Bao Dai's "puppet" image erased, however unpalatable Vietnamese independence might be to many Frenchmen. Pignon, for his part, wanted the United States to dissipate beliefs "widely held in Vietnam" that it would provide practically "unlimited financial and material assistance" to Bao Dai only when the French had totally withdrawn. Pignon's government would only agree to negotiate "supplementary accords" and to sponsor Vietnamese membership in the United Nations.

To break the impasse, Ambassador Bruce urged a "completely cold-blooded" view. Any kind of non-Communist government in Vietnam was desirable, a complete French

withdrawal was unrealistic, and no French government, "either
now or in the future," could survive the granting of complete
Vietnamese independence. Indeed, the French people did not

> feel any consciousness of having . . . griev-
> ously oppressed the native population or having
> exploited it for their own exclusive benefit.
> On the contrary, they take pride in having,
> by their own account, led, with a vast expendi-
> ture of effort, blood and treasure, a congeries
> of backward and ignorant peoples toward a state
> of enlightenment. . . .

However bigoted, this sentiment was real and could not be
disregarded; Washington had to accept the Bao Dai solution as
it was.

     Moreover, in December 1949, the National Security Council
reported that Southeast Asia was the "target of a coordinated
offensive directed by the Kremlin."

> The extension of Communist authority in China
> represents a grievous political defeat for us.
> If Southeast Asia also is swept by Communism, we
> shall have suffered a major political rout the
> repercussions of which will be felt throughout
> the rest of the world, especially in the Middle
> East and in a then critically exposed Australia.

Prophetically, the report concluded that the advantage was
likely to rest with the side which succeeded "in identifying
its own cause with that of the Asian peoples . . . rather than
attempting by direct or impatient methods to control them."
(3)

     In France, the Left had already taken up new positions on
Indochina. While the Communists, as we have seen, intensified
their anti-war campaigns, the Socialists continued to retreat
from the positions taken by Mollet in his letter to Premier
Queuille in January. In July, the SFIO congress called only
for "negotiations with all elements of the Vietnamese people
without any exclusion" but did not specifically mention Ho Chi
Minh. A few days later, Daniel Mayer told the cabinet that the
SFIO would basically allow the Bao Dai solution to come to
fruition. Auriol said any other solution was inconceivable.
(He also tried to reassure Bao Dai that the Elysée Accords
were susceptible to further elaboration.) Moch hoped only
that Bao Dai would propose national elections. With this
settled, Ramadier and Auriol invoked France's right to receive
assistance in its struggle against Communist expansionism.
One Socialist dissenter, Alain Savary, a Counselor of the
French Union, however, greatly upset Auriol when he reported
that everyone in Vietnam was taken up with Ho Chi Minh's
mystique, even the Vietnamese middle class, and that everyone
wanted France to get out, even if in stages.

     With the Chinese Communist victory in the fall of 1949,
most Socialists felt an internationally-supervised truce in

Vietnam was imperative. The MRP's Coste-Floret much preferred
that Bao Dai establish himself as a legitimate monarch, muzzle
the press, and postpone all talk of a popular consultation.
At an important cabinet meeting in September (five days after
the eruption of the Generals' Affair), he forced the
embarrassed and intimidated SFIO ministers to accept his
proposals in astonishing silence. (4)

In the three-week political crisis which followed
Queuille's resignation in October, Indochina was, once again,
only a peripheral issue. Jules Moch, who failed to form a new
government, had proposed to bend the Bao Dai experience "in
the direction of negotiations" (was he including Ho Chi Minh?)
and a truce in Vietnam. Finally, Georges Bidault formed a new
ministry in which René Pleven replaced Ramadier at Defense,
and Jean Letourneau replaced Coste-Floret at Overseas France.
Taking a hard line, the Premier declared that no peace
conditions could ever permit France to renounce its "presence"
in Indochina. (5)

On the last day of 1949, nine months after the Elysée
Accords, the French signed "Supplementary Conventions" with
Bao Dai which turned over various features of internal
administration. Le Monde hailed it as "an important event" in
the history of French policy in East Asia, and some 50,000
people celebrated in the streets of Saigon. However, France
still retained important powers (even the control of customs
had not been settled), and most Vietnamese, even Baodaists,
remained skeptical. Indeed, some 150,000 people, mostly
students, demonstrated in Saigon against Bao Dai, "a marked
opposition" which worried Acheson. Meanwhile, the DRV planned
for a "general counter-offensive" and insisted on a complete
French military withdrawal as a precondition for any
settlement. Ho Chi Minh renewed his appeals for international
recognition. On 18 January, the People's Republic of China
was the first to respond positively. (6)

Ten days later, the French National Assembly again took
up the Elysée Accords in the most heated debate of the entire
war. The Right attacked the Accords as an "abandonment" of
the "national patrimony," the end of the Empire, and the loss
of the French position in the world.

> Fascinated by the mirage of equality, little by
> little, the majority of the people we are pro-
> tecting will demand their independence. . . .
> But they will learn quickly, at their expense,
> that France has assured them the most precious
> of all goods -- liberty! . . . They will be
> angry with us for having lacked clairvoyance and
> firmness. . . . France, having thoughtlessly
> emancipated her underaged children, will be
> deprived of their work, their energy and their
> youth. She will find herself alone in the
> frightening jungle of the contemporary world.

Letourneau scoffed at such "colonial romanticism." Other
right-wing deputies accepted the Accords conditionally, as the
best means to preserve French "accomplishments" in Indochina

and elicit Allied support. Frédéric-Dupont denounced, at great length, the PCF's "treacherous" anti-war activities, Témoignage chrétien's atrocity stories, Paul Rivet's socializing with DRV representatives, and the Socialists' "two-faced" attitude.

The Communists then provided most of the debate's virulence. For a full two hours Jeannette Vermeersch (Thorez's wife) attacked the government's Indochina policies. When she called Bao Dai a French "collaborator," as he had once been a "Japanese valet," the President of Assembly said she was "insulting the nation." When she said that French "law" and "justice" in Madagascar, Vietnam, and other areas were only instruments of slavery, the President called her "out of order." Voices on the right shouted: "Why do you send women to the tribune to say this? Are there not any men among you?" When she read from letters of French soldiers telling of atrocities committed, not only by former German SS in the Foreign Legion, but also by "officers of the Expeditionary Corps," Philippe Farine said she was "talking like Doriot" (who had led the PCF's anti-colonial campaigns in the 1920's).

Then Vermeersch charged that "the Vietnamese people did not shell Marseille, but you shelled Haiphong" (Farine interjected that "Thorez had signed the orders") and that, in burning Vietnamese villages, the French were "committing the same kind of atrocities" the Nazis had done at Oradour-sur-Glane and Ascq. While the Communists applauded, Jean Catrice called her "unworthy of being a Frenchwoman" and other deputies shouted: "Enough! Enough smut! Enough rubbish! Get out of here!"

Thereupon, Vermeersch thumbed her nose. The President: "Madame, you have no right. . . ." Vermeersch: "They insulted me!" Amidst prolonged uproar, the ministers and a number of deputies left the hall. The Communists chanted: "Off to the banquet! Go and collect your checks!" The President: "Madame, I tell you very politely that, when you say the French have done the same things as at Oradour, you intolerably insult both this Assembly and the Nation." Abderrahme-Chérif Djemad replied: "You did such things at Sétif and Djelfa" (in May 1945). Vermeersch: "I ask only, did we or did we not shell Haiphong? Do we or do we not burn Vietnamese villages?" The President, in turn, asked: "Is it not also true that the Vietminh have buried some Frenchmen alive?" adding, "Madame, I never believed a woman capable of such hatred." Vermeersch: "Yes, I hate. I do when I think of the millions of workers you exploit. Yes, I hate the majority of this Assembly!"

Finally, Vermeersch saluted those "courageous" and "conscientious" soldiers who refused to go to Vietnam and declared that the Communists would prevent further troops or arms being shipped to Vietnam. (Frédéric-Dupont interjected: "And so the sabotage will continue!") When she had finished, the ministers returned. When Pleven called her "hysterical and ignominious," the Communists called him a "bastard," a "cad," and several other unpleasant epithets. When an MRP deputy called André Marty "le mutin" ("deserter"), Vermeersch thought she had heard "putain" ("prostitute"). "Who said

that? Who dared insult me like that?   Nobody   answers!   You
cowards!" It was some time before the Assembly settled down.

Vermeersch had also supported   the   immediate,   complete,
and unconditional repatriation of the Expeditionary Corps (not
just negotiations   and   a   truce),   complete   independence for
Vietnam, and the   conclusion   of bilateral accords between two
independent and sovereign states (not just the preservation of
the   French   Union). Other Communist speakers   praised   French
soldiers who were "making contact" with the Vietminh, recalled
the "glorious example" of the Black   Sea   Mutiny   as   well   as
Anatole France's admonition that a   soldier   had   a   right   to
disobey criminal orders, and urged those young men refusing to
go   to   Indochina   "to   reinforce   their   unity   and   action."
Abderrahme-Chérif Djemad   alleged   that   there   was   an entire
brigade of North African deserters fighting for the Vietminh.

Another   major   uproar   occurred when René   Arthaud   (PCF)
accused Pierre de Chevigné   of   having   the   blood   of   80,000
Madagascans on his hands.   When Letourneau defended the former
High   Commissioner's   actions   as "beneficial   to   France   the
Republic,"   the   Communists denounced the entire "regime of mud
and blood!"   When de Chevigné tried to say   that "the majority
of the victims were killed by   the   rebels   because   they   had
remained   faithful   to   France,"   André   Marty   called   him   a
"swine," Jean Pronteau said he had "defiled   the   mission   of
France," and Arthaud said he   had   insulted the corpses he had
"piled up."   When de Chevigné said there was now perfect peace
in Madagascar, the Communists shouted: "Yes, the   peace   of   a
cemetery!"   And they chanted: "En Haute Cour! En Haute   Cour!"
until   he   was   forced   to   step   down.   There was an   awkward
silence on Socialist and government benches.   No one took de
Chevigné's version   of events seriously, and no one challenged
the figure   of 80,000 dead.   The embarrassed ministers quickly
changed the subject.

Finally, after   three   days   of   impassioned   debate, the
Assembly voted 401 to 193 to ratify the Elysée Accords, with a
Socialist amendment   calling for the "free consultation of the
Vietnamese   people   under   the control   of   neutral   observers
chosen in agreement with the   parties   involved."   (Did   this
include the DRV?) The Communists cried: "Down   with   the   war!"
Coste-Floret cried: "Long live the peace!"   (7)

Ambassador Bruce commented that the Communists

even   more   blatantly   than usual   displayed their
complete subservience   to Moscow and their avowed
intentions   to betray   French national   interests
. . .   to delay, frustrate and sabotage the shipment,   not only   of arms   and French   soldiers to
Indochina,   but also   of American   military materials to France.

The   day   after   the   debate, the   Soviet   Union   formally
recognized the DRV, saying that it was doing nothing more than
France itself   had   done   in   March   1946.   Acheson   was   both
surprised and   delighted, for the Soviet action "should remove
any illusions as to the 'nationalist' nature of   Ho Chi Minh's

aims." However, Ho Chi Minh also asked for, and received, recognition from Tito's Yugoslavia, itself anxious to escape from diplomatic isolation. Finally, on 7 February, the United States and the United Kingdom alone bestowed de jure (not de facto) recognition on Bao Dai's government as an "Associated State of the French Union." (8)

NOTES

Notes have been grouped according to topic.

1. Foreign Relations of the United States (FRUS), 1949, VII (FE), Caffery, 16 March, pp. 12-14; SOS Acheson to Saigon/Hanoi, 10, 20 May, pp. 23-25, 29-30; Ogburn (SEA), T/S, 17 May, pp. 27-28; MacArthur (WE), 24 May, pp. 30-32; Bruce (Paris), 29 June, pp. 65-66.

For a detailed discussion of the State Department debate, see Robert M. Blum, Drawing the Line: The Origin of American Containment Policy in East Asia, New York, 1982, pp. 108-124. On the "Ho Chi Minh: An Asian Tito" thesis, urged on the State Department by Harold Isaacs and Paul Mus in 1949, see, also, United States-Vietnam Relations, 1945-1967 (Pentagon Papers) Book I, Part I-C, Washington, 1971, pp. 1-30.

2. FRUS, 1949, VII, Stanton (Bangkok), 28 December, p. 115; Henderson (New Delhi), 21 June, pp. 61-62; Acheson to New Delhi, 30 June, p. 67; Butterworth (AssistantSOS/FE), Nehru's Memorandum on Indochina, 20 October, pp. 92-94; Bliss (London), 9 November, pp. 94-95; FRUS, 1950, VI (FE), Stanton (Bangkok), 12, 19 January, pp. 694, 697; Acheson to Bangkok, 17 January, p. 697.

3. FRUS, 1949, VII, Butterworth/British officials, 9 September, pp. 76-79; Holmes (London), 9 September, pp. 79-80; O'Sullivan/British official, T/S, 28 September, pp. 83-89; Paris Embassy to SOS, 10 November, pp. 95-97; SOS Acheson to Paris, 1 December, pp. 101-102; Bruce, 11 December, pp. 105-110; "The Position of the United States with Respect to Asia," 23, 30 December 1949 (NSC 48/1-2), Pentagon Papers, VIII, pp. 225-272, especially pp. 248, 253, 257.

4. Vincent Auriol, Journal du septennat, Vol. III, 1949, Paris, 1977, 20 July, nn. 28, 61 (July), 23 September, pp. 334-335; Paul Coste-Floret, "Communication . . . sur la situation politique dans les Etats associés d'Indochine," 13 September 1949, ibid., Annexe IV, pp. 290 (Savary), 302-304, 334-335, 491-517, 590, 592-593; R. E. M. Irving, The First Indochina War, London, 1975, pp. 69-70.

5. Georgette Elgey, Histoire de la IVe République, Vol I, Paris, 1965, pp. 411-412; Roger Quilliot, La SFIO et l'exercice du pouvoir, 1944-1958, Paris, 1972, pp. 333-335.

6. Ellen J. Hammer, The Struggle for Indochina, 1940-1955, Stanford, 1955, pp. 265-267; Philippe Devillers, Histoire du Vietnam, 1940-1952, Paris, 1952, pp. 451-455; Le

<u>Monde</u>, 31 December 1949; FRUS, 1950, VI (FE), Acheson to Saigon, 20 January, pp. 698-699.

7. <u>Journal officiel</u>, <u>débats parlementaires</u>, <u>Assemblée nationale</u> 27-28 January 1950: Adolph Aumeran, pp. 598-601, Frédéric-Dupont, pp. 607-612, Gaston Defferre, pp. 602-605; De Chevigné, pp. 606-607, 623-624, Jeannette Vermeersch, pp. 612-623, Abderrahme Chérif Djemad, pp. 633-634; René Arthaud (PCF), pp. 651-654, Alain Signor (PCF), pp. 655-656, conclusion, pp. 683-697.

8. FRUS, 1950, VI, Bruce, 31 January, DOS Statement, 1 February, pp. 704-705, 711; Gareth Porter, <u>Vietnam</u>: <u>The Definitive Documentation</u>, Stanfordville, N.Y., 1979, pp. 222-223.

X
Crusades
FEBRUARY–DECEMBER 1950

With the outbreak of the Korean War in June 1950, both the French Communists and the French Socialists no longer considered Indochina essentially a colonial affair. For both it had become part of an international crusade.

For many people in France, Korea hardened the belief that Indochina was also a victim of "Communist aggression," ultimately engineered by the Soviet Union. Yet, those people already seriously alienated by the Indochina War found the Korean War distinctly distasteful. Few French observers accepted the thesis of North Korea's "unprovoked aggression," and many of those who did disliked American self-righteousness about the matter. _Esprit_, for example, questioned how the United States, which supported reactionary regimes in Greece and Spain and was rehabilating former Nazi industrialists in Germany, could place men like Bao Dai, Syngman Rhee, and Chiang Kai-shek "in the service of democracy." Some French people feared that the Korean War would spread to Europe, while others worried that the United States would abandon Europe to fight Communism in Asia. Almost everyone was concerned that a new arms buildup would impede economic recovery.

The French Right liked Indochina's link to Korea but feared that the United States would give the latter a higher priority than even Europe. The French Communists, while obviously embarrassed by North Korea's invasion, witnessed a paradoxical upsurge in Stockholm petitions because of enhanced fears of a world war. They could now more easily blame Indochina on "American imperialism" rather than on "French colonialism." Indeed, General MacArthur's belligerency in Korea and Washington's plans to re-arm Germany caused American popularity to reach a low ebb by the end of 1950. The French Socialists, for their part, were generally pleased with the Korea-Indochina parallel. When MacArthur invaded North Korea, some were even momentarily entranced by the idea of a Korea unified by the United Nations, only to draw back when he threatened to take the war into China. After the Chinese entered the conflict, the SFIO consistently advocated a negotiated settlement. Despite these different reactions, the

French government basically supported American actions and policies in Korea, knowing that the United States now would have to help out financially in Indochina. Accordingly, Paris postponed recognition of the new Chinese government and any idea of negotiations with Ho Chi Minh. (1)

Even before Korea, most French Socialists had moved dramatically into the American camp on Indochina, although they did not totally close the door on possible negotiations with Ho Chi Minh. In February 1950, Le Populaire denounced Soviet and Chinese recognition of the DRV as "a step toward world war." To Gaston Defferre the Vietminh were nothing but "agents of Soviet imperialism." Generally, the Socialists now favored an "international," not a bilateral, solution to the conflict and demanded more respect and support from France's allies. Never favoring a guerre à outrance (war to the finish) lest Chinese intervention render the war truly internationalized, they basically sought a truce, mediation, and negotiations involving the United States or, at least, the United Nations. At the SFIO congress in May, a few delegates favored voting against military credits if their government did not change its policies. Others wanted "special directives" to bind the Socialist parliamentarians to the congressional resolutions. A representative from Cochinchina said he was going to join the maquis, along with other members of his federation, because the Party never offered anything more than "belles paroles." (2)

In any event, with the Generals' Affair, the Socialists' ability to influence colonial policies eroded considerably. In February, for the first time since the liberation, they quit the cabinet over a civil service issue, hoping to refurbish their "leftist" image with the electorate. In March, they lost Léon Blum. Ambassador Bruce called his death a "heavy blow" to Franco-American relations, particularly with labor. In June, the Socialists contributed principally to Bidault's downfall. Although they soon returned to the government under René Pleven, they lost their traditional social-economic posts but regained Defense (Moch). The MRP retained control of foreign relations and Indochinese affairs (while other overseas matters went under François Mitterrand). (3)

Meanwhile, the French Communists renewed their direct contacts with the Vietminh. In April, Léo Figuères, Secretary-General of the Union des jeunesses républicaines, travelled to Vietnam (by way of Russia and China), where, in the manner of Edgar Snow's Red Star over China, he reported on (and usually glorified) the Vietminh's food production, factories in the forests, education and literacy campaigns, military training, law and order, and women's and youth organizations. He also wrote about French atrocities (avoiding specific cases) and printed letters of French soldiers disgusted with the war but said nothing about French deserters. Surprisingly, the DRV leaders he interviewed apparently had no comments on the PCF's anti-war campaign, but Ho Chi Minh did convey some new peace proposals. Figuères returned to France to write a number of articles and a book (dedicated to Henri Martin). Defense Minister Moch wanted him arrested in order to restore the army's confidence in the government. Although Figuères eluded the police for a few weeks, Duclos allowed him to be arrested in order to better stimulate the anti-war campaign. In 1951, a military tribunal sentenced him to seven years in prison (later suspended) for "fraternization with the enemy." (4)

About the same time, the PCF debated the extent to which the Peace Movement should be independent of the Party, involve other political parties, include non-proletarian elements, and/or be tied to the struggle for socialism. The Party was particularly concerned that the SFIO itself had not participated directly in the Peace Movement, although many individual Socialists had. No one in the PCF disputed the enormous success of the Stockholm and Henri Martin campaigns, and everyone was proud of no longer being associated with "a regime of mud and blood." The debate concerned strategy, not ideology, and the various "factions" frequently overlapped.

André Marty, for example, favored broad "mass actions" at the base, to include even Catholics and conscientious objectors. Only popular pressure, not political action (i.e., with the Socialists), could end the war. Charles Tillon preferred a somewhat autonomous Peace Movement which would focus on French national issues. Duclos wanted a political front national, possibly to include elements of the bourgeoisie and even Gaullists, as long as the Peace Movement principally served the foreign policy interests of the Soviet Union. Thorez favored a more exclusively Communist-Socialist alliance, focusing on working-class issues, in which the Peace Movement would be as much an instrument of social change as one of service to the Soviet Union. Duclos did not actually oppose the Peace Movement, but Thorez was more tolerant of its independent role and trusted more the former résistants in its ranks.

At the Twelfth PCF Congress at Gennevilliers in April, Duclos succeeded in quietly purging a number of résistant types from the Central Committee. After Thorez suffered a stroke in October, front national became the policy. In December, Duclos announced PCF support for any ministry which endorsed the Stockholm Appeal and negotiations between the two super powers. Radical anti-war activities, e.g., dockers' strikes, virtually disappeared. The Peace Movement lost its "independence" and was dissociated from the struggle for Socialism. (5)

Meanwhile, within two months of the outbreak of the Korean War, the United States pressed its European allies for a massive arms buildup and, in September, dramatically called for the creation of a West German army. Indochina now became linked, not only to Korea, but also to Europe, and the Peace Movement had a target closer to home and more capable of rousing popular sentiment. The Paris government argued that it could not at one and the same time fight in Indochina and contribute effectively to the Western Alliance in Europe. It needed massive American economic and military assistance for Indochina.

American officials continued to worry about the "immeasurable significance" of the Peace Movement. They viewed

it as "the most important political instrument in Soviet hands
for . . . enlisting the support of broad non-Communist masses"
particularly in labor and intellectual circles.   Accordingly,
the State Department urged a "frontal attack" against the
Stockholm Appeal, with care being taken "not to offend the
sensibilities of the countless individuals" who signed in good
faith.   "High-ranking government officials, trades union,
religious and other public opinion leaders" in Europe were to
be encouraged to expose the "fraudulent purposes" of the
petition. "Aggression" (as in Korea) was the crime, not the
"weapons" (i.e., atomic bombs) "that may be used to effect or
deter it."

In France, Bruce reported little enthusiasm for NATO or
MDAP but much fear that the country would be physically
obliterated in a new world war, either by the "conquering"
Russians or afterwards by the "liberating" Americans.
Communist propaganda might make the average Frenchman think
that the United States was contemplating "military aggression
against the Soviet Union for its own selfish ends in an
attempt to conquer the world." At the very least, such an
attitude would neutralize France's "effective participation"
in NATO, give the impression that France was "an unreliable
partner," and force the United States to modify its Western
European policies and re-evaluate its support of France.

After the outbreak of the Korean War, Bruce noted a
"discernable improvement" in the way France received American
policies.   While appreciating that the slogan "No national
security without social security" was not confined to the
Left, he hoped a Socialist Defense Minister (Moch) would make
a new arms program more acceptable to an "economically
underprivileged and already disaffected" working class. (6)

Fearing to aggravate the growing sentiment against the
Indochina War, Washington refrained from insisting too much on
further French concessions to Bao Dai as a precondition for
further American aid. Indeed, some French officials obliquely
threatened to withdraw entirely from Indochina, even at the
risk of causing a "serious political disturbance" in the
Metropole and serious repercussions elsewhere in the French
Union. Auriol told Bruce that he had had the greatest
difficulty in getting his own Socialist Party even to approve
the retrocession of French sovereignty over Cochinchina. (7)

Reports reaching Washington on the military situation in
Vietnam were distinctly pessimistic, and with reason. In the
autumn of 1950, the Vietminh began their "general counter
offensive," beginning with the French posts along the Chinese
frontier.   When the French, at the beginning of October,
evacuated Cao Bang (as General Revers had earlier
recommended), their columns were annihilated. Within two
weeks, they had suffered over 6,000 casualties and had been
driven completely out of northern Tonkin. The Vietminh had
delivered France its worst colonial defeat since Montcalm had
died at Québec in 1759. (8)

In France, Cao Bang crystallized a new opposition to the
Vietnam War, especially in certain non-Communist intellectual
circles. Claude Bourdet's recently founded <u>France-Observateur</u>

now believed that the Vietminh, to whom the Vietnamese people had "entirely rallied," could easily drive the French into the sea with more arms. The independent left-wing journals now generally insisted on exclusive negotiations with Ho Chi Minh, finally rejected the Bao Dai solution, but did not yet demand a total French withdrawal. Only the Trotskyists actually cheered Cao Bang as a victory for the Western proletariat.

Interestingly enough, the independent left did not greatly appreciate the Communists' Peace Offensive. Even _Révolution prolétarienne_ had surprisingly little to say about the dockers' strikes or other proletarian anti-war activities. To _France-Observateur_, the Peace Offensive was too limited, too propagandistic, and actually lacked an imminent sense of war. _Témoignage chrétien_ felt the Stockholm Appeal was too closely tied to Communist interests. The Trotskyists noted, with irony, that even Stalin and Truman could sign it. (9)

On 19 October 1950, a stunned National Assembly debated the responsibility for Cao Bang. The Communists (and at least one Socialist) demanded to know why the government would not respond to Ho Chi Minh's peace proposals (made through Léo Figuères). (Paulette Charbonnel earned an epithet equivalent to "Tokyo Rose" when she read a letter from Ho Chi Minh.) Frédéric-Dupont then accused the Communists of sabotage. He also said the Socialists wanted to leave Indochina in disgrace and that the government had "materially and morally" abandoned the French soldiers. When he concluded that France was fighting a "good cause" with a "bad conscience," some Socialists applauded.

In reply, Premier Pleven denied any evidence of sabotage, conceding only some "faulty packing," and denied that Cao Bang had been due to a lack of equipment or manpower. The Socialists defended themselves by saying that France had concluded agreements, including "complete independence," with an entire people, not just with an individual. At the same time, they denied that the Vietminh was a genuine national liberation movement and claimed that Bolshevism, the "gravedigger of freedoms," intended to enslave the colonial peoples.

Then Pierre Mendès-France intervened for the first time on the Indochina question. A man of independent politics, absent from every cabinet from 1946 to 1954, he had not previously expressed any unusual ideas about the war. Now, however, he believed that France "_had_ _to_ choose." There were only two solutions: to increase greatly the military effort _or_ to negotiate with the enemy. There was no middle way. Since the former would require a tripling of resources and troops (and even then would probably be inadequate), the only realistic solution was to reach an accord, "evidently with those whom we are fighting." (Communists, Socialists, and some Popular Republicans applauded. Some Socialists also applauded when right-wing deputies accused Mendès-France of having adopted the Communist position.) (10)

After a one-month postponement of the debate, the Socialists and the MRP jointly proposed an "international solution" to the Indochina conflict, e.g., assistance from the United States. The SFIO also wanted "international mediation," but the MRP stood by the Bao Dai solution. The Communists replied that "internationalization" would only turn Indochina into another Korea. Mendès-France now said that the only real solution was full independence for Vietnam, free elections under neutral supervision, and the withdrawal of the Expeditionary Corps. "Internationalization" would never end the war, only "neutralization." (The MRP and the Right accused him of defeatism.)

At the end, however, almost everyone but the Communists supported Pleven's plan to reinforce the military effort, get assistance from the rest of the "free world," create a Vietnamese army ("Vietnamization"), and combine military and civilian commands under one person. The man chosen was General Jean de Lattre de Tassigny. (11)

NOTES

Notes have been grouped according to topic.

1. Alexander Werth, France, 1940-1955, Boston, 1966, pp. 470-474; Esprit, August-September 1950, pp. 182-185; Joyce and Gabriel Kolko, The Limits of Power: The World and United States Foreign Policy, 1945-1954, New York, 1972, pp. 565-585 (revisionist interpretations of the Korean War).

2. Le Populaire, 1, 9 February 1950; SFIO, 42e Congrès national, Paris, 26-29 Mai 1950, pp. 458-467. For the continued sympathies of some Socialists for Ho Chi Minh, see Odette Merlat, La Revue socialiste, May 1950, pp. 438-449.

3. Foreign Relations of the United States (FRUS), 1950, III (WE), Bruce, 31 March, 18 July, 1 September, pp. 1368-1369, 1380-1381, 1383-1384; Roger Quilliot, La SFIO et l'exercice du pouvoir, 1944-1958, Paris, 1972, pp. 342-349.

Bruce felt that the Socialists still filled "a great need in the political life of France" and demonstrated "the impossibility of gaining right-wing support at the expense of the left." Although Jules Moch lacked Blum's intellectual and moral leadership, Bruce was pleased that he had "courageously assumed the role of 'policeman,'" and had been appointed Defense Minister.

4. Léo Figuères, Je reviens du Vietnam libre, Paris, 1950; Alain Ruscio, Les Communistes français et la guerre d'Indochine, Paris, 1985, pp. 333-336. Roger Pannequin, Les Années sans suite, Paris, 1976, pp. 181-182; Charles Tillon, On chantait rouge, Paris, 1977, p. 483.

Figuères' was the first direct contact between the PCF and the DRV since L'Humanité correspondent Roger L'Hermitte's visit in 1947. In 1950, Tillon was first asked to go but declined, saying that, as former head of the FTP (many of whom were in the Expeditionary Corps), his appearing to be engaged on the side of the Vietminh might confuse young Communist soldiers being told to "fulfill their revolutionary duty" in Vietnam.

Between 1947 and 1950, at least four other PCF emissaries had contacted the DRV indirectly through Saigon, including three deputies and a lawyer sent to defend Duong Bach Mai. See Ruscio, "Le Groupe Culturel Marxiste de Saigon (1945-1950)," Cahiers d'histoire de l'Institut Maurice Thorez, No. 31, 1979, pp. 203-205.

5. L'Humanité, 24 January, 1 February 1950; André Marty, Cahiers du communisme, March, May 1950, pp. 20-34, 53; Werth, pp. 442-443; Irwin Wall, French Communism in the Era of Stalin, Westport, Conn., 1983, pp. 98-99, 103-111; Marshall D. Shulman, Stalin's Foreign Policy Reappraised, Cambridge, 1963, pp. 203-204.

6. Werth, pp. 481-485; FRUS, 1950, III (WE), Tyler (Paris), 3 February, Bruce, 17 March, 1, 16 September, pp. 1357-1359, 1363-1364, 1384-1387; FRUS, 1950, IV (USSR), DOS, 27 July, Perkins, AssistantSOS (EUR), 22 September, pp. 323-326, 329-330;

Appreciating the anti-war movement in France and the anti-war spirit of the French soldiers, General Giap claimed overwhelming superiority in morale and predicted "major disintegration" in the ranks of the Expeditionary Corps and possibly "many disorders" in the Metropole. See, Vo Nguyen Giap, "Immediate Military Tasks for Switching to the General Counteroffensive" (2 February 1950), Gareth Porter, Vietnam: The Definitive Documentation, Stanfordville, N.Y., 1979, pp. 231-237.

7. FRUS, 1950, IV (FE), Bruce, 17 June, Griffin Report, 2 May, Melby Report, 6 August, DOS (T/S), 16 August, Acheson, 1 September, pp. 797, 821, 843-844, 868-870.

The old conflicts between FE and WE continued. One senior official complained that there had been "no real political reporting" from Indochina since Counsels Reed and O'Sullivan had left. One FE officer found the Paris Embassy's positions "maddening," "uninformed," and "irresponsible" and complained that at least one Embassy official was accustomed

to deriding any expressions of concern over the suppression of nationalist movements in Asia as being the result of a pre-occupation with the 'patter of naked brown feet' (a patter which I should think would by now have drummed its way into the hearing even of the people in Paris).

FRUS, 1950, IV (FE), Obgurn to Butterworth, T/S, 21 March, to Rusk, 18 August, pp. 766-767, 862-864. For a more detailed discussion of State Department deliberations about Indochina in 1950, see Robert Blum, Drawing the Line: The Origin of American Containment Policy in East Asia, New York, 1982, pp. 198-213.

8. Joseph Buttinger, Vietnam: A Dragon Embattled, Vol. II, New York, 1967, pp. 749-750; Bernard Fall, Two Vietnams, New York, 1967, pp. 110-111.

9. France-Observateur, 13 April, 11 May, 2 November 1950; La Vérité, January, May, October, 1950; Révolution prolétarienne, August 1950; Témoignage chrétien, 6 January, 31 March, 1 December 1950.

10. Journal officiel, débats parlementaires, Assemblée nationale (JODPAN), 19 October 1950, Frédéric-Dupont, pp. 6974-6979, Pierre Juge (PCF), pp. 6974-6975, René Arthaud (PCF), pp. 6982-6985, Paulette Charbonnel (PCF), pp. 7007-7009, Pierre Cot, pp. 6985-6987, Daniel Mayer (SFIO), pp. 7001-7002, Mendès-France, pp. 7002-7004; Alain Ruscio,

"Le Mendésisme et l'Indochine: A propos de la politique de
Pierre Mendès-France et de son entourage direct concernant la
question indochinoise de 1948 à 1954," _Revue d'histoire
moderne et contemporaine_, 1982, pp. 324-327.

Actually, Pierre Cot first introduced the "_il faut
choisir_" thesis into the debate, even more succinctly than
Mendès-France.

11. _L'Année politique_, _1950_, p. 229; JODPAN, 22 November
1950, Letourneau (MRP), pp. 7998-8003, Arthaud (PCF), pp.
8011-8017, Hélène Le Jeune (PCF), pp. 8040-8043, Jean
Pronteau (PCF), pp. 8053-8055, Mendès-France, pp. 8043-8046,
Pleven, 8047-8050.

PART THREE
THE LEFT IN OPPOSITION
1951–1954

XI
De Lattre de Tassigny
DECEMBER 1950–JANUARY 1952

In 1951, the military situation in Indochina stabilized as the politics of the war crested. The Paris governments, moving successively to the right, remained committed to prosecuting the war, while a new, independent opposition to the war steadily built up steam.

At the end of 1950, following the disaster at Cao Bang, many French and American officials had feared an imminent collapse in Indochina. Even with a coalition government (Ho Chi Minh-Bao Dai) or internationally supervised elections, an American diplomat warned, Vietnam would "fall to the Commies no less surely, no less slowly, and perhaps more cheaply" than the Eastern European states. General Marcel Carpentier told Auriol that, not only was victory impossible, but there was also "no longer any place for Westerners in Asia."

Then, in the first half of 1951, General Jean de Lattre de Tassigny, a charismatic field commander (and High Commissioner), successively broke four major Vietminh offensives (forcing Giap largely to resume guerilla tactics) and consolidated French positions in the Tonkin Delta. Portraying Indochina as the twin to Korea in the struggle of the free world against Communist expansionism, he greatly raised Washington's hopes, although privately he knew he could not hold on forever. (1)

Meanwhile, in June, French voters elected a new legislature, following a new system of "apparentements" (initially inspired by Léon Blum), which gave the allied "third force" parties a disproportionately large number of seats. With 28 percent of the vote, the Communists remained the leading political party (losing some 400,000 supporters) but received only 103 seats (compared to the 150 they might have expected). With only 14 percent of the vote, the Socialists (losing 650,000 supporters), actually had one more seat than the PCF. All total, the third force parties had almost two-thirds of the seats with only 51 percent of the popular vote. (The Gaullists received 21 percent of the vote and 118 seats.) A "Republic of Contradictions" had replaced the "Republic of Illusions." (2)

For the third force, however, it was a Pyrrhic victory. Socialist membership had now dropped to 100,000, about the level it had been in 1933; Le Populaire had only 27,000 readers. To keep the left-wing from splitting off (possibly joining the Communists) and to preserve the long-term chances of the Party, Mollet now stubbornly refused to join any ministerial coalition. Within a few months, the third force became entirely defunct when the MRP pushed through a law permitting state aid to religious schools. (3)

Paradoxically, as the Socialists were becoming more sectarian, the Communists, under Duclos, searched for a broad front national. Like the Socialists, the Communists hoped that a new strategy would arrest an alarming decline in membership and readership. Late in 1950, the Peace Movement collected over two million signatures against German rearmament, a very sensitive subject in France. However, when the Soviet Union decided to create an East German army, the PCF had to shift abruptly. In May 1951, Duclos promised to support any government committed to a five-power pact (to include China) and, among other items, willing to withdraw from Indochina. The PCF now clearly subordinated working-class demands to the foreign policy interests of the Soviet Union. In the end, front national did help to restore order to the Party but secured it few outside alliances. (4)

The ambiance of deep pessimism which enveloped France at the end of 1951 also rendered radical, sectarian adventures inadvisable. Only the Young Communists still seemed actively interested in politics, while the Young Socialists viewed the SFIO as a bureaucratic machine, without any mystique. Intellectuals sensed a general pourissement (decay), and everyone feared a world war. The one in Indochina seemed to be going on forever, and now the United States was pushing for a European army. Most French people found American suggestions of "roll-back" and "preventive war" quite distasteful.

As the Communists plastered the walls of France with "US Go Home!" even President Auriol found American foreign policy "frightening." "History shows us the danger of encirclements." The French "fault" had been to follow the United States "blindly." The Americans had exhibited "the vulgarest form of anti-Communism." "Pride is awful in the imperialist mind." Esprit described a "falsified world" in which fear and anti-Communism had crushed all independent thought. Le Canard enchainé bitterly satirized at some length a Colliers' article portraying Russian crowds enthusiastically greeting American liberators after an atomic war.

All these attitudes had a paradoxical impact on the Indochina War. In a sense, the general cynicism and lethargy, and a concomitant diminution in dramatic anti-war activities, helped to prolong the war. Yet, the anti-American resentment helped feed the Peace Movement, while the Henri Martin campaign, as we shall see, revived something of the former idealistic, "Resistance-style" fervor. (5)

The French political impasse extended to parliamentary discussions of Indochina. While Frédéric-Dupont insisted that the fall of Tonkin would inevitably lead to the Communist domination of all Southeast Asia, India, Africa, and the entire Islamic world, Edouard Daladier, Mendès-France's close associate, countered that the very continuation of the Indochina War jeopardized French interests in Europe and Africa ("where the future of our country resides"). Neither a total French withdrawal from Indochina or direct negotiations with Ho Chi Minh, on the one hand, nor "Vietnamization" or an internationalization of the war, on the other, would work. A Vietnamese national army would not be ready for years; India refused to recognize Bao Dai; none of the Allies would send troops; and the Chinese were ready to intervene at any time. Daladier saw no way out of the conflict except through an appeal to the United Nations, an armistice, and a popular plebiscite to determine a new Vietnamese government.

Gaston Defferre (SFIO) basically agreed with the need to "internationalize the solution" and admitted that more and more people shared Daladier's viewpoint. However, the Socialists, despite continued reservations about the Bao Dai solution, basically supported the government because Indochina was essentially a struggle between the free world and totalitarianism. Their mot d'ordre remained "neither reconquest nor abandon."

The Communists argued that France no longer had any national interests in Indochina, that even the colonialists were rapidly re-investing elsewhere. French soldiers were dying only because the United States wanted to fight Asian Communism. The only real solution -- the one demanded by the majority of the French people -- was to negotiate with the DRV and withdraw the Expeditionary Corps. (6)

Then, Mendès-France, in a lengthy two-and-a-half-hour economic analysis, argued forcefully that France had to have "the true courage" to reduce its governmental expenses, especially the military budget, and, consequently, change its Indochina policy. The economic crisis only caused Communist propaganda to thrive. The Marshall Plan was at an end, American military aid inadequate, and French production at the 1929 level; whereas other European countries had shown substantial increases, and even a Conservative government had cut the military budget in the United Kingdom. Mendès-France did not want to withdraw entirely from Indochina, but he felt that negotiating directly with the adversary (as the United States was doing in Korea) was preferable to any "international" solution, in which France would only come out the loser.

Most deputies listened to Mendès-France with great attention, and practically all sides (except the Communists) applauded at one time or another. The Socialists particularly liked the linking of Indochina to inflation. However, few politicians were in a mood for a great reorganization or austerity drive, and most deputies feared that negotiations with Ho Chi Minh would play into the hands of the French Communists and disturb the United States. Defense Minister

Bidault, for his part, uttered an angry, defiant, "No!"

Ambassador Bruce observed that France was "rapidly moving toward a crisis." While no French government would adopt a policy of withdrawal "in the near future," "such a decision would be generally greeted by the French public with a sense of emotional relief." Mendès-France's thesis had "gained an increasing number of adherents," the Ambassador noted. "The snowball has started to form, and public sentiment for withdrawal . . . will gain steadily and perhaps at an accelerated rate." The only alternatives were an internationalization of the problem and/or massive American aid. (7)

Finally, at the end of 1951, the impasse extended to the diplomatic and military situation in Vietnam. De Lattre de Tassigny privately welcomed but also feared negotiations with Ho Chi Minh. Thinking that direct talks between two great battle leaders might help, the gGeneral secretly sent a couple of personal emissaries to seek out DRV representatives in Calcutta, but the latter failed to show up. Yet, both the General and Auriol feared armistice proposals emanating from the DRV. To respond positively would mean the collapse of the Bao Dai experiment. To respond negatively would be embarrassing in the eyes of the world and would add fuel to PCF propaganda. Somehow they had to show that a rejection was not France's fault.

Next, de Lattre de Tassigny thought of putting himself at the head of a vast international crusade, necessarily involving the United States. He convinced Pope Pius XII that the very fate of Christianity was at stake in Indochina. He told the American people on television that his only son (Lieutenant Bernard de Lattre de Tassigny, killed in May) had died for them and the free world. If Hanoi were lost, the road would be clear for the Communists all the way to the Suez. The General even established a salient position at Hoa Binh (off the Tonkin Delta perimeter), hoping that the United States would be forced to intervene with troops to save it.

Nothing came of these plans. By the end of 1951, the French war effort in Indochina was slowly dying -- and so was Jean de Lattre de Tassigny, of cancer. Shortly before his death, on 11 January 1952, he confided to General Valluy: "There is only one thing which upsets me: I have never completely understood Indochina." (8)

NOTES

Notes have been grouped according to topic.

1. Vincent Auriol, Journal du septennat, Vol. IV, 1951, Paris, 1975, 9 January, pp. 15-17; Philippe Devillers, Histoire du Vietnam, 1940-1952, Paris, 1952, pp. 457-458; Foreign Relations of the United States (FRUS), VI, 1951 (FE), Heath (Saigon), 29 June, pp. 432-439. See, also, National Intelligence Estimate (NIE-20), 20 March, in Gareth Porter, ed., Vietnam: The Definitive Documentation, Stanfordville,

N.Y., 1979, pp. 350-352.

    2. Auriol, V, 1951, 22 June, pp.   229-230; Alexander
Werth, France, 1940-1955, Boston,   1966,   pp.   541-543;
Georgette Elgey, Histoire de la IVe République, Vol. I, Paris,
1965, p. 518.

    Auriol believed that the PCF had been able to hold its
own in the legislative elections because of the popularity of
the Peace Movement.

    3. Auriol, IV, 1951, 1, 3, 9 August, pp.   383-384,
387-388, 394; Elgey, II, pp. 19-23; Roger Quilliot, La SFIO
et l'exercice du pouvoir, Paris, 1972, pp. 411-413.

    The new government, again under René Pleven, continued to
sponsor and subsidize (with the SFIO's concurrence) Jean-Paul
David's "Paix et liberté," the anti-Communist propaganda
movement. Auriol told David that the government was doing its
best to eliminate Communists from the administration. Mollet
wanted to employ the "full resources of the law against those
who were seeking to undermine the material and moral power of
the nation." See Elgey, II, p. 72; Auriol, VI, 1952, Paris,
1978, 28 February, pp. 135-136.

    4. Irwin Wall, French Communism in the Era of Stalin,
Westport, Conn., 1983, pp. 135-140; Marshall D. Shulman,
Stalin's Foreign Policy Reappraised, Cambridge, 1963, pp.
168-171, 199-212.

    5. Werth, pp. 547-549, 553-561; Elgey, I, pp. 508-509;
Auriol, IV, 1951, 3 September, 15 October, pp. 423, 499.

    6. Journal officiel, débats parlementaires, Assemblée
nationale (JODPAN), 28-30 December 1951, Frédéric-Dupont, pp.
10048-10050, Daladier, pp.   10052-10054, Defferre, pp.
10077-10080, Malleret-Joinville (PCF), pp. 10057-10058.

    When one deputy argued that the war had begun when Ho Chi
Minh had "abruptly attacked Indochina," a Communist deputy
replied that this was "a singular manner of writing history,"
p. 10076.

    7. L'Année politique, 1951, pp.   382-403 (Mendès-France
speech); Werth, pp.   551-553; Auriol, IV, 1951, n. 25
(January), p. 906; FRUS, 1951, VI, Bruce, 26 December, pp.
573-578.

    8. Elgey, II, pp. 447-451; Auriol, IV, 1951, 30 July,
pp. 370-376.

    In order to reinforce Hoa Binh, de Lattre de Tassigny had
to strip the defenses he had so carefully prepared in the
Tonkin Delta. Two months after his death, his successors
ignominiously evacuated Hoa Binh, albeit with the loss of only
one battalion. See Auriol, V, 1952, nn. 65, 178 (February),
pp. 953, 965.

    Bruce reported that "the very same Vietminh regiments
which had been badly mauled" by de Lattre de Tassigny a few

months   previously   had again appeared, "brought   up   to   full
strength, completely equipped, well-officered, and   in   good
fighting   spirit."   FRUS,   1951,   IV   (WE),   no.   3606,   17
December, cited in Porter, p.   386.

XII
Pigeons
JANUARY–DECEMBER 1952

The year 1952 revealed the outlines of a dénouement. De Lattre de Tassigny's death had finally torn the veil of illusions. The evacuation of Hoa Binh in February was a political and psychological disaster. General Clément Blanc, the French Chief of Staff, now knew that a military victory was impossible, even with a Baodaist army and greatly increased American aid. Paris had to either turn the whole affair over to the United States or negotiate with the Vietminh.

Hints and rumors of possible negotiations increasingly circulated. Even Jean Letourneau, Minister of the Associated States, admitted the possiblity of a Korean-style armistice. Although he also said that France would not take the first step, that, with time, "exhaustion" or "lethargy" would force the Vietminh to come to terms, his statements indicated a significant evolution in French policy. Auriol felt Letourneau's remarks lacked all "psychological sense," particularly coming on the heels of Hoa Binh; but even he hoped that a plebiscite in Vietnam would ease a French withdrawal (and forestall a Chinese invasion). When told that Ho Chi Minh might receive a majority, the President replied: "Eh bien, tant pis! At least it will be a way for us to get out." (1)

The anti-war movement had grown significantly beyond the confines of the traditional Left. Although a large number of Catholics did not yet sympathize with anti-colonial causes, Esprit completely supported negotiations with Ho Chi Minh alone, arguing that his movement, akin to the Spanish against Napoléon or the Irish against Britain, had roots too deep to be liquidated. Révolution prolétarienne felt the only way to negate Soviet and Chinese influence in Vietnam was to surrender Indochina "totally and completely" to the Indochinese. Otherwise, colonial wars only fed water to the Stalinist mill.

Mendès-France and Claude Bourdet (through France-Observateur) spearheaded the new opposition, gaining adherents even in classical financial circles and in the national

administration. Although they never comprised a coherent
ideological or political group, these men wanted negotiations
with the Vietminh for essentially economic reasons -- to
remove the war's heavy burden on French productivity -- and
wanted to reconstruct France's colonial relations everywhere
in a more profitable manner.

The Socialists, seriously wounded by his attacks on their
complicity and resignation over Indochina, however, called
Mendès-France a "neo-capitalist," inspired by German and
American notions of modernization, efficiency, and technocracy
for the benefit of the liberal bourgeoisie. The MRP, wounded
even more severely, said he was capitulating to Communism. The
Communists, for their part, felt that the "Mendésistes" lacked
the public appeal of the Henri Martin campaign and the
sensationalism of the various scandals of the "filthy war."

Not since early in 1949 had the Socialists called for
negotiations with Ho Chi Minh. Never had they voted against
the government's policies. Despite reservations about Bao
Dai, they still resolutely wanted an anti-Communist regime in
Vietnam. Although now they were definitively in the opposition
on most other issues, a withdrawal from Indochina, an American
official wired, was not "the price for Socialist support" of
the government. The SFIO dissented less over Vietnam than
religious education, social welfare, and wages.

Nevertheless, the expansion of the anti-war movement
inevitably induced an evolution in Socialist policy. By 1952,
the SFIO had begun to advocate accommodations with nationalist
movements in Tunisia, where they vociferously denounced all
repressive measures. Although their solutions were not
terribly radical (self-administration, autonomy, etc.), the
Socialists were able to express openly and firmly their
traditional anti-colonialism and their overseas liberalism,
most probably because Communists were not nationalist leaders
in Tunisia. They also may have wanted to make up for a "bad
conscience" over Indochina, where Cold War dictates
prevailed. (2)

Then, suddenly, in April 1952, the Socialists decided to
abstain on the military budget. Christian Pineau (SFIO),
having just returned from a parliamentary mission, could find
no ready solution to the Indochina conflict, except
"international negotiations" (including with the Chinese). A
precipitous French withdrawal would lead to a national
insurrection and massacres. A massive increase in the war
effort would aid the "opponents of freedom" (i.e., the PCF) by
increasing inflation. Internationalization of the war would
incite Chinese intervention. Direct negotiations with Ho Chi
Minh, despite his popularity, were not feasible because,
Pineau offered, he had lost much political influence within
the Vietminh.

Gaston Defferre said that the Socialists had
fundamentally disagreed with the government's prosecution of
the war for the past five years ("while waging it," a
Communist deputy interjected) and were, in recent months,
joined by other deputies calling for a "choice." France was
bleeding alone and unfairly in Indochina, whereas the

Anglo-Saxons had a greater interest in stopping Communism in Asia. He meant the Socialist abstention, not as an "act of defiance" but as a "courteous but solemn warning." Although Letourneau argued that it would be highly detrimental, the new American Ambassador, James Clement Dunn, doubted the Socialists' abstention would seriously alter the government's policies. (3)

In 1952, the Communists also took a sectarian turn. Except for the Henri Martin campaign, front national had been only moderately successful. PCF membership continued to drop, and the Party had to endure some of the most intense anti-Communist campaigns in French history. The Communists now linked peace to the struggle for socialism. André Marty spoke of self-determination for the colonial peoples, "up to and including separation from France." Jacques Duclos called for a renewed campaign against the manufacture and transport of war materials for Indochina. In March, he addressed a "brotherly salute" to Ho Chi Minh, assuring him that the working class of France was "au coeur" with the Vietnamese people in checking the French imperialists and delivering severe blows to the American war-makers. Outgoing American Ambassador Bruce called this "treasonable," but L'Humanité said the real traitors were those who were turning France over to the United States.

In April, Thorez wrote from Russia that, through "direct working-class action," the Communists had to "work for the defeat" of the French army in Vietnam. In June, Léon Feix complained that people too easily condemned the "filthy war" without fully realizing the reality behind it. While campaigns against the atomic bomb and German rearmament were important, Indochina was a real war being fought "in the name of France." Declaring that "the enemy is in our own country," he called for a return to the radical anti-war activities of 1949-1950. (4)

Already, in May, the Communists had organized massive demonstrations against General Matthew B. Ridgeway's appointment as SHAPE commander. The police arrested André Stil, editor of L'Humanité, for a provocative anti-Ridgeway article. (The General was being accused of having used bacteriological warfare in Korea.) On 28 May, some 10,000 people demonstrated in Paris and other cities. Two were killed, 230 injured, and 718 arrested, including Duclos. In his car were two dead but still-warm pigeons, which the police claimed had been used to carry messages to the demonstrators. (Although Duclos insisted that Madame Gilberte Duclos had intended to serve the birds that evening aux petits pois, the PCF had actually planned to launch a number of pigeons to symbolize Picasso's famous Dove of Peace.) Although Duclos had not been directly involved in the demonstrations, the police claimed they had caught him in flagrant délit and charged him with having threatened the "internal security of the state."

Not long afterwards, police discovered in a chicken coop in Toulon Communist documents concerning the movement of troops to Indochina and plans to sabotage the naval arsenal. With this the police now charged Duclos, as the acting head of the PCF, with threats against the "external security of the

State." The police may also have wanted to link Duclos to Henri Martin, who had been accused, but acquitted, of plotting sabotage at the Toulon naval base. This would have facilitated a crackdown on the campaign against the Indochina War. Indeed, the police arrested a number of other Communists and seized some PCF publications.

A protest strike on 4 June failed miserably, and Duclos remained in prison for over a month. (He wrote a letter to Auriol recalling some radical incidents in the President's militant youth which the latter found "arrogant," "outrageous," and "insolent.") Finally, on 1 July, the Chambre des mises en accusation (Grand Jury) dismissed the charge of flagrant délit and invoked Duclos' parliamentary immunity against the other charges. A few days later, André Stil was also released.

Even many anti-Communists were relieved. The questionable police methods had outraged intellectuals like Mauriac and Sartre. The Socialists, recalling Hitler's use of the Reichstag Fire in 1933 to outlaw the Communists and eventually all opposition, felt most uneasy about the "Pigeons' Conspiracy." At the same time, they refused to engage in joint action in favor of Duclos, saying that Communists were being hypocritical, complaining about political injustice in France while not denouncing the "purge trials" in Czechoslovakia. Yet, the Socialists consistently refused to support measures to lift Duclos' parliamentary immunity, and that of other PCF deputies, on charges of sabotage and "damage to the moral resistance of the Army and the Nation." (5)

The confusion in the PCF led to the famous Marty-Tillon Affair at the end of the year -- a matter not unrelated to the politics of the Indochina War. Tillon had co-founded the French Peace Movement and wanted to make it an autonomous pressure group, independent of the Party. Marty was cool to the Peace Movement (because it subordinated the goal of Socialism) but, as a Party specialist on Indochinese affairs, was the person most reponsible for the Henri Martin campaign, believing that only mass action could end the Vietnam War. Both men, not incidentally, had opposed the anti-Ridgeway demonstrations. Duclos' arrest, coupled with Thorez's absence, led to a power struggle in the PCF in which Marty was expelled from the Party and Tillon deprived of his official functions. Although differing approaches to the peace issue had only been one of several charges, for our purposes the Marty-Tillon Affair showed that the PCF intended to keep the anti-war campaign from being an independent, radical movement leading to socialism.

Yet, the PCF's approach to the Indochina War did not change significantly. Despite the new "hard line," there were few anti-war demonstrations to match the vehemence of the dockers' strikes two years previously, and the powerful Henri Martin campaign fell squarely within the tradition of front national. At the end of 1952, indeed, a growing chorus of Socialists, Radicals, and others joined voices with the Communists in seeking a way out of the Indochina quagmire. (6)

The Socialists had extended their opposition to the government on a number of issues and had become deeply divided over the idea of a European Defense Community. Hence, they found it too heavy a burden to defend the government on Indochina, especially against the vehement attacks of the Communists. Although Pineau felt that, as long as the Korean War continued, France had to be totally on the side of the West, Edouard Depreux argued that negotiations with the Vietminh would not necessarily lead to a Communist victory. Defferre found it incomprehensible to refuse simultaneously to internationalize the war, negotiate with Ho Chi Minh, or get out entirely.

In any event, developments in Indochina confirmed the Socialists' opposition. First, the government (with Auriol's concurrence) secretly tried to contact Vietminh agents, once through Professor Rivet at the Musée de l'homme. Although nothing came of these démarches (the Vietminh were now intent on a military victory, and the United States adamantly opposed any negotiations), the French parliamentary opposition caught the scent. Then, in the fall and winter of 1952, a major Vietminh offensive into northwest Tonkin inspired new re-examinations. (The Vietminh now had 120,000 men in seven well-equipped divisions against the Expeditionary Corps' 150,000 troops.)

Arthur Giovani (PCF) said that the new defeats were not the result of chance but the result of the war's being profoundly unpopular, costly, and already lost militarily. Certain centrists, including François Mitterrand, feared serious repercussions in North Africa and the rest of the French Union. Almost everybody realized that France could not continue in Indochina and contribute effectively to Europe. While some Socialists felt that a military pull-out or defeat in Vietnam would cause a serious internal crisis in France, most were embarrassed when their own Marcel-Edmond Naegelen demanded the "relève," i.e., the active intervention of the United States. (7)

In November, Alain Savary reported to the SFIO's Comité directeur that France no longer had a chance of winning the war but did greatly risk losing it. Since a pure and simple French withdrawal was politically unfeasible, the only solution was to talk with the Vietminh, a difficult but not impossible dialogue. Accordingly, the SFIO's National Council, on 15-16 November, rejected unequivocally any idea of an American take-over in Indochina, any internationalization of the war, or the withdrawal of the Expeditionary Corps in favor of overtures to Ho Chi Minh. (Auriol disagreed, saying this was tantamount to admitting defeat. France first needed a victory.) A few days later, Savary pushed his proposal in the National Assembly. However, when he said that the SFIO had consistently advocated negotiations with Ho Chi Minh, both the Right and the PCF vigorously challenged him. Savary countered that the Communists had never supported the Socialist motions for a truce, but the Communists produced statements of prominent Socialists who disagreed with the National Council's resolutions.

Ambassador Dunn remained unperturbed by the Socialist position, because he felt few SFIO deputies actually supported it and because it did not advocate withdrawal. The parliamentary debate was indefinitely suspended when the government fell over another issue. (8)

NOTES

Notes have been grouped according to topic.

1. Vincent Auriol, Journal du septennat, Vol. VI, 1952, Paris, 1978, 4, January, 22 February, pp. 10-11, 145, 13 May, pp. 331-332, nn. 65, 178 (February), nn. 73-75, (March), pp. 953, 965, 986-987; Le Monde, 15 March 1952; L'Année politique, 1952, pp. 185, 188, 195, 205.

2. Paul-Marie de la Gorce, Apogée et mort de la IVe République, Paris, 1979, pp. 17-21, 27-35, 62-69; Roger Quilliot, La SFIO et l'exercice du pouvoir, 1944-1958, Paris, 1972, pp. 441-449; Paul Clay Sorum, Intellectuals and Decolonization in France, Chapel Hill, 1977, pp. 49-51; Foreign Relations of the United States (FRUS), 1952-1954, XIII (IC), Bonsal (Paris), 14 March, p. 70; Claude Bourdet, "Pour une trève au Vietnam," France-Observateur, 5 July 1951; Alain Serrières, Esprit, September 1951, pp. 406-411; Révolution prolétarienne, February, December 1952.

See, also, Charles-André Julien (SFIO), L'Afrique du Nord en marche, nationalisme musulmans et souveraineté française, Paris, 1952; Jean Rous, Tunisie . . . attention! Paris, 1952.

3. Journal officiel, débats parlementaires, Assemblée nationale (JODPAN), 9-10 April 1952, Pineau, pp. 2062-2066, Defferre, pp. 2093, Letourneau-Defferre, pp. 2101-2102; Auriol, VI, 1952, 28 March, pp. 242-243, nn. 63, 66 (February), pp. 952-953; FRUS, 1952-1954, XIII (IC), Dunn, 22 April, pp. 103-109.

4. Irwin Wall, French Communism in the Era of Stalin, Westport, Conn., 1983, pp. 141-143, 185; Philippe Robrieux, Histoire intérieure du PCF, Vol. II, Paris, 1981, pp. 297-299; François Billoux, "Organiser et diriger l'action unie des masses pour imposer une politique de paix et d'indépendence nationale," Cahiers du communisme, May 1952, pp. 453-468 (Thorez's message); Jacques Duclos, "Message du Comité central du parti communiste français à Ho Chi Minh," ibid., April 1952; Léon Feix, "Intensifions l'action pour la paix au Vietnam," ibid., June 1952, pp. 593-606; L'Humanité, 13 March 1952; Jeannette Vermeersch, France nouvelle, 2 June 1952; FRUS, 1952-1954, XIII (IC), Bruce, 6 March, p. 63.

The Communists never actually rejoiced over the Vietnamese victories and, after Hoa Binh, addressed their "dolorous salute to the French soldiers" who were "falling in this unjust war" (France nouvelle, 26 February 1952).

5. Alexander Werth, France, 1940-1955, Boston, 1966, pp. 575-581; Jacques Fauvet, Histoire du PCF, Paris, 1977, pp. 428-431; Wall, pp. 143-144; Robrieux, II, pp. 300-309; Quilliot, pp. 430-431; Auriol, VI, 1952, nn. 205-206 (May), p. 1042, 27 June, 1-2 July, pp. 415-416, 420-421; L'Année politique, 1952, pp. 50-51, 75-76.

One of the justices who ordered Duclos' release had his house bombed. The Justice Ministry (and Auriol) reacted negatively to the "political positions" of various magistrates in the Duclos and Henri Martin affairs. The Justice Minister protested that Auriol's pardoning of the anti-Ridgeway demonstrators in November destroyed "the happy effects" of the repression. See Auriol, VI, 1952, nn. 11-12 (July), n. 118 (November), p. 1136, n. 157 (December), pp. 1057-1058, 1156.

6. Wall, pp. 144-147; Robrieux, II, pp. 309-338; Werth, pp. 586-590; Fauvet, pp. 431-441. See also André Marty, L'Affaire Marty, Paris, 1955; Charles Tillon, Un 'Procès de Moscou' à Paris, Paris, 1971; Yves Le Braz, Les Rejetés: L'Affaire Marty-Tillon, Paris, 1974.

7. Quilliot, pp. 465-466; De la Gorce, p. 70; Auriol, VI, 1952, 13 May, 10 October, 5, 26 November, pp. 331-332, 611, 691, 747-748, nn. 36, 67 (August), nn. 79, 208-209 (October), nn. 15-16, 38, (November), pp. 1076, 1079, 1109, 1122, 1126, 1128; JODPAN, 24 October 1952, Pleven, pp. 4391-4392, Giovoni, pp. 4392-4394, Naegelen, pp. 4395-4396.

8. Quilliot, pp. 466-468; De la Gorce, pp. 70-71; Auriol, VI, 1952, 4, 17, 26 November, n. 159, pp. 688-689, 719-720, 747-748, 1139, 11 December, p. 787; L'Année politique, 1952, pp. 284-285, 294-295; JODPAN, 19 November 1952, Savary, pp. 5382-5383, 5385; JODPAN, 19 December 1952, Cermolacce (PCF), pp. 6662-6666, Daladier, pp. 6666-6668, Letourneau, pp. 6668-6672; FRUS, 1952-1954, XIII (IC), Dunn, 24 November, 24 December, pp. 300-301, 330-331.

Daladier argued that France could not claim to be defending Southeast Asia, for most of the countries in that region opposed France's Indochina policy and refused to recognize Bao Dai. Nor was it really fighting Communism, for -- as the recent Chinese experience had shown -- this could not be accomplished by arms but only by land reform and other social measures.

XIII
Henri Martin
1950–1953

Early in 1950, an Alsacian sailor named Charles Heimburger, encouraged by a certain Liebert, an _agent provacateur_, tried rather clumsily to damage, with a mixture of metal dust and straw, the propeller shaft of the the French aircraft carrier _Dixmude_ stationed at Toulon. During World War II, Heimburger had been conscripted into the Nazi army. Although he had eventually deserted, this experience left him seriously disturbed, particularly later on when, as a French sailor, he saw former German SS fighting with the French Expeditionary Corps in Indochina. So, now, he tried to sabotage the _Dixmude_ to prevent it from sailing to Indochina.

On 14 March, French Sea Police in Toulon arrested seven sailors for distributing anti-war tracts. They pointed to Second Master Mechanic Henri Martin as their leader. When, on 5 April, the Sea Police arrested Heimburger for sabotage, he, too, implicated Martin. Under the recently passed law of 8 March against sabotage and demoralization of the armed services in peacetime, Heimburger and Martin risked twenty years' imprisonment. (A formal "state of war" never existed between France and the DRV.)

Henri Martin was born on 23 January 1927 at Rosières, a small industrial town in the Cher in central France, a Communist commune since 1939 (where over 80 percent of the people had signed the Stockholm Appeal). His father was a metal-fitter, militant _cégétiste_ and, since the liberation, a member of the PCF. His mother was a devout Roman Catholic. Martin had started to work in the foundry at age fourteen. Later, he fought with distinction with local Resistance groups (including one made up mostly of Vietnamese workers). In June 1945, he enlisted for a five-year stint in the navy, hoping both to improve his mechanical skills and to liberate Indochina from the Japanese.

World War II was over by the time Martin arrived in East Asia, and he soon realized that he had not come to liberate the Indochinese but to help reconquer them, a <u>prise de conscience</u> well attested to in his letters to his family. Throughout 1946, he recounted a number of atrocities, including the wanton strafing of Vietnamese fishing boats, and felt the French in Indochina were behaving exactly as "<u>les Boches</u>" had in France. On 23 November, on board the <u>Chevreuil</u> off Haiphong, he witnessed, and later graphically described, the terrible shelling of the port city, although he was unaware of the political circumstances surrounding the incident.

Believing that the Vietnamese should be allowed to govern themselves, Martin became convinced that only big bankers and former collaborators (with both the Japanese and Germans) benefitted from the war. He started to read about the demoralization of French soldiers in World War I and, three times (twice after Haiphong), sought to be released from his five-year enlistment. In December 1947, he was shipped back to France and soon stationed at Toulon. Twice thereafter he received promotions (the second one, to Second-Master, as late as November 1949). Everyone considered him to be a model sailor. In July 1949, he began distributing anti-war material. Otherwise, he was just waiting for his enlistment to expire in May 1950.

At the time of his arrest, little was precisely known about Martin's affiliation with the PCF, although almost everyone assumed he was a member. Yet, even during his trial, Sartre was not entirely sure. Only after his release in 1953 did Martin admit to having been a Communist since August 1944. (By the 1980's, he had become Director of the PCF's Central School at Choisy-le-Roi.) Having maintained indirect contact with the PCF while in Vietnam, Martin had become active with the party's Federation of the Var in 1949 and began to publish and distribute anti-war tracts signed by "a group of sailors." Soon André Marty took an active interest in, and strongly encouraged, Martin's endeavors.

The Party leadership probably settled on Martin because, in so many ways, he was the model image of a good French Communist sailor. His extra-legal activities corresponded with the PCF's most radical campaigns, yet never exceeded the limits set by the Party. He was not an anti-militarist but strongly disciplined and claimed to defend the honor of the navy; he was not unpatriotic but convinced that the war was unconstitutional and contrary to legitimate French interests; he was not a deserter or mutineer but hoped to encourage collective protests against the war.

After his arrest, Martin (along with Heimburger) waited in prison until October 1950 to be court-martialed. (The other sailors had been released in May.) At first, few people, not even many Communists, seemed interested in the case. In April, <u>L'Avant-Garde</u>, the Communist youth newspaper, called for the release of the seven sailors. By June, some workers manifested open admiration for and solidarity with Martin. On 14 July, veterans of the Black Sea Mutiny of 1919 carried a

banner calling for his acquittal. Six days later, in
L'Humanité, Marty declared it "urgent that a mass tide rise up
to save the first soldier who proclaims his refusal to
continue the war in Indochina. . . . His immediate release
will be an important blow against the sending of our boys to
Indochina."

In September, Thorez appealed for the release of Martin
and Raymonde Dien. Interest in these cases remained pretty
much confined to working-class and Communist circles, and
Martin defense committees existed only in Toulon and
Marseille. (Indeed, it is arguable that the government, not
the PCF, first wanted to make a national affair out of the
case.) By October, Yves Farge, Emmanuel d'Astier de la
Vigerie, and other peace leaders joined in.

By the time the trial opened on 17 October, the campaign
had jelled, compelling the government to send hundreds of CRS
to Toulon to hold down demonstrations. Martin's eloquence and
integrity in defending himself added to his popularity.
Unlike Heimburger, he was not ashamed, did not ask the court
for mercy, and refused to denounce his associates, but did
adamantly deny any involvement in sabotage.

Government prosecutors introduced several examples of
anti-war tracts distributed at the Toulon Naval Base and on
board the Dixmude. The first, on 6 July 1949, signed by a
"group of sailors," called for the end of the "unjust Vietnam
War." A second, in August, adopting the Communist slogan "Not
another man, not another penny for the filthy war," praised
the soldiers who had refused to board a troop train at Fréjus
and was signed by the (Communist-dominated) "Union de la
jeunesse républicaine de France." A tract in November declared
that sailors had not enlisted to die in Indochina for the big
bankers or planters and that the Vietnamese fight for
independence was akin to the French struggle against the
"Boches."

The boldest ones appeared between December 1949 and
February 1950, calling upon soldiers and sailors to refuse to
board ships for Vietnam. Distributed now about every three
days, all were signed by a "group of sailors." In March, a
"proletarian" tone entered with expressions of solidarity with
the striking dockers. Finally, on 11 March, declaring that
French national defense had been betrayed, a tract demanding
the return of the Expeditionary Corps was signed by "the
Communist Party."

As for the charge of sabotage, Liebert testified that
Heimburger had discussed the idea with Martin beforehand,
making him an "accomplice before the fact." However, under
cross-examination, Heimburger suddenly admitted that Martin
had not been in any way involved -- a retraction which, to one
reporter, exploded in the courtroom "like a bomb." More and
more it appeared that Martin was being prosecuted principally
for being a Communist.

Mounting a counter-attack, the defense tried to put the
war on trial. Although the military judges objected, Martin
and his supporters were able to get into the record accounts

of some of the atrocities they had witnessed in Indochina. Mainly the defense argued that Martin was really a patriot, a bon français (as evidenced by his Resistance record) who refused to fight in an unjust and unconstitutional war. Martin himself said that he was defending the "honor of France," that the real traitors were those who were delivering France to the United States, as Vichy had delivered France to the Nazis.

In the end, the court unanimously convicted Heimburger of sabotage. By a five-to-two vote, it convicted Martin of attempts to demoralize the military but, by a four-to-three vote, acquitted him of sabotage (though the charge still stuck in many minds). The court sentenced both men to five years of solitary confinement, and it was the severity of the punishment that most stirred public indignation.

Many people, of course, drew comparisons to the Dreyfus Affair. In both cases the government feared that its honor was at stake, that a total acquittal or even a light sentence would play into the hands of the opposition. Unlike Dreyfus, Martin may have been guilty of something, i.e., in distributing the anti-war literature. Few people denied this much. However, almost no one believed he merited five years in prison -- a sentence equal to Heimburger's, whose attempted sabotage almost no one endorsed -- especially for saying and doing things which so many people in France were saying and doing. Martin's trial was also that of the Resistance, and his imprisonment ironically coincided with the pardon or release of Charles Maurras, Otto Abetz, Marshal Pétain, and many other former Nazis or collaborators.

After the verdict at Toulon, André Marty, who directed the campaign for the PCF, wanted the defense and the Party to stress more the patriotism of Martin's act and to assert categorically that sabotage was contrary to the policy and principles of the Party. In addition, Marty wanted Martin's release given priority over other peace issues. He suggested that the defense committees be headed 80 percent by non-Communist activists, backed up by "support committees" which drew on all social milieux.

As a result, a truly mass campaign began in earnest in the winter of 1950 and even spread to Eastern Europe as part of the Communists' general Peace Offensive. Most notable was a theatrical performance, the Drame à Toulon, the production of a small group, the Les Pavés de Paris, which, in two years, travelled some 50,000 kilometers throughout France, performing to over 200,000 spectators, usually -- thanks to interventions of the police -- under the most improvised conditions. (Sartre cited it as an outstanding illustration of authentic "popular theatre.")

In May 1951, an appellate court overturned the Toulon judgment (on technical grounds) and ordered a new court-martial in July at Brest (where the CRS were more successful in keeping the demonstrators at bay). This time the court dropped the charge of sabotage, and even the prosecutor implicitly pleaded for a reduced sentence by praising Martin's fine Resistance record. Martin, in turn,

discredited the government's only real witness, Liebert, by
forcing him to admit that he had <u>voluntarily</u> enlisted in the
German navy during World War II.

However, the judges at Brest were more hostile than those
at Toulon. "The war is not on trial. That is an affair of
state. . . . We are not the government. . . . Can anyone
disobey the law because of his individual conscience? Where
would that lead us?" To which Martin replied, "We disobeyed
laws under Vichy and the German Occupation because of devotion
to higher laws," and "the war in Vietnam violates the
Constitution." The defense further challenged the prosecution
to produce a single witness who had been actually
"demoralized" by Martin's tracts.

Most spectators expected an acquittal or a light sentence
(Martin had already spent sixteen months in prison). Even the
right-wing press, grown a little weary of the affair, thought
a three-month jail term would be sufficient. The judges,
however, after deliberating very briefly, unanimously
convicted Martin of having demoralized the army and, again,
sentenced him to five years in solitary confinement. They
allowed Heimburger, who appeared more repentent, to serve his
term as a regular prisoner. Martin's attorney did not appeal
this judgment because a third court-martial, held overseas,
could be expected to be even more hostile. In August 1951,
Martin was transferred to the penitentiary at Melun, south of
Paris.

Martin's sympathizers now realized that only mass
pressure could effect his release, and the Communists sought
by every means possible to popularize his cause. The PCF
press frequently published daily articles, full-page spreads,
and countless pictures of the slogan "<u>Libérez Henri Martin</u>"
painted on walls throughout France. Prominent were accounts of
the tribulations of his family and his fiancée, Simone Le
Balbe, whom he married while in prison. Most significantly,
the campaign spread to include numerous Socialists, Radicals,
Catholics, and even some Gaullists. (When a special Mass was
said for Martin, many people had to call the <u>L'Humanité</u>
offices for information.) The Naval Ministry had to establish
a special office just to handle the protests.

Progressive intellectuals, alienated by the repression of
human rights in the Soviet Union and Eastern Europe, effected
a <u>rapprochement</u> with the Communists over the Martin issue. In
January 1952, Bourdet and Sartre joined thirty other
intellectuals in an open letter to President Auriol (in the
manner of Zola's <u>J'Accuse</u>). When told by Auriol that Martin,
despite a too heavy sentence, would not be released as long as
the Communists continued their campaign, Sartre replied that
it was not a question of politics but of justice. Jean-Marie
Domenach, for his part, argued:

> Communist or not, Second-Master Henri Martin is
> guilty of having distributed tracts which contain
> in substance what we have been saying over again
> and again since 1947. Is it right that he should
> be in prison and we free? And, being free, is it

not right that we do everything possible to
liberate him?

To the editor of Esprit, Martin posed the central question of
the times -- that of conscientious disobedience in the face of
injustice -- actions long hallowed in the Christian tradition
and most recently reinforced by the Nuremberg Tribunal. Even a
certain French General had, in June 1940, disobeyed his
government in the name of honor and national interest.

The League of the Rights of Man and many jurists
questioned the very legality of the trial. Martin's
conviction rested on a law passed by the National Assembly on
8 March 1950, published in the Journal officiel on 11 March
and posted in Toulon only on 19 March, five days after Martin
had been arrested. Since the law could not be applied
retroactively, Martin was probably not guilty of anything.
The March 1950 law, in turn, derived from a wartime decree of
9 April 1940, directed against the Communists during the
period of the Nazi-Soviet Pact.

Both the null-and-void decree and the new law explicitly
condemned "participation in an enterprise of demoralization of
the army for the purpose of harming the national defense"
(emphasis added). However, the government's singling out of
Martin questioned the idea of any "enterprise"; its failure to
produce any soldier or sailor, who, because of Martin, had
refused to go to Indochina, questioned the idea of
"demoralization"; and its repeated insistence that France no
longer had any political or economic interests in Indochina
questioned the idea of any "harm to the national defense."

Martin defense committees sprang up almost everywhere, in
every arrondissement in Paris, in smaller cities, and in
innumerable workplaces. Sometimes they convened daily.
Groups of war veterans, mothers of soldiers, and war widows
formed delegations to various government ministers and
deputies. Martin's cause spread to several other countries,
and his name was well known in both Vietnam and Algeria. In
March 1952, several artists, who had presented "Témoignages
pour Henri Martin" at a major art exposition, were threatened
by the "Voice of America" with being barred from the United
States.

The most spectacular protesters were the many "acrobats
of freedom" who painted slogans or hung banners from chimneys,
watertowers, bridges, and other perilous places. If the
police succeeded in removing them or painting them over, the
affiches tended to appear again and again. The residents of
the Rue Alphonse-Karr in the nineteenth arrondissement in
Paris, for example, battled like this for days before the
police finally gave up and went away. The Martin campaign
also spawned a number of mini-affairs, such as the "Honfleur
Five" and the "Rennes Four," the trials of those who had
staged sympathy protests.

Eventually, the campaign focused on securing a
presidential pardon. As a young Socialist deputy, Vincent
Auriol had campaigned in 1908-1910 on behalf of a soldier
court-martialed for having denounced atrocities committed in

Algeria. More significantly, in 1923, he had campaigned for the release of the Black Sea Mutineers, including André Marty. However, the Henri Martin Affair clearly annoyed him, and he tried to dismiss it as a Communist propaganda campaign.

Although the President refused to receive delegations, he was compelled to respond personally to certain distinguished scholars or clerics, once to a group of fifteen infirm Catholic priests in a sanatorium. (He also complained that Hélène Parmelin's "pernicious" articles in L'Humanité were being "parrotted" (doublée) by certain ecclesiastics "in search of an audience.") In November 1951, during a visit to the Salon d'automne, Auriol had several "offensive" paintings taken down, including one showing dockers at Nice dumping American war matériel into the sea and a portrait of Henri Martin. Auriol later told Jean-Paul David, the anti-Communist propagandist, that the Martin affair was causing "mad havoc" in intellectual circles.

As the 14th of July (1952) approached -- a traditional period for presidential clemency -- both the President of the League of the Rights of Man and Mathilde Martin, the sailor's mother, appealed directly to Auriol. His secretary replied that her son's actions had imperiled the lives of the sons of other "mamas" and that his dossier would not be re-examined until after the "propaganda campaigns" had ceased. Nevertheless, when Auriol reduced Heimburger's sentence (arguing that he had been Martin's victim), the Communists were furious, demonstrated regularly before the President's summer place at Muret, and daily attacked him in Toulouse's Le Patriote du Sud-Ouest. (Auriol wanted the newspaper indicted for "offense to the Head of State.")

When Monsieur and Madame Martin angrily reproached him for having liberated former German war criminals under pressure from their friends and partisans, Auriol wrote in his Journal:

> What a frightful matter. The Communists have taken the son, the mother, and the father and hold them in their claws for their cause, for their propaganda, even if they make them suffer. As for me, I would ruin my prestige and my authority if I obeyed the summons of the Communist Party to pardon Martin. I will do it the day when there are no more sommations. I have said it, and I repeat it, I will do it.

When civil servants in Toulouse also protested, Auriol complained of "cowardice everywhere," that no one would would say that Martin was a "bastard" (salaud) and a convicted "saboteur" (forgetting that Martin had been acquitted of sabotage.)

The Henri Martin campaign peaked in the summer and fall of 1952. Parmelin completed her book (which, when finally published, omitted all but pejorative references to André Marty, the man most responsible for the campaign) and a short film. Meanwhile, Sartre and several other intellectuals worked on their own book (which appeared after Martin's release). Otherwise, the campaign diminished in intensity, with the PCF preoccupied with internal matters.

At long last, early on Sunday morning, 2 August 1953, after a confidential call the evening before from Auriol to the warden, Martin and Heimburger were released, two years before the expiration of the former's term, after having spent three-and-a-half years in prison. So quickly and quietly did Martin leave prison that no one was there to meet him. He simply boarded a train and made his way to the L'Humanité offices in Paris.*

Communists and Deserters

The Henri Martin Affair poses the entire question of the French Communists' attitude toward military service, including conscientious objection, refusals to go to Vietnam, desertion, and active collaboration with the enemy.

Probably somewhere between 2,000 and 5,000 non-Indochinese soldiers deserted the French Expeditionary Corps and passed over to the Vietminh in the nine years of fighting between 1945 and 1954. About two-thirds of these were members of the Foreign Legion, 16 percent were North Africans, 14 percent Metropolitan Frenchmen, and 4 percent Black Africans. An additional 30,000 to 70,000 Baodaists soldiers also deserted. Many deserted for personal reasons, not necessarily because of political sympathy for the Vietminh.

As early as October 1942, Ho Chi Minh called upon French soldiers and Legionnaires to turn their guns away from the Vietnamese guerillas to the Japanese. Although he appealed to a certain Eurasian camraderie, no non-Vietnamese responded until the summer of 1945, when a few French civilians, especially schoolteachers with Marxist or socialist leanings, rallied to the Vietminh cause. The Marxist Cultural Group of Saigon served as a liaison but did not actively encourage desertion. (Many deserters found the Group too timid.)

That fall some Legionnaires who had been in anti-Fascist struggles in Europe began to desert. The most famous was Erwin Borchers, a German citizen born in Alsace and a pacifist, who had deserted the Wehrmacht in 1939, fled to France, and joined the Legion. For the Vietminh, he wrote press articles and later did broadcasts for Radio Berlin. Between 1947 and 1950, at least seven former members of the French Expeditionary Corps served as military advisers. Paul Coste-Floret was disturbed enough to demand their surrender as part of the ill-fated Mus mission in May 1947.

Many deserted for essentially personal reasons. Poor morale constantly afflicted the soldiers of the Expeditionary Corps, who found little moral purpose for a war few believed they could win. Indeed, many developed an increasing admiration for the intelligence, courage, and endurance of the Vietnamese, with whom not a few intermarried. Sympathetic soldiers would begin to "fraternize" with the enemy, give some

information, transfer some supplies, and then possibly
desert.

Others, particularly former <u>Franc-Tireurs</u> <u>et</u> <u>partisans</u>
with proletarian backgrounds, deserted for ideological or
political reasons. Yet, surprisingly few were French
Communists. Those who escaped the anti-Communist purges of the
army had to be extremely careful lest they receive a bullet in
the back. More importantly, the PCF never encouraged
desertion, basically believing that Communist soldiers would
be more useful within the army than outside it. The Party
counseled young members to do "their duty as Communists" in
Vietnam, i.e. indoctrinate politically their comrades,
perhaps even undermine the morale of the "imperialist army,"
or, more immediately, prevent wanton destruction, massacres
and the killing of prisoners.

Yet, the PCF's precepts were contradictory. Thorez was
saying that the French people would never fight <u>the</u> Red Army,
not that they would never fight a Communist-led army in
Vietnam. The republication of André Marty's account of the
Black Sea Mutiny of 1919 was hardly calculated to dissuade
potential deserters. Nor was the PCF's praise, in the press
and National Assembly, for those soldiers who refused to go to
Vietnam. <u>L'Avant-Garde</u>, the Young Communist publication, while
advising young members to go to Vietnam, published photographs
(in 1949) of a group of deserters in the Vietminh camp.

After 1950, only one Communist officer, a certain Captain
Ribera, passed over to the Vietminh. A former FTP, Ribera was
well liked by his men, mostly Moroccans, because he avoided
risky operations. Through interrogating prisoners, he
gradually came into contact with the <u>maquis</u>. He passed some
information but refused to surrender his post. Finally,
warned that he had aroused serious suspicions and would
probably be shot in the back, Ribera arranged for a Vietminh
ambush in which he and some others were able to desert. The
PCF, however, disavowed Ribera's action as "individualistic"
and almost "anarchistic" and insisted that the army could
trust other "Republican" officers.

When the Indochina War ended, some deserters went to
Eastern Europe, while others remained in northern Vietnam,
where they did various kinds of work for the DRV. Not until
1962 were they repatriated to France as part of President De
Gaulle's general amnesty covering both the Indochina and
Algerian wars. In November of that year, forty former
deserters and their Vietnamese wives and children arrived in
Marseille. Some later wanted to go back to Vietnam but were
prevented by the intensification of the American war.**

NOTES

*Sources on the Henri Martin Affair

A. Hélène Parmelin, Matricule 2078: L'Affaire Henri Martin, Paris, 1953, pp. 1–25 (Martin's arrest), pp. 26–35 (role in the Resistance), pp. 36–50 (letters from Vietnam), pp. 51–63 (Haiphong), pp. 64–76 (sabotage of the Dixmude), pp. 77–90 (beginnings of campaign), pp. 91–167 (trial at Toulon), pp. 168–177 (campaign amplifies), pp. 178–246 (trial at Brest), pp. 247–269 (imprisonment and marriage), pp. 276–391 (petitions, delegations, affichages, intellectuals), pp. 392ff. (Auriol).

B. Jean-Paul Sartre et alii, L'Affaire Henri Martin, Paris, 1953, pp. 19–105, 123–139 (Martin's letters, commentaries), pp. 105–111 (Heimburger), pp. 111–123, 139–142 (Toulon trial), pp. 142–160 (Brest Trial), pp. 161–202 (legal questions), pp. 203–238 (appeals for pardon), pp. 243–249 (Domenach).

C. Vincent Auriol, Journal du septennat, Vol. V, 1951, Paris, 1970–1979, 10 November, pp. 536–537 (Salon d'automne); Auriol, VI, 1952, 7 January, pp. 7–8 (reply to Justin Godart), 19 February, p. 135 (Jean-Paul David), 30 April, pp. 294–295 (Abbés for Martin), 9, 28 July, pp. 431, 464 (reply to Madame Martin), 19 August, p. 500 (civil servants), 19 August, p. 507 (Heimburger's pardon), 2 September, p. 524 ("salaud"), 5 September, p. 537, n. 38, p. 1090 ("cowardice"), 23 December, p. 845 (Muret); Auriol, VII, 1953–1954, 13 July, p. 303 (appeal), 3 August, pp. 308–310 (Martin's release).

D. André Marty Archives, Reel 12, contains important letters on campaign tactics, starting on 28 October 1950, Auriol's reply to Madame Mathilde Martin, Marty's correspondence with the Martin family, and considerable correspondence between Marty and Hélène Parmelin in August and September 1952

E. Alain Ruscio, Les Communistes français et la guerre d'Indochine, 1944–1954, Paris, 1985, pp. 266–287. Ruscio's 1,947-page state doctoral thesis (Université de Paris I – Panthéon-Sorbonne, 1984), same title, contains much more detailed information and extensive interviews with participants in the Henri Martin Affair.

F. See also Dominique Desanti, Les Staliniens, 1944–1956, Paris, 1975, pp. 208–209 (intellectuals and the PCF); Theodore Zeldin, The French, New York, 1982, pp. 235–237 (Martin and the PCF Central School); Jacques Varin, "L'Affaire Henri Martin," Cahiers d'histoire de l'Institut Maurice Thorez, March–April 1972; Jacques Doyon, Les Soldats blancs de Ho Chi Minh, Paris, 1973, pp. 146–151; Francis Joucelain, Le PCF et la première guerre d'Indochine, Paris, 1973, pp.

34-39.

Even right-wing deputies could be sympathetic to Martin's plight but preferred to blame the machinations of the PCF. See, for example, Journal officiel, débats parlementaires, Assemblée nationale, 28-30 December 1951, p.   10089.

**Sources on   Communists and Deserters

A. The basic account is Jacques Doyon, Les Soldats blancs de Ho Chi Minh, Paris, 1973, pp.   25-36, 44-54, 59-80, 307-312 (early deserters), pp.   269-303 (PCF's attitude), pp.   373-385 (Ribera), pp.   412-413,   425ff.   (amnesty and return), Annexe II, pp.   504-506 (statistics).

In 1950, Mao Tse-tung asked Léo Figuères   if   there   were Communist formations in the Expeditionary Corps. Stalin asked Duclos the same thing in 1951. See, Figuères, Jeunesse militant, Paris, 1971, p.   208; Duclos, Mémoires, IV, Paris, 1971, p.   332. For PCF advice to young Communist soldiers, see l'Avant-Garde, 12-18 October 1949.

B. For more statistics on deserters, see Henri Azeau,   Ho Chi Minh, dernière chance, Paris, 1968, pp.   305-308,   and André Marty, L'Affaire Marty, Paris, 1955, p.   279.

Azeau has unpublished official figures giving 1,373 Legionnaires, 338 North Africans,   288 Metropolitan French and 78 Africans as having deserted the Expeditionary Corps in addition to some 30,610 Indochinese.

In October 1954, André Marty, as a deputy, learned from the Defense Minister that 5,568 soldiers and sailors had been court-martialed in absentia for serious offenses during the Vietnam War and presumably may have been deserters.   See Journal officiel, 6 October 1954.

C. On the Marxist Cultural Group of Saigon (MCG), see Alain   Ruscio,   Les Communistes français et la guerre d'Indochine, 1944-1954, Paris, 1985, pp.   315-331, and his "Le Groupe Culturel Marxiste de Saigon (1945-1950)," Cahiers d'histoire de l'Institut Maurice Thorez, No. 31, 1979, pp. 187-208.

Notable members of the MCG were Louis Caput, the Socialist, Henri Lanoue, the syndicalist, and Jean Chesneaux and Georges Bouderel, later distinguished professors of Oriental history.

D. On the morale of the Expeditionary Corps, see Paul-Marie De la Gorce, L'Après-Guerre, Paris, 1978, pp. 351-356.

On the French government's concern with desertions (among Baodaists) and the questioning of war aims by members of the Expeditionary Corps, see Auriol, VI, 1952, 24 March, 7 April, pp.   223-224, 260.

A former deserter, a skilled worker, told this author that he had gone to Vietnam at age 18. One day, he was guarding a group of civilians who asked him why he had come there. When he could not think of a good reason, they asked him why did he not release them and join the <u>maquis.</u> Later in the day, he put down his rifle and did so. After amnesty, he returned to France with his Vietnamese wife and two children (he spoke fluent Vietnamese), only to visit his French family; he then planned to go back to Vietnam, a prospect interrupted by the American bombing of northern Vietnam.

XIV
Mendès-France and Ho Chi Minh
JANUARY–NOVEMBER 1953

In 1953, the politics of the Indochina War unravelled significantly. Although Paris and Washington still planned for victory, the Vietminh maintained the military (and diplomatic) initiative. In France, the opposition to the war grew and crystallized beyond the traditional Left, and Pierre Mendès-France narrowly missed becoming Premier.

A poll in the spring showed that only 15 percent of the French people still supported a military solution, as opposed to 27 percent in 1950 and 37 percent in 1947. Thirty-five percent favored negotiations with the Vietminh, up from 24 percent in 1950 and 15 percent in 1947. An additional 15 percent advocated abandoning Indochina completely. Disturbed by the Vietminh's continued military successes and the increased demands of the Associated States, enjoying the fruits of post-war economic prosperity, continually ill-informed about events in Indochina, and weary of Cold War tensions, most people now wanted an end to the war. Stalin's death in March, an armistice in Korea in August, and the explosion of a Russian hydrogen bomb made a détente everywhere more imperative. Yet, the Paris government continued the Indochina policies of its predecessors. President Eisenhower said that the French were no longer pursuing a "colonialist" venture, and NATO (in December 1952) included Indochina in the defense of the free world. Although Mollet vaguely insisted on prompt negotiations with the Vietminh, the Socialists, in January, once again supported the military budget. Only the Communists voted against it. (1)

American assessments of the situation in Indochina remained pessimistic, due to the fact that the Bao Dai solution still had not gotten off the ground and that the Vietminh were extending their control throughout Vietnam. By mid-1954, a National Intelligence Estimate held, the French Union's political and military position might "deteriorate very rapidly," even if the Vietminh had not achieved "a final military decision" by that time. Even a continued military stalemate, Secretary of State John Foster Dulles feared, would

have the "most undesirable political consequences."   To
obviate these prospects, Washington insisted that Paris come
up with a plan to destroy the "principal enemy forces" within
approximately two years and appoint a "bold and aggressive"
French military leader or else lose any further assistance.
(2)

As the year progressed, France's difficulties only
multiplied. In April, the Vietminh moved into Laos. Premier
René Mayer and Letourneau called this a violation of an
international frontier and wanted to appeal to the United
Nations. Washington agreed.   Foreign Minister Bidault,
however, argued that any UN action, if not immediately vetoed
by the Soviet Union, would weaken French influence over the
Associated States,   expose France to Arab and Asian
denunciations in the General Assembly, implicitly give an
international status to the Vietminh, allow the United States
to assume the military direction of the war, and invite
Chinese military intervention.

Next, the Associated States began to fall out.   In
Cambodia, Prince Norodom Sihanouk threatened to make "common
cause" with the Vietminh if France did not concede his country
full sovereignty over all military, judicial, and economic
matters -- demands which unleashed a new wave of anti-war
protests in the French press. In Vietnam, the Baodaists
wanted genuine independence, free national elections, and an
end to the war.   Vietnamese Socialists demanded immediate
negotiations with the Vietminh. (3)

Mayer first responded by secretly sending envoys to meet
with Vietminh representatives in Rangoon. Although both sides
favored bilateral discussions, nothing developed.   Next, Mayer
named General Henri Navarre as the new Commander-in-Chief in
Indochina to prepare militarily the conditions for an
honorable withdrawal, although publicly he was to come up with
a plan for ultimate victory. Finally, to quell the growing
public revulsion against the "filthy war," Mayer dramatically
devaluated the Indochinese piastre and set up a parliamentary
commission to study the associated scandals.   Letourneau
resigned in protest, and the Baodaists, besides lamenting a
loss of income, feared that Paris' unilateral action was a
first step toward a "liquidation" of the war. (4)

Meanwhile, anti-war sentiment in France sharply
expanded. Philippe Devillers' Histoire du Vietnam, 1940-1952
and Paul Mus' Vietnam: Sociologie d'une guerre provided some
desperately needed accurate information. In April 1953, a new
voice, Jean-Jacques Servan-Schreiber, charged that certain
political groups, with vested financial interests, were
"conspiring" to keep the war going. His new journal,
L'Express, whose heterogeneous collaborators included Mauriac,
Malraux, and Camus, advocated serious changes overseas (except
in Algeria). In its very first issue, Mendès-France wrote that
the French negotiating position in Indochina was better two
years ago than the last year, better then than at present, and
probably better now than a year hence.

Ambassador Douglas Dillon felt that "L'Humanité could not
have done better" than L'Express. He now feared that demands

for negotiations or withdrawal "might well reach serious proportions" and that the anti-war campaign, "no longer the case of the fairly isolated voice of Mendès-France," might be expected "to fall on more responsive ears."

The intellectual onslaught continued. Le Monde complained that, while France was exhausting itself in Indochina, Germany would become the leading power in Europe. Raymond Aron said Indochina could be justified only in terms of worldwide anti-Communist diplomacy, not French interests. Bourdet contrasted Ho Chi Minh's successful agrarian reform program with the reactionary landowners behind Bao Dai.

Sartre noted with irony that France was fighting for the freedom of the Indochinese peoples to choose a non-Communist government because one could not be free and a Communist at the same time; for a Communist, by definition, was a slave, and no sane person would freely choose Communism. Therefore, to give the Vietnamese freedom was to assure that they did not become Communist. French methods, admittedly not very honorable, were at least a hundred times less horrible than those of Communists; and all the present crimes of a democracy could not equal the horror of the future crimes of a hypothetical Soviet domination. (5)

Anxiety finally reached official levels. Paul Devinat told Auriol that the Vietminh, appearing "everywhere but nowhere," were treating the Expeditionary Corps as a "punching ball," much as the Resistance had handled the German army. Another official declared flatly that negotiations with Ho Chi Minh, possible then, "will be necessary tomorrow." Minister of War Pierre de Chevigné admonished his colleagues to "stop acting like children," for they did not have a "shadow of a chance" of achieving a "decent solution" in Indochina. Paul Reynaud called the continued bloodletting in Indochina "a crime against France." (He recommended a "yellowing" of the Expeditionary Corps.) Auriol himself refused to stand for re-election partly because of Indochina. (6)

The Communists and Socialists now challenged the government on a whole range of issues, including the pardon of the Alsacian volunteers involved in the Oradour massacre of June 1944. The Socialists, even more than the Communists, denounced repressive practices in Morocco. The Communists (and about half the Socialists) attacked the proposed European Defense Community.

On Indochina, the Socialists were less clear and unified. At their congress in May, proponents of direct negotiations with the DRV, such as Louis Caput and the Federation of the Seine, again emerged forcefully, while pro-Baodaists, such as André Bidet, argued that the Associated States only needed more independence and more responsibility for their own defense. A few Socialists even hoped that, with American aid, a military victory might still be possible. Most, however, favored a truce, followed by negotiations (with almost anybody) and free elections. (7)

Despite the expanding opposition, the PCF remained politically isolated. It had lost two-thirds of its membership since 1947; its press was curtailed (<u>Ce Soir</u> disappeared in March); and a number of officials were arrested (including Stil and Benoît Frachon) on charges of endangering "the external security of the State" (which, in most cases, meant speeches or articles against the Indochina War).

Nevertheless, the PCF did benefit from the détente following Stalin's death. (Indeed, in the National Assembly, in March, only two deputies refused to rise in homage to the war leader; and French flags were lowered to half-mast -- except overseas where Frédéric-Dupont felt it would insult French soldiers fighting Communism.) The Socialists refused to endorse the more virulent forms of anti-Communism which, according to Christian Pineau, had "no other bases than hatred and the desire to curry favor with certain domestic and foreign interests." In return, the PCF moderated its tone, but not its positions, on Indochina; the Henri Martin campaign diminished greatly; and <u>L'Humanité</u> reported only a few minor dockers' protests against the war. (8)

In the spring, the Left did well in the municipal elections, whereas the Gaullists lost half their supporters, causing the RPF (<u>Rassemblement populaire français</u>) to disband. Then a decline in real wages spurred a series of strikes, and, in May, the Communists and Socialists combined to help overthrow the Mayer government.

Auriol then turned to Mendès-France, who, in his investiture speech, invoked "prudence and discretion" on the subject of Indochina. He said nothing about negotiations, nor did he repudiate the idea of internationalizing the war, causing both the regrouped "Gaullists" and Communists serious reservations. Emmanuel d'Astier de la Vigerie called his "obscure" statements a step backward, a parliamentary maneuver "unworthy of a man of your quality."

The result was that the Communists refused to vote for Mendès-France. Although <u>Le Populaire</u> accused the PCF of preferring verbal propaganda and signature campaigns to seizing "an opportunity to act," the Socialists themselves were divided over the Radical candidate. (Ultimately, they voted for him but refused to join his cabinet.) The MRP, the Right, and the "Gaullists," on the other hand, feared Mendès-France really intended to abandon Indochina (and were nervous about his designs for North Africa). In the end, he failed by thirteen votes.

Even if the PCF (ignoring his anti-Communist remarks) had abstained, Mendès-France still would not have had a constitutional majority. By being ambiguous, he had simply aroused too many fears on too many issues. In any event, a Mendès-France government, at this time, probably would not have lasted long enough to have achieved a peace settlement in Indochina. (9)

The new Premier, the conservative Joseph Laniel, would not say with whom, when, or on what basis he might negotiate on Indochina. Among his ministers, Bidault insisted on strict adherence to the French Union (as did Auriol), whereas François Mitterrand was willing to grant commonwealth status, and Paul Reynaud favored complete independence in order to be able to relinquish the burden of the war to the Baodaists. Laniel would only agree to relinquish some French functions and to deal with the Associated States through diplomatic, inter-governmental channels.

Neither the Cambodians nor the Baodaists were satisfied. A Vietnamese National Congress in October called for total independence and the renegotiation of all treaties with France. Vietnam, the Congress resolved, would no longer participate in the French Union "in its present form." The motion elicited a great deal of resentment in France. To Auriol it was "scandalous, an act of frightening ingratitude." To Consul Donald Heath (Saigon), it was "the product of emotional, irresponsible nationalism." (10)

In France, the Socialists forced a major debate in November (in which Mendès-France did not participate). After the Baodaist Congress, Alain Savary argued, France could no longer claim to be preserving the French Union, nor stopping aggression (as in Korea) because Indochina was basically a civil war, nor defending Southeast Asia against the Chinese (who could easily bypass Hanoi), nor (after the Korean armistice) participating in an international crusade against Asian Communism. While talks with Moscow and Peking might be helpful, France had to negotiate directly with Ho Chi Minh. Although he did not think the Vietminh were genuine nationalists or all that popular (Boutbien called them "Stalinist fanatics"), Savary believed Ho Chi Minh was no more "Peking's puppet" than Mao Tse-tung had been "Moscow's puppet." (Nor, for that matter, he added, were French soldiers "American mercenaries.")

In the same debate, Daladier complained of France's "deplorable complacency," if not "servility," toward the United States. The Communists argued that the war would cost France all its independence, if it did not end in an atomic conflict. Jean Pronteau prophetically forecast, at the very least, a thirty-year war. Right-wing and centrist deputies, for their part, several times challenged the Communists and Socialists to defend their earlier ministerial records on Indochina. Laniel minimized the significance of the Baodaist Congress but said he was open to peace proposals emanating from "Ho Chi Minh and his team."

Alhough the Premier appealed to the Socialists not to harm French morale and encourage the enemy, the SFIO moved for immediate negotiations with the adversary. Defferre believed that, despite "some touching accents," Laniel really intended to send the Contingent (the regular army) to Indochina to continue the war (as a precondition for receiving more American aid). At the same time, Defferre did not want the Socialist position confused with the PCF's desire for a Vietminh victory.

In the end, the Assembly rejected a Socialist motion (330 to 250), and a Communist one, in favor of one calling for unspecified negotiations, the development of a Vietnamese army, and international support. A third of the Radicals joined the SFIO and PCF in voting against this motion.

Ambassador Dillon commented that only the Communists and Socialists had a party policy on Indochina, that "everyone was in favor of 'negotiations' but only the Communists said with whom, when and how," and that Mendès-France had avoided the subject by being absent. (11)

Having listened from the gallery to Laniel's overtures, Svante Löfgren, a correspondent for the Swedish Expressen, immediately transmitted five questions to Ho Chi Minh. In reply, the DRV President said that the withdrawal of the Expeditionary Corps was no longer a prerequisite for negotiations, any talks should be essentially between France and Vietnam, and any constructive proposition leading to a cease-fire was welcome. To Auriol, it was both a "maneuver" and a "bombshell," and the Baodaists panicked. However, Laniel dismissed Ho Chi Minh's proposals as "unofficial." Privately, he still hoped for a victory. As part of his plan (somewhat revised), General Navarre had just dropped six battalions at an abandoned Japanese-built airfield in a remote spot in western Tonkin called Dien Bien Phu. (12)

NOTES

Notes have been grouped according to topic.

1. Paul Clay Sorum, Intellectuals and Decolonization in France, Chapel Hill, 1977, p. 10 (opinion poll); L'Année politique, 1953, pp. 188-189, 207-208; Vincent Auriol, Journal du septennat, Vol. VII, 1953-1954, Paris, 1970-1979., n. 73 (March), p. 720.

2. United States-Vietnam Relations, 1945-1967 (Pentagon Papers), Washington, 1971, Book IX, SOS Dulles to Paris, 19, 26, 27 March 1953, UnderSOS Bedell Smith to Paris, 24 April 1953, National Intelligence Estimate (NIE-91), 4 June 1953, pp. 15-20, 31, 44-55; Foreign Relations of the United States (FRUS), 1952-1954, XIII (IC), Franco-American Discussions, Washington, 30 March 1953, pp. 440-452.

3. Georgette Elgey, Histoire de la IVe République, Vol. II, Paris, 1968, pp. 456-461; Ellen J. Hammer, The Struggle for Indochina, 1940-1955, Stanford, 1955, pp. 289-297; Auriol, VII, 1953-1954, 15, 22 April, pp. 119, 127-128, n. 86, p. 735.

4. Elgey, II, pp. 456, 461-462; R. E. M. Irving, The First Indochina War, London, 1975, pp. 107-111; Auriol, VII, 1953-1954, n. 27 (January), 16 March, nn. 60, 127 (May), 8 August, pp. 89-91, 316-320, 690, 742, 748; Georges Chaffard, Les Deux guerres du Vietnam, Paris, 1969, pp. 143-162 and Jacques Raphaël-Leygues, Pont de liaises: Mission en Indochine, Paris, 1976.

The parliamentary commission to study the piastre scandal did not report until the end of the war, revealed little not already known, attributed no precise responsibilities, but severely reprimanded Letourneau's failure to halt the traffic. (Letourneau had also defended the Expeditionary

Corps' trafficking in opium on the grounds of "military imperatives.") An unsuccessful attempt was made to link Auriol's son, Paul, to the piastre scandal.

5. Paul-Marie De la Gorce, Apogée et mort de la IVe République, Paris, 1979, pp. 75-79; Elgey, II, pp. 130-134; Sorum, p. 56; Hammer, pp. 299-300; Auriol, VII, 1953-1954, n. 90 (April), p. 736; France-Observateur, 19 March 1953; Les Temps modernes, August-September 1953 (a special issue on Indochina), pp. 400-401; FRUS, 1952-1954, XIII (IC), Dillon, 30 April, 23 May, pp. 530-532, 579-581.

6. Elgey, II, p. 132; Auriol, VII, 1953-1954; 23, 26 February, 17 April, pp. 60-61, 66, 124.

7. Elgey, II, pp. 113-117 (Oradour), De la Gorce, pp. 46-50 (Morocco), 112-116, 138-145 (EDC); SFIO, Bulletin intérieur, May 1953, pp. 3, 15, 28-29, July 1953, p. 11; Le Populaire, 10, 20 February, 7 April, 2 May 1953; Louis Caput, Pour le rétablissement de la paix en Indochine, Paris, (September) 1953.

Caput had tried unsuccessfully to contact DRV representatives in Hong Kong in 1948.

8. Alexander Werth, France, 1940-1955, Boston, 1966, p. 605; Elgey, II, p. 127; Auriol, VII, 1953-1954, pp. xviii-xix, nn. 25 (March), pp. 713-715; L'Année politique, 1953, p. 27; L'Humanité, 12, 26 January, 12 February, 24 March 1953; Maurice Kriegel-Valrimont, "La Paix au Vietnam par la négociation avec Ho Chi Minh," Cahiers du communisme, June 1953, pp. 721-732.

9. Elgey, II, pp. 134-136; Werth, pp. 608-614; Auriol, VII, 1953-1954, 22 May 1953, n. 143 (May); n. 4 (June), pp. 188-189, 751, 755; Journal officiel, débats parlementaires, Assemblée nationale (JODPAN), 3-4 June 1953, Mendès-France, pp. 2907, 2968; D'Astier de la Vigerie, pp. 2961-2962; Duclos, pp. 2971-2974; Le Populaire, 6-7 June 1953.

When Moch hinted that popular pressure might force the Socialists to form a government with the Communists, Auriol vigorously objected and urged the Socialists to return to a conservative cabinet.

Mendès-France (and certain observers) believed that Auriol, underestimating the central importance of Indochina, had called on him only with the intention to clear the way for a center-right Premier. In September, in Washington, Mendès-France told Dulles that he had never favored immediate negotiations with the Vietminh. See FRUS, 1952-1954, XIII (FE), 11 September 1953, pp. 796-797.

10. Hammer, pp. 301-307; Auriol, VII, 1953-1954, 17 October 1953, pp. 468-469; FRUS, 1952-1954, XIII (FE), Heath, 17 October 1953, p. 836.

11. JODPAN, 20, 23, 27 October 1953, Laniel, pp. 4393-4394, 4602-4607; Savary, pp. 4394-4395, 4562-4564; Giovoni (PCF), pp. 4395-4396, 4542-4545; Boutbien (SFIO),

pp. 4548-4550; Kriegel-Valrimont (PCF), pp. 4566-4569; Daladier, pp. 4577-4579; Defferre (SFIO), pp. 4608-4610; FRUS, 1952-1954, XIII (FE), Dillon, 28 October 1953, pp. 853-855.

12. Auriol, VII, 1953-1954, 30 November 1953, p. 522, nn. 84 (November), 5-8 (December), pp. 823-824; Elgey, II, p. 469; L'Année politique, 1953, pp. 303-304; Le Populaire, 1, 2 December (responded quite positively to Ho Chi Minh's overtures).

XV
Dien Bien Phu and Geneva
NOVEMBER 1953–JULY 1954

The last eight months of the Indochina War witnessed a veritable avalanche -- a heavy military defeat invited a major change in French politics which, in turn, rapidly led to peace in Indochina. The French Left rode the crest of the anti-war movement but had little imprint on the final peace settlement.

With the ambiance of détente at the end of 1953, the PCF tried to reintegrate itself somewhat into the French political arena, becoming distinctly conciliatory on a number of issues. Thus, for example, when over four million workers went out on strike in August 1953 (the largest number in post-war France) -- essentially a "Communist army led by Socialist and Catholic generals" -- neither the PCF nor the CGT sought any political advantages. They were much more concerned to find allies to block the proposed European Defense Community (EDC). In the same vein, in December 1953, the PCF supported the right-wing Socialist Marcel Naegelen for the presidency, despite his record of repression as Resident-General in Algeria, because he was opposed to the EDC. On Indochina, the PCF, with a few notable exceptions, generally eschewed demagogy in favor of more reasoned analyses.

The Socialists, however, were little affected by détente and, albeit deeply divided over the EDC, little interested in an alliance with the PCF. On Indochina, they clearly marked their distance, wanting peace but not on terms advantageous to the DRV. In the spring of 1954, Alain Savary (in place of Pierre Cot) undertook an official mission to the DRV, a trip interrupted when more fruitful international discussions appeared on the horizon. (1)

A Four-Power Conference at Berlin in January agreed to a Five-Power Conference on Korea and Indochina at Geneva in April. Hoping to encourage France to reject the EDC, the Soviet Union offered to mediate with the DRV. Neither Bidault (who wanted to avoid the DRV) nor Washington (which wanted to avoid the Chinese) were anxious for these talks but were forced to go along because of domestic (French) and international pressure for a settlement. Indeed, on 22 February, Prime Minister Nehru urged an immediate cease-fire in Vietnam.

When both both the Communists and Socialists endorsed Nehru's proposal, the National Assembly was forced into a week-long debate. The PCF accused the Laniel government of "maneuvers and false solutions," while the SFIO complained that France was surrendering its independence to the United States. Laniel, however, rejected any bilateral negotiations with the Vietminh, who, he insisted, had to evacuate most of the areas under their control. (He also reminded the Socialists of the positions their ministers had taken in the early years of the war.) Then, Mendès-France touched off a storm when he called for immediate and direct negotiations with Ho Chi Minh. However cruel or unfair, this was the only real solution. He also suspected the government was using Geneva as an alibi, secretly hoping it would fail and the United States would be forced to intervene militarily in Indochina. Although Laniel survived a vote of confidence by sixty-two votes, his majority was shrinking. (2)

Immediately after the debate, on 13 March, the Vietminh launched their long-awaited assault on Dien Bien Phu, and, within two days, had effectively sealed the fate of the fortress, although a massive airlift permitted the defenders to hold on. (Despite all the talk of the heroic "French" defenders, a third were Legionnaires, including many Germans, and the bulk were colonial troops, mostly North Africans, Black Africans and Indochinese -- an "extraordinary mixture of colors and races.") For the next two months, the battle essentially developed into a brutal artillery duel. General Giap probably postponed a final assault to magnify the psychological impact of the French defeat on the eve of the Geneva Conference, while Paris hoped that a prolonged defense might inspire American intervention. When Dien Bien Phu finally fell on 7 May, the Vietminh had suffered over 8,000 casualties, while the French had lost 5,000 (about 5 percent of the Expeditionary Corps). The Tonkin Delta defenses were now untenable, and the road to Hanoi open. The Baodaist army collapsed, and about half went over to the Vietminh. (3)

Dien Bien Phu symbolized the beginning of the end of the French Empire. (The Trotskyists called it the "Stalingrad of colonialism.") During the battle, the French Communists never called for strikes or demonstrations of solidarity with the Vietminh forces (for which the Trotskyists condemned them). Nor, when the garrison fell, did they yield to "atrocious rejoicing" (as the Socialists charged). Amidst right-wing calls of "murderers," their deputies did refuse to rise in homage to the defenders, but on the grounds that the government had no right to salute those soldiers they had had killed. The fall of the fortress, L'Humanité wrote, simply showed the insanity of trying to reconquer a people "taking the cause of their independence into their own hands." The men who fell at Dien Bien Phu would still be alive if Laniel had accepted Ho Chi Minh's peace proposals in November 1953. Claude Bourdet, for his part, dismissed any undue sentimentality over the defeat. Valluy, not Giap, had started the war; Ho Chi Minh, not the French, had made all the peace overtures; and French forces, not the Vietnamese, had destroyed villages and burned people to death with napalm. (4)

The Geneva discussions on Indochina started immediately after the fall of Dien Bien Phu. Both sides agreed on the need for an armistice but disagreed over "regroupment zones." Pham Van Dong called for the complete evacuation of the French Expeditionary Corps, the total independence of Vietnam (with some vague ties to the French Union), and national elections. The Chinese supported him, but the Russians suggested international control and collective guarantees. Although Bidault tried to stall (while he secretly negotiated with the Americans to intervene militarily), the Communist side knew that his days as Foreign Minister were numbered and that the French military situation in the Tonkin Delta was collapsing. (5)

In France, Dien Bien Phu had reduced Laniel's majority to two votes. After a three-week respite (because of concern for the safety of the Expeditionary Corps), the Socialists and Communists renewed the attack at the beginning of June. The former strongly opposed the sending of the Contingent, since Indochina was not a case of "national defense," or any internationalization of the war. The Communists accused Bidault of playing "an insane game," of working with the United States to undermine the Geneva negotiations and prepare for World War III. Bidault could only dismiss these charges as so much "soap opera."

Then Mendès-France entered the breach, charging that Laniel still looked to total victory (witness his appointment of Frédéric-Dupont as Minister of the Associated States), while implying that proponents of negotiations were "bad Frenchmen" or "Moscow's agents." Mendès-France then accused Bidault of having nearly started a world war, "playing poker" with millions of lives, in total disregard for the French parliament. The government had alienated itself from the people and needed to be changed entirely.

Laniel could only reply that the opposition, under the sway of the Communists, was preparing for an "Asian Munich." The Communists retorted that his government constituted the "gravediggers of France." The Assembly, as a whole, refused confidence by a vote of 306 to 293. About half the Radicals and most of the "Gaullists" had joined the opposition. The "Republic of Contradictions" was finished. (6)

President René Coty now quickly turned to Mendès-France. In his investiture speech, on 17 June, he called for an immediate cease-fire but also for the maintenance of the French presence in East Asia (possibly protected by the Contingent.) Then he dramatically announced that if he did not achieve peace at Geneva within thirty days, i.e., by 20 July, he would automatically resign. He also said he would not accept the votes of the Communists or anyone who had "directly or indirectly espoused the cause of those whom we fight." (An MRP deputy queried if he would also discount PCF votes in a contest over the EDC.)

NOTES

Notes have been grouped according to topic.

1. Alexander Werth, France, 1940-1955, Boston, 1966, pp. 631-633; Irwin Wall, French Communism in the Era of Stalin, Westport, Conn., 1983, pp. 177-178; Roger Quilliot, La SFIO et l'exercice du pouvoir, 1944-1958, Paris, 1972, pp. 501-502; Paul-Marie de la Force, Apogée et mort de la IVe République, Paris, 1979, p. 82; Georgette Elgey, Histoire de la IVe République, Vol. II, Paris, 1968, p. 468.

The conservative René Coty, who refused to take a clear stand on the EDC, became the new President of the Fourth Republic.

2. Elgey, pp. 465, 477-478; L'Année politique, 1954, pp. 11-13; Journal officiel, débats parlementaires, Assemblée nationale (JODPAN), 5, 9 March 1954, Giovoni (PCF), pp. 709-711; Gilbert de Chambrun (Progressiste), pp. 711-713; Mayer, pp. 707-709; Lussy (SFIO), pp. 756-766; Laniel, pp. 713-715; Mendès-France, pp. 758-761; Foreign Relations of the United States (FRUS), 1952-1954, XIII (IC), Dillon, 6, 10 March 1954, pp. 1097-1099, 1103-1105.

3. Werth, pp. 667, 671-672; Elgey, II, pp. 491-492, 526-527; Bernard B. Fall, "Dien Bien Phu: A Battle to Remember," New York Times Magazine, 3 May 1964, in Marvin E. Gettleman, editor, Vietnam: History, Documents and Opinions, New York, 1970, pp. 133-142.

4. L'Humanité, 8 May 1954; Le Populaire, 10 May 1954; La Vérité, 9-22 April, 14-27 May 1954; France-Observateur, 13 May 1954; L'Année politique, 1954, pp. 27-29; JODPAN, 11-14 May 1954, Pronteau-Laniel exchange, p. 2336; Gilbert de Chambrun (Progressiste), pp. 2338-2340; Waldeck Rochet (PCF), p. 2340; Louis Vallon (PCF), p. 2341.

5. Philippe Devillers and Jean Lacouture, Vietnam: De la guerre française à la guerre américaine, Paris, 1969, pp. 164-183 (Geneva), pp. 164-183; Elgey, II, pp. 533-539, 545-546.

6. Elgey, II, pp. 548-550; Werth, pp. 673-675; JODPAN, 1-2, 9, 12 June 1954, Pronteau (PCF), pp. 2744-2749; Malleret-Joinville (PCF), pp. 2780-2781; Guyot (PCF), pp. 2860-2862, 2980-2981; Bidault, pp. 2844-2849; Mendès-France, pp. 2849-2855; Laniel, pp. 2871-2873; SFIO and PCF motions, p. 2873.

At the PCF Congress early in June (the first since 1950), Indochina was not a major preoccupation. See Wall, pp. 170-178.

7. Werth, pp. 676-681; Jacques Fauvet, Histoire du PCF, Paris, 1977, pp. 450-452; L'Année politique, 1954, pp. 40-45; JODPAN, 17 June 1954, Mendès-France, pp. 2992-2994, 3000-3003; Billoux (PCF), pp. 2999-3000; d'Astier de la

Vigerie, p.   3004; Waldeck-Rochet (PCF), pp.   3006-3007.

8. Werth, pp.   682-685; Devillers and Lacouture, pp. 261-318; Donald Lancaster, "Power Politics at the Geneva Conference," in Gettleman, pp.   146-163; text of the Accords and Final Declaration, ibid., pp. 164-188; Robert F. Randle, Geneva 1954, Princeton, 1969; Dwight D. Eisenhower, Mandate for a Change, New York, 1963, p. 372; Ellen J. Hammer, The Struggle for Indochina, 1940-1955, Stanford, 1955, pp. 313-314, 333-337; George C. Herring, America's Longest War: The United States and Vietnam, 1950-1972, New York, 1979, pp. 38-42.

9. Werth, pp.   685-686; L'Année politique, 1954, pp. 412-415; JODPAN, 22-23 July 1954, Mendès-France, pp. 3533-3537, 3579-3584; Gilbert de Chambrun (Progressiste), pp. 3539-3540; Waldeck-Rochet (PCF), pp. 3573-3575; Lussy (SFIO), pp. 3544-3545; Frédéric-Dupont, pp. 3540-3543.

10. La Vérité, 22 January-4 February, 1-14 October 1954; Le Populaire, 22 July 1954; L'Humanité, 21 July 1954; Maurice Kriegel-Valrimont, "Une Victoire des forces de paix qui en appelle d'autres," Cahiers du communisme, August-September 1954, pp.   987-996; Alain Ruscio, "Le Mendésisme et l'Indochine," Revue d'histoire moderne et contemporaine, No. 2, 1982, pp. 334-342 (a critical view).

Conclusion

Over ten years have passed since the end of the Second Indochinese War, over twenty since the end of the Algerian War, and over thirty since the end of the First Indochinese War. Recriminations are scarcer, but still a serious debate continues over the colonial policies of the French Left, particularly those of the Communists.

Right-wing critics accuse the French Communists of having actively encouraged colonial revolts. Yet, while a part of the government, they urged moderation upon the overseas nationalists, who, for their part, were less inclined to radical action while the Left had some influence in Paris. Nor did the Communists ever favor an immediate or complete dismantling of the Empire, only its liberalization. The Right also says that, while in the opposition, the Communists engaged in extra-legal and unpatriotic activities. Yet, the Communists always prescribed definite limits and never advocated desertion or sabotage. Moreover, they could, in many respects, not unreasonably claim to be defending the true interests of France, which the other political parties were betraying.

Left-wing critics accuse the Communists of having endorsed, however passively, the principal measures which led to war in Indochina. If they had, instead, voted against military credits or even resigned from the ministry in protest, they might have inhibited the war's prosecution at an early date. Certainly, the Communists shared enough of the colonial consensus not to want Indochina to rotate entirely out of the French orbit. They also clearly subordinated the interests of the colonial peoples to those of their Metropolitan constituents -- normally not an unreasonable position, except for a Communist Party.

Nevertheless, the Communist ministers only marginally affected Indochina policies, they never demanded less than what Ho Chi Minh was asking for, and they did resist the war currents as much as feasible (within the parameters of their overall strategies). Their resigning might not have prevented the other parties from effectively prosecuting the war, as was

proved later on when they were active in the opposition.
Their resigning at an earlier time might also have advanced
the Cold War in France, without salubrious consequences for
the French working class, Soviet foreign policies, or the
aspirations of the Vietnamese revolutionaries.

Left-wing critics further charge that the Communists were
deficient in the opposition. For example, they took a full
two years to oppose the Indochina War meaningfully (basically
because the Soviet Union was still little interested in the
conflict). They never called a general strike against the war
and they never called for the fraternization of French troops
with the Vietminh. Their Peace Offensive, moreover,
essentially promoted the status quo between the super-powers,
not Third World liberation movements which might upset that
balance of power. Finally, the Communists might have
shortened the Vietnam War -- and on terms more favorable to
the Vietminh -- if they had kept up their radical activities
in the last years of the war.

Communist defenders counter that the working class was
too weakened and too demoralized (and too little sensitive to
colonial issues) to engage in more vigorous anti-war
activities. Indeed, the government had demonstrated quite
convincingly that it could handle massive strikes, even of a
domestic nature (and a symbolic one on behalf of Jacques
Duclos failed abysmally). "Fraternization with the enemy" was
difficult to inspire in a volunteer army which was rapidly
purging its Communist officers. The Peace Offensive, even if
mostly concerned with a world war, did heighten the
unpopularity of the Vietnam War. In the Henri Martin Affair,
moreover, the Communists showed they could deviate from
principal Soviet concerns to focus exclusively and massively
on the Indochina War itself.

The Communists did briefly try to resuscitate the
anti-war movements in 1952 but were compelled to back off
during the détente that followed Stalin's death. In any
event, lacking any kind of an alliance with the Socialists,
they were in no position to impose the terms of a peace
settlement. And, we must remember that on paper, at least,
Geneva did not appear to be disadvantageous to the DRV.
Finally, the French Communists benefitted greatly from the
fact that the objective situation in Vietnam (on which
American documentation is so instructive) so accurately
reflected their position, permitting them to be effective with
almost any combination of anti-war tactics they chose.

The French Socialists found themselves in a much more
awkward position. Right-wing critics correctly accuse them,
not of being "subversive," but of undermining the unity of
governments trying to prosecute the war. Although a majority
of the SFIO backed a politique de force and the Bao Dai
solution, the Party was sufficiently divided that its support
appeared most reluctant. In the Generals' Affair, moreover,
the Socialists were most provocative, seeking not only to
change Indochina policies but also to displace their political
opponents in directing the war.

Left-wing criticism is less nuanced. Committed to an unswerving anti-Communism, both in Vietnam and France, the Socialists simply bore a heavy and unequivocal responsibility for the origins and continuation of the war. Their claims to have consistently opposed the war are much less convincing than Communist denials of ministerial responsiblity. Indeed, the SFIO never officially participated in any major anti-war activities and never actually voted against military credits for the war until March 1954, only a few months before the end of the war. The Socialists could never bring themselves to associate with the PCF on Indochina (except on a few parliamentary motions) and, even at the end, still hoped for a non-Communist government in Vietnam.

Yet, the Socialists were actually more politically incapacitated than the Communists. Deeply divided on many issues, in serious decline in membership and at the polling booth, the SFIO lost much effectiveness as a governmental party and never recuperated its effectiveness in the opposition. Imbued with the mission civilisatrice and a weak anti-colonial tradition, the SFIO was loathe to see France lose any of its overseas presence. Continually buffeted by the Right and the Left, the SFIO could not resist the pulls of the Cold War and, except for some hesitating steps in the last two years, was unable to chart an independent course on Indochina. Finally, and perhaps most importantly, the correlation between Socialist policies and the objective situation in Vietnam was always quite precarious.

The Communists and the Socialists, of course, acted not in isolation but in the context of the Cold War. Neither party had complete discretion in determining its Indochina policies, and both had to wage a number of battles on other fronts. On a variety of other crucial issues, the United States and the Soviet Union made their own demands, kept the Communists and Socialists embroiled with one another, and thus greatly complicated the French Left's approach to Indochina. At another level, the French Communist-Socialist feud over Indochina reflected a bitter and intense political rivalry, a desperate competition for constituencies, a scramble for governmental influence, and, to some extent, even a class conflict. At whatever level the analysis, the net result was an interminable Vietnamese tragedy.

Bibliographical Essay

The French National Archives, Ministry of Overseas France (Paris/Aix-en-Provence), and the Military Archives (Vincennes), have made available some documents (through 1946), notably parts of the Moutet Papers and some information related to the Interministerial Committee on Indochina. The French Communists have released some internal documents, usually minutes of Central Committee meetings, to their own historians. The Socialists reveal their internal deliberations through the minutes of the Comité directeur, the Bulletin intérieur, and President Vincent Auriol's Journal du septennat, 1947-1954, six volumes, Paris, 1970-1978. (Vol. IV, 1950, has not yet appeared). Aided by excellent editorial notes, this Journal provides copious insights into the politics of the Fourth Republic. The parliamentary debates, reported verbatim in the Journal officiel de la République française, are particularly rich sources of the positions and opinions of the participants, as is the Communist and Socialist press. L'Année politique is a good annual digest of political events and contains some important texts. Despite their vast number, Communist and Socialist memoirs have shed little light on party policies toward the Vietnam War. Personal interviews have been more helpful. American government material, both published and unpublished (now available through 1954), on France and Indochina is abundant and also includes a fair amount on the French Communists and Socialists and the Peace Offensive.

The literature on the French Left, the Cold War, the First Indochinese War, and related topics is, of course, enormous. Listed below are only some of the more useful references. Others are cited only in the notes.

For some telling left-wing criticisms of the PCF's policies on the First Indochina War, see Jacques Doyon, Les Soldats blancs de Ho Chi Minh, Paris, 1973; Francis Joucelain, Le Parti communiste français et la première guerre d'Indochine, Paris, 1973; Grégoire Madjarian, La Question coloniale et la politique du Parti Communiste français, 1944-1947, Paris, 1977; Madjarian, Crise de l'impérialisme colonial et mouvement ouvrier, Paris, 1977; and Jacob Moneta, editor, Le Parti communiste français et la question coloniale, 1920-1965, Paris, 1971 (documents).

For right-wing criticisms, see, principally, Edouard Frédéric-Dupont, Comment la France a-t-elle perdu l'Indochine, Paris, 1955; and "La Trahison communiste: Pour comprendre les événements d'Indochine," Bulletin de l'Association d'études et d'informations politiques internationales, June 1954.

The PCF, however, has not been without able defenders. See Léo Figuères, Ho Chi Minh: Notre camarade. Souvenirs de militants français, Paris, 1970; Figuères, Je reviens du Vietnam libre (notes de voyage), Paris, 1950; Monique Lafon, editor, Le Parti communiste français dans la lutte contre le colonialisme, Paris, 1962 (documents); Hélène Parmelin, Matricule 2078: L'Affaire Henri Martin, Paris, 1953; Jean Surêt-Canale, "La Politique anti-colonialiste dans l'histoire du Parti Communiste français," Cahiers d'histoire de l'Institut Maurice Thorez, March-April 1972; Jacques Varin, "L'Affaire Henri Martin," ibid.; Charles Fourniau and Alain Ruscio, "Le PCF face au déclenchement de la première guerre d'Indochine," ibid., Nos. 19, 22, 1976-1977; and, especially, Alain Ruscio's Les Communistes français et la guerre d'Indochine, 1944-1954, Paris, 1985.

Other studies include Bernard Fall, "Tribulations of a Party Line: The French Communists and Indochina," Foreign Affairs, April 1955; Edward Rice-Maximin, "The French Communists and Indochina, 1945-1954," Contemporary French Civilization, Spring 1978; and Phan Van Ban's sympathetic "Les Rapports entre le Parti communiste français et la révolution vietnamienne," Nghien cuu lich su, Hanoi, February 1961 (Khiem Nguyen graciously provided a translation).

The only comparable studies so far on the Socialists are Owen Roberts, "The French Socialist Party and Its Indochina Policy, 1946-1951," Ph.D. Dissertation, Columbia University, 1955; and Edward Rice-Maximin, "The French Socialists and the First Indochinese War, 1945-1954," French Colonial Studies/ Etudes coloniales françaises, Vol. III, 1979.

On the colonial policies of the French Left in the inter-war period (1919-1939), see, principally, William B. Cohen, "The Colonial Policy of the Popular Front," French Historical Studies, Spring 1972; Enrica Collotti-Pischel, L'Internationale communiste et les problèmes coloniaux, 1919-1935, Paris, 1968; William Duiker, The Comintern and Vietnamese Communism, Athens, Ohio, 1975; Daniel Hémery, "Aux Origines des guerres d'indépendence vietnamiennes," Le Mouvement social, October-December, 1977; Thomas Adrian Schweitzer, "The French Communist Party and the Colonial Question, 1928-1939," M.A. Thesis, University of Wisconsin, 1968; and Manuela Semidei, "Les Socialistes français et le problème colonial entre les deux guerres (1919-1939)," La Revue française de sciences politiques, December 1968.

On the French Communists in general, see, notably, Frédéric Bon et alii, Le Communisme en France, Paris, 1969; Stéphane Courtois, Le PCF dans la guerre, Paris, 1980; Dominique Desanti, Les Staliniens, 1944-1956, Paris, 1975;

Jacques Fauvet, Histoire du Parti communiste français, de 1920 à 1976, Paris, 1977; Annie Kriegel, Les Communistes français: Essai d'ethnographie politique, Paris, 1968; Alfred J. Rieber, Stalin and the French Communist Party, 1941-1947, New York, 1962; Philippe Robrieux, Histoire intérieure du Parti communiste français (1920-1983), four volumes, Paris, 1981-1984 (massive); Robrieux, Maurice Thorez: Vie secrète et vie publique, Paris, 1975; George Ross, Workers and Communism in France: From Popular Front to Eurocommunism, Berkeley, 1981; Ronald Tiersky, The French Communist Party, 1920-1972, New York, 1974; Unir (anonymous Party dissidents or police agents), Histoire du Parti communiste français, three volumes, Paris, ca. 1960; and Irwin M. Wall's excellent French Communism in the Era of Stalin: The Quest for Unity and Integration, 1945-1962, Westport, Conn., 1983.

Testimonies of leading Communists include Jacques Duclos, Mémoires: Sur la brèche, 1945-1952, Paris, 1971; Léo Figuères, Jeunesse militante, Paris, 1971; Benoît Frachon, Au Rythme des jours, Vol. I (1944-1954), Paris, 1967; Archives André Marty (especially, Reels 9 and 12); Maurice Thorez, Oeuvres, Vols. XXX-XXXIII (1944-1947), Paris, 1960-1965; and Charles Tillon, On chantait rouge, Paris, 1977. Most other memoirs have not been very helpful. The Communist press includes Cahiers du communisme (previously, Cahiers du bolchévisme, Central Committee); France nouvelle (weekly); L'Humanité (daily); Ce Soir (evening), and La Vie ouvrière (CGT).

On the French Socialists in general, see Léon Blum, Oeuvres, Vols. VI, VII (1945-1950), Paris, 1958-1963; Joel Colton, Léon Blum, Paris, 1967; B. D. Graham, The French Socialists and Tripartism, 1944-1947, London, 1965; Jean Lacouture, Léon Blum, Paris, 1975; Daniel Ligou, Histoire du socialisme en France, 1871-1961, Paris, 1962; and, especially, Roger Quilliot's La SFIO et l'exercice du pouvoir, 1944-1958, Paris, 1972. Again, most of the many Socialist memoirs have not been very helpful. The principal SFIO publications are Bulletin intérieur (internal documents and proceedings of the annual congresses); La Pensée socialiste (1946-1947, left-wing dissidents); Le Populaire (daily); and La Revue socialiste (theoretical monthly).

On the independent Left, see Claude Bourdet, L'Aventure incertaine: De la Résistance à la Restauration, Paris, 1976; Daniel Guérin, Au Service des colonisés, 1930-1953, Paris, 1954; Guérin, Ci-git le colonialisme, Paris, 1973; Pierre Naville, Questions du socialisme, Vol. I, Guerres d'Asie: Vietnam et Corée, Paris, 1966; Jean-Paul Sartre, Situations V: Colonialisme et néo-colonialisme, Paris, 1964; Sartre et alii, L'Affaire Henri Martin, Paris, 1953; and Paul Clay Sorum, Intellectuals and Decolonization in France, Chapel Hill, 1977.

Independent journals and newspapers consulted include Les Cahiers de la Ligue des droits de l'homme; Combat: Esprit (Personalist, Catholic); Franc-Tireur; France-Observateur (Bourdet); Force ouvrière (syndicalist); Le Monde (daily); Révolution prolétarienne (Pierre Monatte/Anarcho-Syndicalist); Témoignage chrétien (Catholic); Les Temps modernes (Sartre); and La Vérité (Trotskyist).

On French politics in general, see Paul-Marie de la Gorce, L'Après-Guerre: Naissance de la France moderne, Paris, 1978; De la Gorce, Apogée et mort de la IVe République, 1952-1958, Paris, 1979; Dominique Desanti, 1947: L'Année où le monde a tremblé, Paris, 1975; Georgette Elgey, Histoire de la IVe République (1945-1954), two volumes, Paris, 1965, 1968 (intimate political revelations); Jean Lacouture, Mendès-France, Paris, 1982; Pierre Olivier Lapie, Histoire de la IVe République, Paris, 1970 (a Socialist's account); D. Bruce Marshall, The French Colonial Myth and Constitution-Making in the Fourth Republic, New Haven, 1973; Alain Ruscio, "Le Mendésisme et l'Indochine," Revue d'histoire moderne et contemporaine, No. 2, 1982; David Schoenbrun, Ainsi va la France, Paris, 1957; Tony Smith, "The French Colonial Consensus and People's War, 1946-1958," Journal of Contemporary History, December 1974; Alexander Werth, France, 1940-1955, Boston, 1966 (a classic); and Gordon Wright, The Reshaping of French Democracy, New York, 1948.

On United States foreign policy, see Robert M. Blum, Drawing the Line: The Origin of American Containment Policy in East Asia, New York, 1982; Robert M. Blum, "The United States and Vietnam, 1944-1947: A Staff Study Based on the Pentagon Papers," U.S. Senate, Committee on Foreign Relations, 3 April 1972; Joyce and Gabriel Kolko, The Limits of Power: The World and United States Foreign Policy, 1945-1954, New York, 1972; Walter LaFeber, America, Russia, and the Cold War, 1945-1971, New York, 1972; Yonosuke Nagai and Akira Iriye, editors, The Origins of the Cold War in Asia, New York 1977; Edward Rice-Maximin, "The United States and the French Left, 1945-1949: The View from the State Department," Journal of Contemporary History, October 1984; E. Rice-Maximin, "The French Communists, the United States and the Peace Movement of the Cold War, 1948-1952," Proceedings of the Twelfth Annual Meeting of the Western Society for French History, 1984, Santa Barbara, Calif., 1985; and Foreign Relations of the United States, Washington, 1968-1982 (State Department documents, on Indochina through 1954, on France through 1951).

On Soviet (and Chinese) foreign policy, see, especially, King C. Chen, Vietnam and China, 1938-1954, Princeton, 1969; Charles B. McLane, Soviet Strategies in Southeast Asia, Princeton, 1966 (Lenin and Stalin); Stuart Schram and Hélène Carrère d'Encausse, Marxism and Asia, London, 1969; Marshall D. Shulman, Stalin's Foreign Policy Reappraised, Cambridge, 1963; Josef Stalin, Le Marxisme et la question nationale et coloniale, Paris, 1949.

On the First Indochinese War, the French sources most frequently consulted are Lucien Bodard, La Guerre d'Indochine, three volumes, Paris, 1963 (military history); Jean Chesneaux, Contribution à l'histoire de la nation vietnamienne, Paris, 1955; Chesneaux et alii, Tradition et révolution au Vietnam, Paris, 1971; Philippe Devillers, Histoire du Vietnam, 1940-1952, Paris, 1952 (the basic account); Devillers and Jean Lacouture, Vietnam: De la guerre française à la guerre américaine, Paris, 1969; Bernard Fall, Le Vietminh: La République démocratique du Vietnam, 1945-1960, Paris, 1960; Jean Lacouture, Ho Chi Minh, Paris, 1967; Paul Mus, Vietnam: Sociologie d'une guerre, Paris, 1952; Nguyen The-Anh,

Bibliographie critique sur les relations entre le Vietnam et l'Occident, Paris, 1967; Pierre Rousset, Le Parti communiste vietnamien, Paris, 1975; Alain Ruscio, "Le Premier mois de la guerre," Cahiers d'histoire de l'Institut de Recherches Marxistes, No. 17, 1984 (November-December 1946, documents); Jean Sainteny, Histoire d'une paix manquée: Indochine, 1945-1947, Paris, 1953, 1967; and Andrée Viollis' classic Indochine S.O.S., Paris, 1935.

The English sources most frequently consulted are Joseph Buttinger, Vietnam: A Dragon Embattled, two volumes, New York, 1967; Concerned Asian Scholars, The Indochina Story, New York, 1970; William Duiker, The Communist Road to Power in Vietnam, Boulder, 1981; Richard Falk, The Vietnam War and International Law, two volumes, Princeton, 1968-1969; Bernard Fall, editor, Ho Chi Minh on Revolution, 1920-1966, New York, 1967; Marvin E. Gettleman, editor, Vietnam: History, Documents and Opinions, New York, 1970; Ellen J. Hammer, The Struggle for Indochina, 1940-1955, Stanford, 1955; R. E. M. Irving, The First Indochina War, London, 1975 (sympathetic to MRP); Harold Isaacs, No Peace for Asia, New York, 1947 (journalist's account); Walter LaFeber, "Roosevelt, Churchill and Indochina, 1942-1945," American Historical Review, December 1975; David G. Marr, Vietnamese Tradition on Trial, 1920-1945, Berkeley, 1981; Gareth Porter, editor, Vietnam: The Definitive Documentation of Human Decisions, Stanfordville, N.Y., 1979 (includes Vietnamese documents); Edward Rice-Maximin, "The United States, France and Vietnam, 1945-1950: The View from the State Department," Contemporary French Civilization, Fall 1982; George Rosie, The British in Vietnam: How the Twenty-Five Year War Began, London, 1971; Archimedes L. A. Patti, Why Vietnam? Prelude to America's Albatross, Berkeley, 1980 (OSS); United States, Department of Defense, United States-Vietnam Relations, 1945-1967 (Pentagon Papers), twelve volumes, Washington, 1971; and William Appleman Williams et alii, America in Vietnam: A Documentary History, New York, 1985.

Index

Abbott, George, U.S. Consul, 66, 70

Abd-el-Krim, 3

Abetz, Otto, 126

Accords (treaties): Bay of Along (1948), 66-67, 69, 71; bilateral, 36, 96, 100, 140; Elysée (1949), 70-72, 85, 91-94, 96; Geneva (1954), 29, 89, 145-147, 151; March 1946, 28-30, 34, 36, 38, 42-43, 45, 48, 54, 71, 73n.7, 96; supplementary (1949), 92, 94

Acheson, Dean, Secretary of State, 41n.8, 44, 47, 70, 77, 91-92, 94, 96-97

Affichages, 111, 127-128

Africa/Africans, 14, 112, 130, 133n.B, 144, 147

Alduy, Paul (SFIO), 70-71

Alessandri, Jean, General, 86

Algeria/Algerians, 3-4, 16, 21n.6, 65, 78-79, 95-96, 128-129, 131, 136, 143; dockers, 78-80; Statute (1947), 65; War (1954-1962), ix-x, 66, 131

Algiers, 14-15, 79

André, Max (MRP), 36, 74n.13

Angeletti, Yves (PCF), 39

Anti-colonialism/imperialism, ix, 4, 21n.6, 55, 78-79, 95, 116-117

Anti-Communism: France, 14, 49, 53, 56-58, 70, 75, 111, 114n.3, 117-118, 131, 137, 152; Vietnam, 14, 117-118, 138, 152

Anti-war: activities/ sentiment (Vietnam War), ix-x, 25, 29, 51n.9, 66, 70, 78-80, 83n.9, 84n.10, 85, 95, 100-03, 105n.6, 111, 116-119, 122n.5, 124-125, 135-137, 143, 151-152; demonstrations/ strikes, 25, 56, 66-67, 78-82, 94, 125-126, 144, 151; literature, 79-80, 123-128.

D'Argenlieu, Georges Thierry, Admiral, 24, 26-29, 33n.12, 36-37, 42-45, 47

Arthaud, René (PCF), 96

Artists, 126, 128-129

Arms trafficking, 38

Aron, Raymond, 46, 51n.9, 137

Assemblies: Cochinchina, 27;
  Constituent (France),
  26-27, 35, 39, 46;
  Consultative (Algiers),
  14-15; French Union, 39,
  70-71; Provisional
  (France), 15, 17

Assembly National (France):
  sessions, (22 December
  1946) 45, (March 1947),
  48-49, 57, (November 1947),
  58, (June 1948), 84n.11,
  (July 1948), 68-69,
  (January 1949), 76, (March
  1949), 40-41n.5, 71-72,
  (June 1949), 78, (January
  1950), 40-41n.5, 44,
  74n.13, 94-96, 131, (March
  1950), 80, (Generals'
  Affair, 1950), 88-89; 89,
  (October-November, 1950),
  103-04, (December, 1951),
  112-113, (October-November
  1952), 120-121, (March
  1953), 138, (November
  1953), 139-140, (March
  1954), 144, (June 1954),
  (July 1954), 147; (piastre
  scandal, 1954), 89;
  commissions, 56, 85, 88-89,
  117, 136, 140n.4; law, 8
  March 1950, 80, 128

Assimilationism, 4, 14, 16,
  34, 39

Associationism, 4, 15-16, 36,
  46

Associated States (Indo-
  china), 5, 71, 97, 135-137,
  139, 147

D'Astier de la Vigerie,
  Emmanuel, 82n.2, 125, 138

Atlantic Charter, 15

Atrocities (Vietnam War), 23,
  67, 95, 100, 117, 124, 126,
  128, 131, 145

Auriol, Paul (son/Vincent),
  140-141n.4

Auriol, Vincent: Bao
  Dai/Baodaists, 53-55, 93,
  139; Blum, 14, 44, 58;

Bullitt, 55; Cochinchina,
  102; election, 46; German
  SS, 83n.7; Ho Chi Minh/DRV,
  53-54, 113, 116, 120, 140;
  Madagascar, 65; Marie
  declaration, 69; Henri
  Martin, 128-130;
  Mendès-France, 138; PCF,
  114n.2, 141n.9; pessimism,
  110, 137; USA, 111; PCF,
  114n.2; pigeons'
  conspiracy, 119, 122n.5;
  PCF-SFIO, 141n.9; Jean
  Rous, 55; SFIO dissidents,
  70-71; USA, 111

L'Avant-Garde (PCF), 124, 131

Le Balbe, Simone
  (fiancée/Henri Martin), 127

Bao Dai: abdication, 19; as
  alternative, 36; diplomatic
  recognition, 72, 91-92, 97
  112, 122n.8; Elysée
  Accords, 70-72; Geneva
  Accords, 146-147;
  government of, 92, 97, 110;
  Hadong, 54; independent
  left, 56; Japanese coup,
  17; Korea, 99; landowners,
  137; as mediator, 65, 71;
  MRP, 94; negotiations with,
  48, 65, 71, 139; PCF, 25,
  57, 95; popular support,
  53; Revers, 86-87; SFIO,
  48, 67, 93, 117, 137; USA,
  44, 69, 91-93, 97, 102

Bao Dai solution, 51n.9,
  55-56, 59, 65, 67, 70, 86,
  87, 93-94, 103-04, 112-113,
  135, 147, 151

Baodaists; 73n.7, 89, 94,
  136, 139-140, 146; army,
  29, 85, 104, 112, 116, 130,
  133n.D, 139, 144

Berlin, 75-76, 130, 143

Belloir, Gérard (PCF), 81

Bidault, Georges, 18, 24, 27,
  35-37, 39, 42-44, 47, 53,
  87-88, 94, 100, 112-113,
  136, 138, 143, 145

Bidet, André, 137

Billoux, François (PCF), 49

Black Sea mutiny (1919),
    78-79, 95-96, 124, 129, 131

Blanc, Clément, General, 116

Blum, Léon, 4-5, 14, 24,
    35-36, 38, 44-46, 53-54,
    58, 67-69, 100, 104n.4, 110

Bollaert, Emile, High
    Commissioner, 47, 49,
    53-54, 70, 73n.7

Bolshevism, 4, 28-29, 103.
    See also USSR

Bonaparte: Napoléon, 48,
    74n.9, 116; Louis-Napoléon,
    74n.9

Bonnet, Henri, Ambassador, 18

Bonté, Florimond (PCF), 15

Borchers, Erwin, 130

Bouderel, Georges, 133n.C

Boulier, Jean, O.P., 81

Bourdet, Claude, 55, 76, 102,
    116, 127, 137, 144-145

Boutbien, Léon (SFIO), 46,
    55, 68, 139

Bradley, Omar, General, 78

Brazzaville, Conference of
    (1944), 14-15, 17

Brest, 79, 126-127

Brest-Litovsk, treaty of,
    1918, 29

Bruce, David, Ambassador, 81,
    92-93, 96, 100, 102,
    104n.3, 112, 114n.8, 118

Bullitt, William C., 54-55,
    67

Byrnes, James F., Secretary
    of State, 24

Cabinet, French (meetings),
    43-44, 47-48, 52-53, 69,
    87, 94

Cachin, Marcel (PCF), 76

Caffery, Jefferson,
    Ambassador, 21n.21, 41n.8,
    45, 51n.14, 53-54, 58,
    68-70, 72, 74n.9, 77, 81,
    82n.2, 83n.9, 92

Cambodia, 26, 136, 139, 146

Camus, Albert, 51n.9, 136

Le Canard Enchainé, 111

Cao Bang, battle of, 102-03

Caput, Louis (SFIO/Vietnam),
    26, 73n.7, 86, 133n.C, 137,
    141n.7

Carpentier, Marcel, General,
    110

Catholics: France, 12-13, 28,
    33n.12, 36, 46, 51n.9, 56,
    67-68, 81, 85-86, 101, 116,
    123, 126-129; Missions, 36;
    Vietnam, 31n.1, 67, 85

Cédille, Jean, Colonel, 23

Central Committee (PCF), 49,
    78, 101, 146

Central Intelligence Agency
    (CIA), 58-59

Césaire, Aimé (PCF/
    Martinique), 39

Charbonel, Paulette (PCF),
    103

Chesneaux, Jean (MCG), 133n.C

Cherbourg, 79

De Chevigné, Pierre, 96, 137

Chiang Kai-shek, 17, 67, 99

China/Chinese, 1-2, 17-19,
    28, 43, 48, 55, 57, 70-71,

91-93, 99, 122n.8;
Nationalists (Kuomintang),
5, 17-19, 23, 26, 28, 87
People's Republic (PRC),
79, 86, 94, 111-112,
116-117, 136, 143, 145-146

Christianity, 4, 81, 85, 113,
128. See also Catholics.

Civilization/Civilizing
Mission, 2, 4, 11, 39, 46,
55, 93, 96, 152

Cochinchina, 17, 23, 25,
27-29, 34, 36-38, 42,
45-48, 54, 70, 72, 85, 100

Cogniot, Georges (PCF), 76

La Colombe (Dove of Peace,
Picasso), 77, 118

Colonial consensus, ix, 4-5,
11, 14, 150

Colonial trusts, 13, 15-16,
30, 35, 37, 45

Combat, 56

Combat pour la paix, 77

Combattants de la liberté, 76

Cominform, 57, 69

Comintern (Communist
International): 2, 4-5, 38

Communism: ix, 51n.9, 71, 75,
137; Asian, 91-93, 99, 112,
117-118, 122n.8, 138-139

Communists, French (PCF):

Colonial politics (general):
Algeria, 16, colonial
question, 1, 13-14, 35, 37;
Comintern, 3; Constitution,
35, 39; Madagascar, 52;
Morocco, 137; Popular
Front, 4-5, 7n.7;
post-liberation, 11-13,
15-16; Rif War, 3, 6n.5,
6-7n.6, 78-79 world
Communism, 30

Domestic politics:
anti-Communism, 114n.3;

autocritique, 78;
Cominform, 57; Congresses,
(1945), 15, (1947) 53,
(1950) 101; Constitution,
34, 40; détente (1953),
143; integration,
political, ix, 12-13;
isolation, 12, 57-59, 70,
75, 82, 137; Mendès-France,
138, 146; military budget
(1948), 69; ministry, 12,
35, 52-53, 114n.3;
municipal elections, 12,
57-58; Oradour, 137;
opportunism, 6n.5, 15;
outlawing of, 58, 71-72,
76, 119; parliamentary
elections, (1946) 42-44,
(1951), 110, 114n.2;
political bureau, 49; RDR,
68; Resistance/liberation,
12-14, 20n.2; sectarianism,
118-119; SFIO, 12-13, 27,
36, 44, 59n.3, 75, 101,
111, 119, 141n.9, 143,
151-152; strikes (1947),
58-59; USA, 35, 40n.3, 47,
58, 68, 70

Indochina: adventurism,
20n.2, 77, 111; anti-war
activities, 25, 84n.10, 56,
67, 113; Bullitt, 55;
conclusion, 150-152; DRV,
25-26, 37-38; desertion,
130-131, 133n.A; Dien Bien
Phu/Geneva, 144, 147,
148n.6; Generals' Affair,
88-89; Haiphong-Hanoi,
43-47; Henri Martin,
123-130, 133n.F;
historiography, ix-x; Hoa
Binh, 121n.4;
individualism, 78, 80, 131;
ICP, 6n,2, 32n.6; Korea,
99; legality, concern for,
12, 40n.3, 80, 82, 124,
150; MCG, 26;
Mendès-France, 117;
negotiations (1946), 28,
30, 32n.8, 36-38, 42;
parliamentary debates
(March 1947), 48-49, (March
1949), 71-72, (June 1949),
78, (January 1950), 95-96,
(October 1950), 103-04,
(December 1951), 112-113,
114n.6, (October 1952),
120, (March 1954), 144,
(June 1954), 145-146; peace

offensive, 75-82, 101, 103, 111, 118-119; post-liberation, 11, 17-18, 25; sabotage, 84n.11; Tran Ngoc Danh, 66; uprisings (1930), 3

Communists (other):

Algerian, 3, 16; American, 32n.6; Belgian, 30, 49; British, 30; Chinese, 38, 44, 74n.10, 78, 91, 93; Dutch, 30; European, 30, 53, 57; former, 80-81; Indonesian, 30; Italian, 30, 49; Polish, 76; Vietnamese, 5, 6n.4, 14, 19, 24-26, 28, 30, 37-39, 41n.8, 44, 47-48, 54-56, 65, 72, 91-93; other, 66, 81

Confédération générale du travail (CGT), 13, 25, 32n.8, 52, 58-59, 68-70, 79-80, 123, 143

Confédération française des travailleurs chrétiens (CFTC), 69, 143

Congresses: Asian Women, 78; Peoples against Imperialism, 55; Vietnamese National, 139

Conseil national de la résistance (CNR), 14

Conscientious objection, 96, 101, 124, 127-128, 130. See also Disobedience

Coste-Floret, Paul (MRP) 57, 69, 85-87, 93, 96, 130

Cot, Pierre, 35, 48, 82n.2, 106n.10, 143

Coty, René, President, 145, 148n.1

Cuisinier, Jeanne (SFIO), 55, 67

Daladier, Edouard, 112, 122n.8, 139

Dalat, Conferences of (1946), 36-37

David, Jean-Paul, 114n.3, 129

Day of Resistance to Dictatorship and War, 83n.4

Debès, Colonel, 43

Dechezelle, Yves (SFIO), 55

Decoux, Jean, Admiral, 17

Defferre, Gaston (SFIO), 72, 100, 112, 117, 120, 139

De Gaulle, Charles, 11-12, 14-15, 17-18, 21n.11, 25, 27, 39, 47, 49, 53, 74n.9, 88, 128, 131. See also Gaullists

Delahoutre Commission (Generals' Affair), 88-89

Délégation des Gauches, 32n.6

Democratic Republic of Vietnam (DRV): delegation (Paris), 37-38, 48, 66, 70, 95; diplomatic recognition, 11, 29-30, 66, 79, 94, 96-97, 100; elections (1946), 27-28, 32n.11, 37, 55; establishment, 19, 23-24; Fontainebleau, 34, 36-37, 42; Geneva, 146-147, 151; isolation, 29, 97; literacy campaign, 23, 66-67, 100; March Accords, 28-30; negotiations with (actual/proposed), 13-14, 25, 28-30, 32n.8, 36-39, 42-48, 52-53, 55, 58, 66, 69, 72, 73n.7, 87, 103, 112-113, 116-117, 120, 135-137, 141n.9, 144; PCF/SFIO, 25-26, 46, 48, 67, 100, 104n.4; popular support, 23-26, 28, 46, 48, 53-56, 65, 69-70, 72, 92-93, 117, 146-147; diplomatic recognition 94, 96-97, 100; USA, 24, 41n.8, 44, 54-55. See also Ho Chi Minh, Vietminh

Détente, 135, 138, 143, 146, 151

Devinat, Paul, 137

Disobedience, 76, 79, 95–96, 125, 128–131. See also Conscientious objection

Drame à Toulon, 126

Dreyfus, Alfred, 126–127

Demoralization: France, 114n.3; French military, 66, 80, 88, 105n.6, 123–124, 127–128, 130–131, 133n.D, 139; French working class, 58–59, 70, 151

Department of State (DOS): embassies (Paris), 53, 69, 77, 81, 105n.7; (others), 81; EUR/FE/SEA, 18, 44, 91, 105n.7; Fontainebleau, 38–39; PCF, 51n.14, 53; peace movement, 77, 81–82, 83n.5, 101–02; policies: (1945), 18, (1947), 54–55, (1948), 69, (1949), 91–93, 97n.1; Vietnamese Communism/USSR, 44, 74n.10. See also individual ambassadors and consuls.

Depreux, Edouard (SFIO), 120

Desertion, 12, 53, 96, 100, 123–124, 130–131, 133n.B,D, 150

Devillers, Philippe, 28, 136

Dien, Raymonde, 79, 125, 147

Dien Bien Phu, battle of, 140, 144–145

Dillon, Douglas, Ambassador, 136–137, 140

Djemad, Abderrahme-Chérif, 95–96

Dockers. See Workers

Domenach, Jean-Marie, 55, 127–128

Doriot, Jacques (Doriotiste), 21n.6, 95

Duclos, Jacques, 27, 48–49, 53, 69, 72, 76, 101, 111, 118–119, 122n.5, 133n.A, 146, 151

Dulles, John Foster, Secretary of State, 135, 141n.9, 146

Dunn, James Clement, Ambassador, 118, 121

Duong Bach Mai, 48, 104n.4

Eisenhower, Dwight, President, 135, 146–147

Elections: France, cantonal (1949), 69, 75; constituent, 26–27, 35; legislative, (1946) 42, (1951) 110–111, 114n.2; municipal, (1945), 12, (1947), 57, (1953), 138; Vietnam, January 1946, 27–28, 32n.11, 37, 55; proposed, 69, 93–94, 96, 104, 110, 112, 116, 136–137, 145–147. See also Referenda.

Engels, Friedrich, 1

Esprit, 51n.9, 55–56, 99, 111, 116, 127–128

Estates General of French Colonization, 36

European Defense Community (EDC), 137, 143, 145–146, 148n.1

L'Express, 136

Expressen, 140

Farge, Yves, 4, 76–77, 81, 82n.2, 125

Fascism, 4–5, 11, 14, 21n.6, 130, 146

Feix, Léon (PCF), 118

Figuères, Léo (PCF), 100-01,
    103, 104n.3, 133n.A, 147

Filthy war (la sale guerre),
    67, 79, 88, 117-118, 125,
    136

Fontaine, André (SFIO), 46,
    50-51n.8

Fontainebleau, Conference of
    (1946), 36-39, 40-41n.5,
    72, 74n.13

Force ouvrière, 58, 68-69,
    143

Foreign Legion, French, 19,
    50-51n.8, 60n.6, 95,
    130-131, 133n.B, 144, 147

Frachon, Benoit (PCF/CGT),
    79, 138

France, Anatole, 96

France-Nouvelle, 57

France-Observateur, 102-03,
    116

Franc-Tireur, 55, 71

Franc-Tireurs et partisans
    (FTP), 11, 38, 41n.6, 78,
    104-05n.4, 131

Fraternization, 2-3, 96, 101,
    130, 151

Free French, 14, 18

Frédéric-Dupont, Edouard,
    71-72, 95, 103, 112, 138,
    145, 147

Fréjus, 79, 125

French Right/Conservatives,
    ix-x, 11, 28, 45, 47-49,
    65-66, 69, 71, 78, 86,
    94-95, 99, 103-04, 104n.3,
    110, 120, 127, 133n.F, 139,
    144, 150-152

French Union, 11, 15, 17,
    29-30, 36-37, 46, 56,
    65-67, 69, 71, 96-97, 102,
    120, 135, 138-139, 145, 147

Front national/Front français
    (PCF strategy), 13, 70, 75,
    77, 83n.6, 101, 111,
    118-119

Gallagher, Philip E., Major
    General, 24

Gandhi, Mahatma, 72

Gaullists, 28, 35, 45, 49,
    52, 57, 65-67, 69-70, 72,
    76, 88, 101, 110, 127, 138,
    145-146

Gauchistes, ix-x, 6n.5, 56,
    75, 84n.10, 150-152

Generals' Affair, 86-89, 94,
    100, 151

Geneva, Conference of (1954),
    143-146. See also Accords,
    Geneva

Germany/Germans, 12, 19, 27,
    29, 46-47, 49, 50-51n.8,
    58, 60n.6, 77, 81, 99, 101,
    111, 124, 127, 129-130,
    136-137; Gestapo, 46, 86;
    SS, 69, 78, 83n.7, 95, 123,
    144; Nazi Germany, 12, 46,
    60n.6; rearmament, 77-78,
    111, 118

Giap, Vo Nguyen, General, 29,
    36, 41n.6, 45, 105n.6, 110,
    144

Gilson, Etienne, 76

Giovani, Arthur (PCF), 120

Gouin, Félix (SFIO), 27, 29,
    53

Gracey, Douglas, General, 23

Greece, 48, 99

Grew, Joseph C. (DOS), 18

Guadeloupe, 34

Guillon, Jean (PCF), 78

Guiana, French, 34

Guérin, Daniel, 4

Guesdes, Jules, 79

Hadong, 54

Haiphong, 26, 43-46, 48,
    50n.2, 54, 67, 83n.9, 95,
    124

Haiti, 48

Hanoi, 19, 44-46, 66, 113,
    139, 144

Heath, Donald, U.S. Consul,
    139

Heimburger, Charles, 123-126,
    129-130

L'Hermitte, Roger (PCF), 46,
    104n.4

Herriot, Edouard, 39

Histoire du Vietnam, 1940-
    1952 (Philippe Devillers),
    136

Hitler, Adolph/Hitlerians,
    15-16, 72, 119

Hoa Binh, 113, 114n.8, 116,
    121n.4

Ho Chi Minh: agrarian
    reforms, 137; Bao Dai, 66;
    Blum, 54, 58, Cochinchina,
    36; Comintern/ICP, 3, 5,
    38; DRV, 19-20; elections,
    (1946), 116, (1956),
    146-147; exclusion of,
    47-48, 52-53; desertions
    to, 130; Hanoi-Haiphong,
    43-46; independent left,
    56, 103, 116, 144-145, 147;
    de Lattre de Tassigny, 113;
    Leclerc, 28; PCF, 3, 39,
    100, 118, 150; negotiations
    with (actual/proposed), 19,
    28-29, 37, 42, 112-113,
    117, 120, 139, 144; Nehru,
    92; parliamentary debates
    72, 114n.6; PCF, 3, 39,
    100, 118, 150; peace

solutions, 110, 140, 144;
    Revers, 86-87; Sainteny,
    19, 28-29, 33n.12; SFIO,
    14, 54, 58, 65, 67, 70-71,
    93-94; recognition of,
    96-97; USA, 24, 31n.4,
    41n.8, 55, 91-93, 97n.1;
    USSR, 66; Vietminh, 16. See
    also DRV, Vietminh.

Honfleur Five, 128

Hong Kong, 65, 73n.7, 141n.7

Horst Wessel Lied, 50-51n.8

L'Humanité, 12, 27, 37, 38,
    45, 68, 75-76, 88, 104n.4,
    118, 125, 127, 129-130,
    136, 138, 144. See also
    Press (PCF).

Ile de France, 56

Imperialism (colonialism):
    American, 30, 56-57, 77,
    80, 99, 111; British, 23,
    25, 55; European, 1-2, 92;
    French, 16, 26, 36, 39,
    54-56, 78, 99, 131; Soviet,
    56, 92, 100; Western, 15,
    77

Independence: Associated
    States, 137; France, 46,
    57, 75, 139, 144; overseas,
    1-2, 4, 14, 16, 34, 39 57,
    91, 118; Vietnam, 5, 18-19,
    23-25, 30, 31n.1, 36-38,
    44, 54-56, 65-67, 86, 92,
    96, 103-04, 125, 136, 139,
    144-146

India, 1, 30, 92, 112

Indochina: Associated State,
    34; federation (De Gaulle),
    17, 25, 36; French
    sovereignty (USA), 24;
    trusteeship (Roosvelt), 18;
    unity (Moutet), 26. See
    also Vietnam

Indochine S.O.S. (Andrée
    Viollis), 7n.8

Indochinese Communist Party
(ICP), 5, 6n.4, 16-17, 26,
32n.6

Indochinese War, Second
(American), x, 66, 77, 131,
133-134n.D, 146

Indonesia (Dutch East
Indies), 26, 30, 92

Intelligentsia, 46, 51n.9,
68, 76, 102, 119, 127-130,
137

Interests, French national,
ix, 47, 54, 56-57, 83n.6,
89, 96, 101, 112, 124, 128,
137

International solution/
internationalization
(Vietnam War), 70, 100,
103-04, 110, 112-113, 117,
120, 138-139, 145

Interministerial Committee on
Indochina, 38, 42-44, 50n.2

Ireland, 1-2, 116

Isaacs, Harold, 25-26

Islamic civilization/world,
2, 16, 112

Italy, 30, 77, 81

J'Accuse (Emile Zola), 127

Japan/Japanese, 2, 11, 17-19,
23-26, 28, 57, 60n.6, 67,
72, 77, 95, 123-124, 130

Jaurès, Jean, 2, 79

Joliot-Curie, Frédéric (PCF),
77

Jouhaux, Léon, 58

Kriegel-Valrimont, Maurice
(PCF), 88

Korea/Korean War, 57, 99,
101-02, 104, 110, 112, 116,
118, 120, 135, 139, 143

Labor, Department of (USA),
81

Labor movement. See Trade
Unions, Working Class

Labrouquère, André (SFIO), 29

Lacoste, Robert (SFIO), 69

Lambert, Saravane, 49, 72

Laniel, Joseph, 138-140,
144-145

Lanoue, Henri, 133n.c

Laos, 26, 136, 146

De Lattre de Tassigny:
Bernard, Lieutenant, 113;
Jean, General, 86, 104,
110, 113, 114n.8, 116

League of the Rights of Man
(Ligue des droits de
l'homme), 32n.8, 56,
128-129

Lebanon, 21n.6, 25, 37

Leclerc, Philippe, General
(Comte de Hautecloque),
24-25, 28, 33n.12, 36, 43,
45, 47, 85

Lendemains (MCG), 26

Lenin, Vladimir Ilyich, 2

Letourneau, Jean, 74n.13, 94,
96, 116, 118, 136,
140-141n.4

Lewis, John L., 70

Liberals/progressives, 26,
28, 56, 70, 76-77, 79, 81

Liberation (France), 11-12,
20n.2, 25, 39-40, 49, 58,
100, 123

Liebert, 123, 125, 127

Life, 55

Lofgren, Svante, 140

Lovett, Robert (DOS), 58

Lozeray, Henri (PCF), 15, 36

MacArthur, Douglas, General,
  24, 99

McCarthyism, 146

Madagascar, 52, 57, 65, 95-96

Malraux, André, 136

Malleret-Joinville, Alfred
  (PCF), 78

Mao Tse-tung, 133n.A, 139

Marie, André, 69

Marseille, 58, 78-79, 95,
  125, 131

Marshall, George C.,
  Secretary of State, 47,
  53-54, 66, 68

Marshall Plan (European
  Recovery Program), 53, 59,
  75, 112

Martin: Henri, 79-80, 82, 88,
  100-01, 111, 118-119,
  122n.5, 123-130, 133n.F,
  138, 147, 151; Monsieur et
  Madame (parents), 123, 129

Martinique, 34

Marty, André, 20n.2, 78,
  95-96, 101, 118-119,
  124-126, 129, 133n.B

Marx, Karl/Marxism/Marxists,
  1-2, 19, 36, 130

Marxist Cultural Group
  (Saigon), 26, 50n.2, 73n.7,
  130, 133n.C

Mass action, 67, 78, 80, 101,
  118-119, 125, 127

Mast, Charles, General, 86-88

Matricule 2078 (Hélène
  Parmelin), 129

Mauriac, François, 46, 51n.9,
  119, 136

Maurras, Charles, 126

Mayer, Daniel (SFIO), 14, 36,
  48, 69, 93

Mayer, René, 136, 138

Mendès-France, Pierre/
  Mendésistes, 103-04,
  106n.10, 112-113, 116-117,
  135-137, 139-140, 141n.9,
  144-147

Mercier, André, 17

Military budget/credits, 27,
  48-49, 68-69, 78, 100, 112,
  117-118, 135, 150, 152

Military defeatism, 77, 104,
  118

Military Defense Assistance
  Pact (MDAP), 77, 102

Mitterrand, François, 77,
  100, 120, 138

Moch, Jules (SFIO), 38, 58,
  70, 76, 87, 89, 93-94, 100,
  102, 104n.3, 141n.9

Moffat, Abbott Low (DOS),
  38-39, 44

Mollet, Guy/Molletistes, 36,
  53, 55, 71; letter, 71-72,
  93, 111, 114n.3, 135

Monatte, Pierre, 56

Le Monde, 67, 76, 79, 88, 94,
  137

Monnerville, Gaston, 17

Morlière, Louis, General, 43

Morocco/Moroccans, 3, 34,
  131, 137. See also Rif War

Moscow Foreign Ministers
  Conference (1947), 47, 52

Mounier, Emmanuel, 51n.9

Moutet, Marius, 4, 16, 26-27,
  30, 34, 37-39, 42-43,
  45-48, 52, 57, 73n.13

Mouvement de la paix, 77

Mouvement républicain
  populaire (MRP): Bao Dai
  solution, 59, 65, 93;
  constituent assembly, 27;
  Generals' Affair, 85-89;
  High Commissioner, 70; High
  Commissioner, 70; Ho Chi
  Minh, negotiations with,
  28, 36, 74n.13; inter-
  ministerial committee, 38;
  legislative elections, 42;
  Mendès-France, 117, 138;
  municipal elections (1945),
  12-13; overseas ministry,
  57; parliamentary debates:
  (March 1947), 49, (March
  1949), 72, (January 1950),
  95, (October- November
  1950), 103-104, (November
  1953), 139, (June 1954),
  145-147; Patti, 25;
  politique de force, 45;
  SFIO, 36, 67.

Munich, treaty of (1938), 28,
  145

Mus, Paul, 53, 130, 136

Musée de l'homme, 40-41n.5,
  120

Naegelen, Marcel-Edmond
  (SFIO), 65, 120, 143

National Council for the
  Defense of Peace and
  Freedom, 76

National Defense Committee,
  42

National Intelligence
  Estimate (USA), 135

National Security Council
  (USA), 93

Nationalism: Asia, 29,
  105n.7; France, ix-x, 11,
  82, 82n.2; overseas, 2, 57,
  150; Tunisia, 117; Vietnam,
  4-5, 11, 16-17, 26, 47, 54,
  65, 67, 71, 91, 96, 139

Navarre, Henri, General, 136,
  140

Navy: French, 78, 123-124;
  German, 127; Ministry of,
  127

Nazi-Soviet Pact (1939), 12,
  14, 128

Nazism, 81, 95, 99, 123-126

Nehru, Pandit, 92, 144

Nenni, Pietro, 77

Netherlands, 26, 29-30

Neutralism, 75-76, 92

Nguyen Ai Quoc. See Ho Chi
  Minh

Nguyen Van Thinh, 42

Nguyen Van Xuan, 65-67, 71,
  85, 87

Nice, 79, 129

Noguères, Henri (SFIO), 55

North Africa, 3, 5, 37, 65,
  96, 120, 130-131, 133n.B,
  138, 144, 147. See also
  Algeria, Morocco, Tunisia.

North Atlantic Treaty
  Organization (NATO/Western
  Alliance), 75-77, 101-02,
  135

Nuremberg Tribunal, 128

Occupation (France), 13, 46,
  58, 127

Office of Strategic Services
  (OSS), 18-20, 24

Opium, 23, 88, 140-141n.4

Oradour, 78, 95, 137

O'Sullivan, James, U.S.
  Consul, 44, 54, 60n.6,,
  105n.7

L'Ouverture, Toussaint, 48

Overseas: deputies, 5, 13,
  39, 49, 52; Ministry of,
  27, 52, 57, 74n.13, 85-86,
  94

Pacifism, 2, 76-77, 130

Pacte colonial, 15-16

Paix et liberté, 114n.3

Paris (city), 80, 128

Parliament, French. See
  Assembly, National

Parti Communiste français
  (PCF). See Communists,
  French.

Pasteur, 79

Le Patriote du Sud-Ouest, 129

Patriotism, ix, 11, 79, 88,
  124-126, 150

Patti, Archimedes L. A.,
  Major (OSS), 18-19, 25

Les Pavés de Paris, 126

Peace: ballot, 78; caravans,
  78; movement/offensive,
  75-82, 82n.2, 101-03, 111,
  114n.3, 118-119, 125-126,
  138, 151; national day, 78;
  partisans, 82; proposals
  (Ho Chi Minh), 24, 100,
  103, 139. See also Anti-war

La Pensée socialiste, 55

Pétain, Philippe, Marshal,
  13, 126

Peyré, Roger, 85-89

Pham Van Dong, 36, 145

Philip, André (SFIO), 4

Philippines, 57, 92

Piastre, 71, 87-89, 136,
  140n.4

Picasso, Pablo, 77, 82, 118

Pigeons, Conspiracy of,
  118-119

Pignon, Léon (MRP), 70,
  85-88, 92

Pineau, Christian (SFIO),
  117, 120, 138

Pius XII, Pope/Vatican,
  31n.1, 75, 113.

Pivert, Marceau, 4, 68, 83n.4

Pleven, René, 94-95, 100,
  103-04, 114n.3

Poland, 1, 76

Politique de force, 33n.12,
  43, 45, 69, 151

Le Populaire, 14, 26, 38, 45,
  55, 66-67, 70-71, 100, 111,
  138

Popular Front: government,
  1936-1938, 4-5; 13-14, 16,
  76-77; PCF strategy, 27,
  77, 83n.6

Popular Republicans. See MRP

Potsdam, Allied Conference of
  (1945), 23, 25

Le Premier choc (André Stil),
  80

Pronteau, Jean (PCF), 96, 139

Proletariat, See Workers/
  Working Class

Press: French (general), 45,
  76, 87, 89, 136; French
  left, 71, 89, 102-03;
  French right, 45, 127; PCF,
  12, 43, 46, 71, 75, 79,

111, 118-119, 131, 138;
liberal, 79; SFIO, 67, 111;
Soviet, 57, 92; Vietnamese,
94. See also listings of
individual journals and
newspapers

Quakers, 81

Queuille, Henri, 69, 71, 77,
86, 87, 93-94

Racism/paternalism, 4, 15-17,
21n.11, 30, 35, 39,
40-41n.5, 92-94

Radical Party, 4, 27, 32n.8,
39, 47, 65, 69, 86-87, 119,
127, 138, 139, 145

Ramadier, Paul, 14, 46,
48-49, 52-53, 55, 57-58,
69, 76, 78, 85-87, 89,
93-94

Rassemblement démocratique
révolutionnaire (RDR),
67-68, 83n.4

Rassemblement populaire
français (RPF), 138. See
also Gaullists

Red Star over China (Edgar
Snow), 100

Reed, Charles, II, U.S.
Consul, 44, 54, 105n.7

Referenda: France, 27,
32n.32, 35, 39;
Cochinchina, 29, 34, 36-38;
Vietnam, 69, 71. See also
Elections

Religious groups/leaders,
76-77, 102. See also
Catholics, Quakers

Rennes Four, 128

Reynaud, Paul, 48, 69, 137,
139

Resistance: France, 11-14,
27, 38, 47, 55, 81, 86-87,

101, 111, 123, 125-126,
137; Vietnam, 17, 19, 37,
55, 65

Réunion, 34

Revers, Georges, General, 38,
53, 79, 85-88, 102

Revolution/revolts: anti-
colonial, ix, 2-5, 12, 14,
16, 23, 26, 36, 52, 57,
150; Asia, 1-2; Europe,
1-3; France (1789), 2, 24,
37; France (post-1944), 12,
20n.2, 27, 47, 58, 70, 77;
social, 36, 56; Vietnam, 5,
11, 23, 25-26, 28, 30, 56,
117, 147, 151

Révolution prolétarienne, 56,
83n.9, 103, 116

Rhee, Syngman, 99

Ribera, Captain, 131

Ridgeway, Matthew, General,
118-119, 122n.5

Rif War, 3, 6n.5, 6-7n.6,
78-79

Rivet, Paul (SFIO), 6, 36,
36n.5, 40-41n.5, 55, 72,
74n.13, 95, 120

Robeson, Paul, 77

Rochet, Waldeck (PCF), 146

Roosevelt, Franklin Delano,
President, 18

Rosenberg, Julius and Ethel,
146

Rosenfeld, Oreste (SFIO), 30,
38, 70-71

Rous, Jean (SFIO), 55-56, 68

Ruscio, Alain, 41n.6, 50n.2,
83n.9, 84n.10

Sabotage, 38, 79-80, 84n.11,
88, 95-96, 103, 118-119,
123, 125-126, 129, 150

Sadoul, Jacques, 28

Saigon, 19, 23-26, 28, 42-45,
    50-51n.8, 66, 86, 88, 94,
    104n.4

Sailors, French, 3, 38, 79,
    123-125, 128, 133n.B, 147

Sainteny, Jean, Commissioner,
    19, 25, 28-29, 33n.12,
    44-45

Salan, Raoul, General, 60n.6

Salon d'automne, 129

Sarraut, Albert, 28

Sartre, Jean-Paul, 30, 46,
    55, 67-68, 76, 83n.4, 119,
    124, 126-127, 129-130, 137

Savary, Alain (SFIO), 93,
    120, 139, 143

Scandals, 71, 86-89, 94, 100,
    117, 136, 140n.4, 151

Schuman, Robert (MRP), 58, 69

Schumann, Maurice (MRP), 72

Second International, 1-2

Section française de
    l'Internationale ouvrière
    (SFIO). See Socialists,
    French

Servan-Schreiber,
    Jean-Jacques, 136

Sihanouk, Norodom, Prince,
    136

Socialism/Socialist
    (general), ix, 1, 4, 27,
    36, 68, 75, 81-82, 101,
    118-119, 130

Socialists, French (SFIO):

colonial politics (general):
    Algeria, 4, 65, 143;
    Brazzaville, 15-16;
    Madagascar, 52; Morocco,
    6-7n.6, 137; overseas
    mministry, 52; post-1944,

16, 39; pre-1939, 1-5,
    6-7n.6; Tunisia, 117

domestic politics:
    anti-Communism, 114n.3,
    119, 138; arms buildup,
    102; comité directeur,
    13-14, 46, 55, 68, 71, 120;
    congresses, 13-14, 55, 67,
    100; constituent assembly,
    27, 34, 40; dissidents, 36,
    55, 68, 70, 93; EDC, 120,
    137, 143; schism, 3;
    internal crises, 35-36, 55;
    left-wing, 4, 27, 67-68,
    83n.4, 111; legislative
    elections, 42, 110;
    Mendès-France, 117, 138,
    146; ministry, 44, 49, 111;
    national council, 53, 71,
    120; Oradour, 137;
    parliamentarians, 13-14,
    52-53, 55, 100;
    post-liberation, 12-14;
    PCF, 27, 51n.14, 52-53, 57,
    59n.3, 119, 141n.9; RDR,
    68; sectarianism, 111,
    117-118; strikes, 58-59,
    69-70; third force, 65,
    67-69, 71, 77, 110-111;
    USA, 35, 57-58, 104n.3;
    unity/PCF, 12-13, 27, 36,
    75, 101, 119, 143, 151-152

Indochina: abstention,
    117-118; Bao Dai solution,
    53-54, 65-67, 112; Bay of
    Along Accords, 66-67;
    Caput, 73n.7; Cochinchina,
    102; conclusion, 151-152;
    congresses, 66-67, 100,
    137; Dien Bien Phu, 144;
    Generals' Affair, 85,
    87-89; Hanoi-Haiphong,
    42-43, 45-46; Henri Martin,
    127; historiography, x;
    Korea, 99-100; liberation,
    11, 17, 26;MCG, 133n.C;
    negotiations (1946), 30,
    32n.8, 36-38; parliamentary
    debate (March 1947), 48-49,
    50n.14, (July 1948), 68-69,
    (March 1949), 72, (January
    1950), 95-96, (October
    1950), 103-04, (December
    1951), 112, (April 1952),
    117-118, (November 1952),
    120, (January 1953), 135,
    (November 1953), 139,
    (March 1954), 144, (June

1954), 145-146; peace
movement, 77, 82, 101;
positions (1949), 93-94,
(1950) 100, (1951-1952),
117, 120; Rivet, 40-41n.5;
SFIO divisions, 38, 55-56,
137; Socialists/Vietnam,
25-26, 73n.7; USA, 18

Socialists, Vietnamese, 23,
136

Ce Soir (PCF), 12, 43, 138

Soldiers/troops: Algerian,
78; Allied, 112; French, 3,
11, 46, 49, 53, 56, 58, 66,
72, 95-96, 100, 103,
104-05n.4, 105n.6, 112,
121n.4, 125, 128, 130-131,
133n.B, 138-139, 144, 147;
German, 60n.6, 78

Solosieff, Stephane, 19

Soviet Union (USSR):

General: Allied intervention
(1919), 78; Bolshevik
Revolution, 2; colonial
policies, 3-4, 21n.6,
30-31; Europe, 71; foreign
policy, 12, 26, 30-31, 111,
151; Germany, 27, 111;
Korean War, 99; Marshall
Plan, 53; reconstruction,
30; repression, 127;

France: entente, 12, 49;
independent leftists,
55-56, 68; liberation, 12;
PCF, 83n.6; peace
offensive, 75-77, 81-82,
82n.2; strikes (1947), 59

Indochina: Bao Dai, 65;
conclusion, 152; DRV/Ho Chi
Minh, 24-26, 28, 44, 47;
DRV/recognition, 79, 66,
69, 74n.10, 96-97, PCF,
ix-x; Geneva, 143, 145-146;
ICP, 6n.4; Sartre, 137;
Southeast Asia/Indochina,
19, 21n.11, 36, 54-55, 57,
91-93, 116; United Nations,
136; USA, 30, 96

Spain, 45, 99, 116

Stalin, Josef/Stalinism: ix,
12, 17, 72, 76, 103,
133n.A, 135, 138, 151;
Stalin Prize, 80;
Stalingrad, Battle of, 76,
144; Stalinists, 56, 72,
91, 116, 139

Stanton, Edwin, Ambassador,
92

Stavisky Affair, 89

Stil, André, 80, 118-119, 138

Stockholm Appeal, 81-82, 88,
99, 101-03, 123

Strikes, domestic (France),
38, 52, 55, 58, 69, 75, 81,
119, 138, 143; general, 3,
53, 78

Subversion, ix-x, 3, 56, 79,
151

Syria, 4, n.6 21, 25, 37

Témoignage chrétien, 95, 103

Témoignages pour Henri
Martin, 128

Les Temps Modernes, 30. See
also Sartre, Jean-Paul

Téri, Simone (PCF), 37

Thailand, 92

Thorez, Maurice: colonial
question, 15, 39;
deserters, 131; Henri
Martin, 125; Ho Chi
Minh/DRV, 24-25, 37, 48;
Indochina, 41n.6, 47-48,
95, 118 Madagascar, 52;
Marty-Tillon, 119;
ministry, 27, 35, 42-43,
46, 49, 52-53; peace
movement, 76, 101; return
of, 12, 20n.2; USSR, 57,
76; Vietnam (1930), 3, 6n.5

Tillon, Charles, 20n.2,
21n.6, 27, 38, 41n.6; 43,

76, 78, 82n.2, 101,
104-05n.4, 119

Tito, Josef (Titism), 69, 75,
77, 91, 97, 97n.1

Tonkin: 17, 23, 28, 37,
73n.7, 85, 102, 112, 120,
140; Delta, 66, 85, 110,
113, 114n.8, 144-145

Toulon, 79, 118, 123-128

Toulouse, 129

Tours, 79

Tran Ngoc Danh, 66

Treason, 25, 71-72, 81,
87-89, 95, 118, 126

Tripartism, 27, 29, 44,
46-47, 49, 52

Trade unions (labor
movement): France, 13, 53,
58-59 68, 70, 76-77, 102,
133n.C; overseas/Vietnam,
4-5, 16; USA, 67, 82. See
also individual unions,
e.g., CGT

Trotsky, Leon/Trotskyists: 3,
15, 55; French Trotskyists,
4, 26, 30, 52, 56, 68, 77,
83n.9, 103, 144, 147

Truce (armistice/cease-fire/
Vietnam), 14, 43, 45, 78,
93-94, 96, 100, 112, 116,
120, 137, 140, 144-145

Truman, Harry S., President,
24, 48-49, 54-55, 81-82,
103; Doctrine, 48

Tunisia, 34, 87, 117

Union des jeunesses
républicaines de France,
12-13, 100, 125

Union française, mission de
France (Paul Alduy), 70

United Kingdom, 5, 18-19,
23-26, 29-30, 76, 92, 97,
112, 116, 146

United Nations, 24-25, 44,
67, 75, 77, 92, 99-100,
112, 136

United States:

France: army, 12; Cominform,
57; economic/military aid,
35, 53, 139, 147; European
army, 111; influence on
government, 118, 126, 139,
144; municipal elections
(1947), 57-58; PCF, 27, 35,
53; peace offensive, 76;
RDR, 68; SFIO, 35;
Stockholm appeal, 81-72,
102; union leaders, 58-59

Indochina: anti-colonialism,
17; Asian nationalism, 28;
Bao Dai, 65, 97; Cold War,
47; conclusion, 152;
crusade, 113; Bullitt,
54-55; DRV/Vietnamese
Communism, 24, 26, 120;
economic/military aid,
91-92, 102, 116, 137;
foreign policy, x;
Generals' Affair, 87-89;
Geneva, 143, 145, 147;
Henri Martin, 128;
Indochina policy
(1940-1945), 17-19, 24-25,
28, (1947), 54-55, (1948),
68, (1949), 91-93, (1953),
135-136; Indonesia, 30;
PCF, 67; 69; 81-82; rélève,
116, 120

Valentino, Paul (SFIO/
Guadeloupe), 17

Valluy, Jean, General, 43,
66, 85-86, 113

Van Co, 86, 89

Vermeersch, Jeannette, 78,
95-96

Veterans, 81, 128

Vichy (French regime): 14,
  18, 28, 126-127; Vichyites,
  34, 37, 45

La Vie ouvrière, 79

Vietminh (League for the
  Independence of Vietnam):
  formation, 16; World War
  II/revolution, 17-19. See
  also DRV, Ho Chi Minh

Vietnam: division of, 23, 26,
  146-147; northern, 23,
  133-134n.D; southern, 23,
  146-147; territorial
  integrity, 30, 37, 146-147;
  unity, 54, 66, 71, 146-147

Vietnam: Sociologie d'une
  guerre (Paul Mus), 136

Viet Nam Quoc Dan Dang
  (VNQDD)/pro-Chinese
  Vietnamese, 5, 27-29

Vietnamization, 104, 112,
  137, 139

Voice of America, 82, 128

Wall, Irwin, 7n.7, 51n.14,
  82n.2, 83n.6

War matériel/weapons:
  manufacture and transport,
  3, 45, 78-80, 95-96, 118,
  129; nuclear, 77-78, 81,
  102, 111, 118, 135, 139;
  trafficking, 38

Wilson, Woodrow, President,
  31n.4

Withdrawal/repatriation
  (French forces), 3, 29, 48,
  67, 85, 92-95, 102-04,
  112-113, 116-117, 120-121,
  125, 136-138, 140, 145-146

Women, 76, 78, 128

Workers/working-class
  (proletariat): Algerian,
  78; building, 79-80;
  Catholic, 81; dockers, 26,
  38, 44, 56, 78-82, 83n.9,
  88, 101, 103, 119, 125,
  138, 147; European, 1-2;
  French, 3, 12, 14, 25, 26,
  44, 49, 51n.14, 52-53,
  55-58, 66-68, 70, 74n.9,
  75, 78-79, 81-82, 101-02,
  111, 118-119, 124-125, 131,
  133-134n.D, 151; miners,
  38, 69-70, 77; munitions,
  79; overseas, 5; railway,
  78-80, 147; steel, 25, 79;
  Vietnamese, 56, 66, 123;
  Western, 103

World Council of
  Intellectuals for Peace, 76

World Peace Congresses:
  76-77, 81, 83n.4,

World War I, 2, 124; World
  War II, 3, 11-12, 14-17,
  19, 37, 123-124, 126; world
  war (prospective), 76,
  99-100, 102, 111, 139, 145,
  151

Yalta Conference (1945), 18

Yen Bay (uprising, 1930), 5

Young Communists, 104-05n.4,
  111, 124, 131

Young Socialists, 55, 111

Youth, 76, 78

Yugoslavia, 76, 97

Zhdanov, Andrei, 57

Zola, Emile, 127

About the Author

EDWARD RICE-MAXIMIN is Supervisor of the International Student and Scholar Office, North Texas State University. His articles have appeared in the *Journal of Contemporary History, Contemporary French Civilization,* and *French Colonial Historical Studies.*